Politics and Digital Literature in the Middle East

Nele Lenze

Politics and Digital Literature in the Middle East

Perspectives on Online Text and Context

Nele Lenze
Gulf University for Science and Technology
Kuwait, Kuwait

ISBN 978-3-319-76815-1   ISBN 978-3-319-76816-8 (eBook)
https://doi.org/10.1007/978-3-319-76816-8

Library of Congress Control Number: 2018941842

© The Editor(s) (if applicable) and The Author(s) 2019
This work is subject to copyright. All rights are solely and exclusively licensed by the Publisher, whether the whole or part of the material is concerned, specifically the rights of translation, reprinting, reuse of illustrations, recitation, broadcasting, reproduction on microfilms or in any other physical way, and transmission or information storage and retrieval, electronic adaptation, computer software, or by similar or dissimilar methodology now known or hereafter developed.
The use of general descriptive names, registered names, trademarks, service marks, etc. in this publication does not imply, even in the absence of a specific statement, that such names are exempt from the relevant protective laws and regulations and therefore free for general use.
The publisher, the authors, and the editors are safe to assume that the advice and information in this book are believed to be true and accurate at the date of publication. Neither the publisher nor the authors or the editors give a warranty, express or implied, with respect to the material contained herein or for any errors or omissions that may have been made. The publisher remains neutral with regard to jurisdictional claims in published maps and institutional affiliations.

Cover credit: iStock / Getty Images Plus

Printed on acid-free paper

This Palgrave Macmillan imprint is published by the registered company Springer International Publishing AG part of Springer Nature.
The registered company address is: Gewerbestrasse 11, 6330 Cham, Switzerland

Acknowledgements

It is a great pleasure to thank everyone who helped me write my first monograph successfully.

First and foremost I want to express my gratitude to my PhD advisor Stephan Guth. His help, guidance, supervision, support, and patience from the preliminary to the concluding level encouraged me to stay on track. I am grateful for the help and support of my second supervisor Peter Gendolla.

Looking back, I am very thankful for all I have received throughout these years from the kind people around me. I am truly indebted and grateful for the invaluable support on both an academic and a personal level during the writing process by Mona Abdel-Fadil and Sarah Jurkiewicz.

I would like to show my gratitude for the moral support and friendship of Peggy März, Teresa Pepe, Jens Borgland, Russell Craig, Lotte Fasshauer, Heather Mae Ellis, Florian Holzhauer, Jon Nordenson, Stefanie Scharf, Nithin Mathew, Peter Bitschene, Claudia Lenze-Bitschene, Sahar Khamis, and Deborah Wheeler. A special thanks goes to Charlotte Schriwer and Patrick Sin whose endless supply of baked goods kept me fuelled. For feedback on the manuscript, I thank Edison Yap Zong Yao and Roman Ziqing Chen.

My gratitude also goes to the financial, academic, and technical support of the University of Oslo that provided the necessary financial support for this research.

Contents

1 Beginnings: How to Read Arabic Literature Online? 1
2 Style and Media Make-Up of Digital Literature 15
3 Socio-Political Expressions Through Language and Narration 25
4 Participatory Culture 47
5 Who Are the Actors? Portrayal of Heroes 79
6 Challenges of Online Distribution 113
7 Concluding Thoughts 139

Bibliography 147

Index 171

About the Author

Nele Lenze is a visiting assistant professor at the Gulf University for Science and Technology in Kuwait; prior to that she was a senior research fellow and managing editor at the Middle East Institute at the National University of Singapore. She holds a PhD in Middle East Studies and Media Studies from the University of Oslo where she lectured on the Arab online sphere. She obtained her master's from Freie University Berlin. Lenze co-edited *Media in the Middle East: Activism, Politics, and Culture* (2017) with Charlotte Schriwer and Zubaidah Abdul Jalil, *Converging Regions: Global Perspectives on Asia and the Middle East* (2014) with Charlotte Schriwer, as well as *The Arab Uprisings: Catalysts, Dynamics, and Trajectories* (2014) with Fahed Al-Sumait and Michael Hudson.

List of Tables

Table 4.1 Example of a story that was reposted several times in different forms in various repostings 71
Table 6.1 Reposting of a story since 2006 132

CHAPTER 1

Beginnings: How to Read Arabic Literature Online?

INTRODUCTION

The majority of current research on Arabic-speaking countries is focused on the political-economy and state domination or co-optation. This book shows that literature is a part of cultural expressions that contribute to societal growth. Throughout this monograph, I outline the text and context of online literary developments in Egypt, Lebanon, and a few Gulf states, while occasionally adding examples from other countries.

Text and context are essential parts of this monograph. All close-readings and in-depth examples of literary online texts are from various countries of the Gulf; for detailed analyses of Egypt's and Lebanon's digital literary field, I rely on text analyses performed by fellow researchers. The datasets of original sources of online literature on which this book is based have been downsized according to specific criteria such as frequency and typicality in representation—this shows the interdiscursivity, uniqueness, and redundancy in the selection of examples. It is not a large-scale collection of original sources and focuses on aspects that make online literature what it is. However, I use detailed case studies on the macro level and apply linguistic analysis as well as context analysis: changing social, historical, and political contexts are analysed and connections among fields of action, genres, discourses, and text are highlighted using a selection of relevant conceptual tools.

© The Author(s) 2019
N. Lenze, *Politics and Digital Literature in the Middle East*,
https://doi.org/10.1007/978-3-319-76816-8_1

The chapters are arranged according to how digital text is perceived, starting with a look at the outer shell—its *make-up and visual* components. This is followed by what strikes the reader most after reading a first selection of texts: *language and narration* are notable in that they immediately render the communicative part of digital literature visible. These features are highlighted in the chapter on *participation culture* that introduces more aspects of interactivity which distinguishes digital literature from printed publications. Participation is activated through an emotional or intellectual connection to stories and poems. An important part of identification is through the protagonist, or main "hero" of the story—this aspect is elucidated in the subsequent chapter on *portrayal of heroes*. Within the analysis of heroes' portrayal, it becomes obvious that *constraints and challenges* are part of the overall writing and distribution process. Discussing these issues helps one understand the genre in its political context.

As part of the text analysis, I discuss visual aspects as well as sociopolitically relevant issues that are brought up in a number of text, often represented through narration and the portrayal of main characters. This portrayal is a relevant aspect of my reading of short stories, especially the relationship between individual identities in contrast to collective ideals. The chapter *Narration and Language* analyses a variety of perspectives on text. It is important for reading the sources because it reflects stylistic and aesthetic distinctions that are apparent in literary texts from the region. Tarek El-Ariss points out that "forms of techno-writing" undergo structural and linguistic transformation.[1] These changes apply to the script as well as language use of English, dialect, and Modern Standard Arabic (MSA). A way to look at the media make-up is to discuss its aesthetics. Distance and perspective are two important aspects of literary texts published online.[2]

As for the reading of context, I look at the media make-up of the text, discussing participation culture as well as issues of publishing restrictions.

---

[1] Tarek El-Ariss, *Trials of Arab Modernity: Literary Affects and the New Political*, 2013, p. 145.

[2] Aesthetics is the focus of Christopher Funkhouser's work. Christopher *Funkhouser*, "Digital Poetry: A Look at Generative, Visual, and Interconnected Possibilities in its First Four Decades", in Ray Siemens and Susan Schreibman (eds.), *Companion to Digital Literary Studies*, Oxford 2008, http://www.digitalhumanities.org/companion/view?docId=blackwell/9781405148641/9781405148641.xml&chunk.id=ss1-5-11&toc.depth=1&toc.id=ss1-5-11&brand=9781405148641_brand, last accessed January 27, 2012.

The chapter *Participatory Culture* draws on a different methodological approach because, here, forums and blogs are analysed by identifying their function for readers and writers.

Within this introductory chapter, I would like to guide the reader through some essential pointers on theory as well as on socio-political circumstances in the countries that are part of literary and contextual analysis. Comprehending the theoretical approaches adopted in this book is key to appreciating the general framing of the issue at hand.

Reading Text in Theoretical Context

While every chapter in this book introduces its theoretical framework separately with respect to the issue being examined, it is useful to provide a summary of the theoretical approaches adopted in the book in order to establish a clear direction of thought. The interdisciplinary analysis of the texts includes theory and practices that are problem-oriented. The theoretical approaches used in this book consist of two types: on the one hand, theories that deal with literature in general, and on the other hand, theories related to digital culture.

I should note one important definition for the texts I read within my analysis. Despite most texts in this monograph being taken from non-official and established sources such as publishing houses, they carry an aesthetic significance as representatives of popular culture. Reuven Snir's definition of what literature is helps to understand the choices I made in my selection.

> A literary text may be defined as any text that in a given community has been imbued with cultural value and that allows for high levels of complexity and significance in the way it is constructed. At the same time, the designation 'literary text' points not to an inherent property of certain kinds of objects, but rather to a quality assigned by people involved in producing, reading and analysing those objects. Texts perceived as literary by one culture or community are seen as non-literary by another.[3]

My study of digital literature focuses on interactions, texts, and contexts of short texts that are published not only in forums and blogs, but also on other digital platforms.

---

[3] Reuven Snir, Modern Arabic Literature: A Theoretical Framework, 2017, p. 13.

Looking at Literature

Earlier research on printed Arabic literature serves as the theoretical base for my findings. Scholars such as El-Ariss, Sabry Hafez, Stephan Guth, Angelika Neuwirth, Andreas Pflitsch, and Christian Junge provide in-depth analysis of postmodern Arabic writing. For the Gulf region in particular, Gail Ramsay is an active researcher of online text. For blog literature in Egypt, Teresa Pepe's insights serve as a great resource.

Delving more into specificities of the literariness of my sources, the findings of the following researchers serve as a solid foundation for my study. The question of modernity and postmodernity has been heavily discussed in recent years. Guth analyses changes in contemporary Arabic literature and discusses a countering modernity as well as a "reviving literary heritage" as the main findings of his work on culture and identity in post-1980s literature in the Arab world.

Neuwirth is one of the editors of *Arabic Literature: Postmodern Perspectives*.[4] Her research on contemporary literature deals with ideas of *memory and identity* and *collective memory*; this is valuable for my research because identity representation in the form of the heroes' portrayal is an essential part of my discussion of short stories published online. Individual identity can be seen in contrast to collective ideals, as will be presented in the chapter on portrayal of heroes.

Ramsay is one of the few scholars who has conducted research on Arabic literary blogs. She studies short stories (in print) from the United Arab Emirates (UAE) and Oman, and issues of globalisation in the Gulf as well as the "post-structural concepts of cultural representation".[5] In her recent monograph *Blogs & Literature & Activism* she studies Egyptian literary blogs. This work draws on Pepe's thoughts on autofictionality in Egyptian literary blogs—a remarkable and important examination of literary writing online. Ramsay works on the connection of literary texts and

---

[4] Angelika Neuwirth, Andreas Pflitsch, and Barbara Winckler (eds.), *Arabic Literature: Postmodern Perspectives*, London 2010. Translated from the original German version: *Arabische Literatur, postmodern*, München 2004.

[5] Gail Ramsay, "Global Heroes and Local Characters in Short Stories from the United Arab Emirates and the Sultanate of Oman", in Paul Starkey, Boutros Hallaq & Stefan Wild (eds.), Middle Eastern Literatures, Vol. 9 (Number 2) August 2006, pp. 211–216; Gail, Ramsay, "Globalisation and Cross-Cultural Writing in the United Arab Emirates and Oman", in Gunilla Lindberg-Wada, Stefan Helgesson, Margareta Petersson, Anders Pettersson (eds.), Literature and Literary History in Global Contexts: A Comparative Project, Vol. 4, Berlin, New York 2006, pp. 241–277.

activism, a unique approach to studying Arabic literary production on the internet; this is especially relevant throughout the Arab Uprisings, as political messages and art were closely connected during this time. Ramsay avoids the trap of strong comparisons to European traditions and looks at blogs as a form of inner-Egyptian resistance.

Pepe offers an in-depth analysis of the literariness of Egyptian blogs in her discussion on the term *adab*. In her paper she points to literary critics who find blogging to be "devaluing the prestige of *adab* in high literature".[6] Her analysis is of great importance as it contextualises terminology and criticism in Egypt. Another significant contribution by Pepe is her situating of the literary quality of Egyptian blogging within the context of a bigger transformation of literature.[7]

El-Ariss makes clear the need to renegotiate "Western" literary theory when it is applied to Arabic texts because an interpretation of the cultural, literary, and historic background and context is essential.[8] This is because the Eurocentric model does not take into account the peculiarities and transformations within Arab political and social reality—especially considering the changes after and during the Uprisings of 2011. Instead, El-Ariss suggests carefully exploring Arabic texts within its manifestation.[9]

El-Ariss also warns of earlier research on Arabic literature in which "texts [are treated] as sites of resistance to or deployment of Western cultural models, thereby engaging modernity as a narrative of complicity with a hegemonic West, which suppresses, one way or another, Arab–Islamic tradition and practices".[10] Both points are particularly salient given how these analyses continue to be employed today. In the same manner, Pflitsch examines the contrast of cultural heritage and Western modernity, emphasising that a Western perception of Arabic literature is often "oriented on exotic allures" and, just like Marilyn Booth, finds that diversity and quality

---

[6] Teresa Pepe, "Improper Narratives: Egyptian Personal Blogs and the Arabic Notion of Adab", *LEA—Lingue e letterature d'Oriente e d'Occidente*, vol. 1, n. 1 (2012), pp. 547–562, p. 558.

[7] Teresa Pepe, "When Writers Activate Readers. How the autofictional blog transforms Arabic literature", Journal of Arabic and Islamic Studies 15 (2015): 73–91, p. 75.

[8] Tarek El-Ariss, *Trials of Arab Modernity: Literary Affects and the New Political*, 2013, p. 150.

[9] Ibid., p. 11.

[10] Ibid., p. 10.

are often disregarded.[11] It is important to keep the debate on Orientalism—made popular by Edward Said—in mind when dealing with texts from the Arabic-speaking world, as preconceptions should not be applied to studying any topic. As El-Ariss points out, when applying European theories on Arabic texts, the local context is relevant and should be reflected. To this end, I make sure to underscore the individuality of literary texts published in online forums and blogs. He also points out how the legitimacy of the literary canon is questioned with the new publications[12]—a theme that is picked up repeatedly in academic evaluations of new and digital literature.

Common to all these scholars is their emphasis on the dichotomy between heritage or memory and global influence, as well as on self-presentation or identity presentation. The following section describes methods and theories that are adopted to outline the distinctions of online literature in the Gulf. Because this field has not been well researched, I decide to use a collection of theoretical approaches to avoid losing valuable nuances which would have otherwise been lost if I were to use a more restricted set of theories. My choice of methods derives from my research question about the distinctive aspects that recur in my sources.

Examining Digital Culture

For a closer look at *Participation Culture*, I will draw on the findings of Louis Leung because they help to identify the process of interaction and communication.[13] David Gauntlett's findings are also vitally relevant[14]: he argues that new media has changed the way that the audience perceives content. With new media, the audience are no longer passive recipients of content—they are now able to actively voice their opinions and interact with and challenge other points of view.

---

[11] Andreas Pflitsch, "The End of Illusions: On Arab Postmodernism", in Angelika Neuwirth, Andreas Pflitsch, and Barbara Winckler (eds.), *Arabic Literature: Postmodern Perspectives*, London 2010, pp. 25–40, p. 36.

[12] Ibid., p. 151.

[13] Louis Leung, "User-generated content on the Internet: an examination of gratifications, civic engagement and psychological empowerment", in *New Media & Society*, London 2009, pp. 1327–1347, p. 1328 f.

[14] David Gauntlett, *Participation Culture, Creativity, and Social Change*, November 29, 2008, http://www.youtube.com/watch?v=MNqgXbI1_o8&feature=related, last accessed November 11, 2011.

Kristina Riegert finds that from a media studies perspective the local context has to be considered while analysing online content. Media differs in authoritarian, transitioning, and democratic settings.[15] She introduces Joke Hermes' concept of cultural citizenship. Studying cultural citizenship means trying to understand public opinion that is built on shared identity among the audience.[16]

Gerard Genette provides a methodological approach to the actual literary source texts. He coined terms that are relevant for the analysis of narration. His method is suitable for examining the voice of the narrator as well as narrative moods. Apart from the importance of seeing texts in an autonomous nature his ideas on narration help explain my sources. Especially important for literary online texts are his identification of a *narrative instance* (referring to the actual moment and context of narration) and *narrative levels* (looking at the acts narrated to the act of narration itself).

The chapter *Challenges of Online Distribution* is discussed against the background of views on the internet as a public sphere. This is necessary since I analyse censorship as well as the redistribution of text. Both are social functions that influence the dynamics of literary stories that are posted on blogs and in forums. The debate on the internet as a public sphere is long and Riegert concludes that it is usually ultimately rejected.[17] This is mostly due to the medium not fitting the defined characteristic of a traditional public sphere. Sarah Jurkiewicz calls this space a counter-public[18] which means it is not necessarily a public sphere but rather a public space for new ideas and identity—opening spaces for counter discussions.

The brief introduction to a selection of critical and theoretical tools of my own analysis of the source selection offers an overall arch that frames the monograph. As an interdisciplinary approach, this variety in themes and perspectives analysed helps mapping out critical issues within Arabic

---

[15] Kristina Riegert, "Understanding Popular Arab Bloggers: From Public Spheres to Cultural Citizens", *International Journal of Communication* 9(2015), 458–477, p. 459.

[16] Ibid., p. 461.

[17] Kristna Riegert, "Understanding Popular Arab Bloggers: From Public Spheres to Cultural Citizens", *International Journal of Communication* 9(2015), 458–477, p. 460.

[18] Jurkiewicz, S. 2011a. "Blogging as Counterpublic? The Lebanese and Egyptian Blogosphere in Comparison". In Social Dynamics 2.0: Researching Change in Times of Media Convergence, edited by N. C. Schneider and B. Gräf, 27–47. Berlin: Frank & Timme, p. 27.

literature on the net. With providing political and economic context, this chapter presents a foundation of reading the monograph.

Critical discourse analysis (CDA) helps analyse the settings of literary texts. CDA is interdisciplinary and examines language as a social practice. Even if it is more often used for analysing political discourse, I will apply a selection of tools from CDA to my sources. CDA is vital because it draws on the analysis of separate discourses that form a public reflection on a single subject. I use the term "discourse" as defined in CDA: a form of language use in writing and speech that is seen as a "social practice" and shows social identities.[19] This method is needed to analyse selected discourses in a variety of stories. When we take Ruth Wodak's discourse-historical approach into consideration for analysing literature online, we offer a closer look at the text and unveil underlying nuances of great analytical salience. One important factor of CDA is dealing with power imbalances that can be expressed in hegemonic identity narratives. These are manifested in the literary texts, which I discuss in the chapter on "heroes" and the chapter on narration. This power imbalance is expressed through an asymmetric relationship between social actors. In no way is the literality of the text merely reduced to sociological accounts of a representation of *all* Arabs, as El-Ariss warns. Rather, the analysis of power dynamics is in addition to examining the literary features of the texts. El-Ariss cautions that the binaries of tradition versus modernity as well as Islam versus the West have "reduced texts to sociological accounts and elided their literary complexity". In this way they are "treated as an objective representation of Arab culture and Islam or as the 'true word' of the native informant."

Instead of dealing with binaries such as East and West as means of comparing literary texts, I will look at how online literature developed in

---

[19] CDA sees discourse—language use in speech and writing—as a form of "social practice". Describing discourse as social practice implies a dialectical relationship between a particular discursive event and the situation(s), institution(s), and social structure(s) that frame it: the discursive event is shaped by them, but it also shapes them. That is, discourse is socially constitutive as well as socially conditioned—it constitutes situations, objects of knowledge, and the social identities of and relationships between people and groups of people. It is constitutive both in the sense that it helps to sustain and reproduce the social status quo and in the sense that it contributes to transforming that status quo. Since discourse is so socially consequential, it gives rise to important issues of power. Discursive practices may have major ideological effects—that is, they can help produce and reproduce unequal power relations between (for instance) social classes, women and men, and ethnic/cultural majorities and minorities through the ways they represent things and position people (Fairclough and Wodak, 1997: 258).

comparison to earlier printed text, and how Lebanon, Egypt, and a selection of Gulf countries turn out to all have unique ways of using the medium.

In order to avoid generalising and stereotyping, I find it essential to introduce a brief summary of the circumstances in which the literature under consideration is produced. These contextualise the theories and differentiating and common developments in a global context.

POLITICAL DEVELOPMENT

In the outline on theoretical approaches, one stream of thinking leads to an analysis of reading texts within its contexts but without instrumentalising it as a representation of political dissent. The short introduction into a socio-political background here merely serves as an essential foundation for reading literary works within their own contexts. It is imperative to differentiate among the contexts of Egypt, Lebanon, and the Gulf countries in their engagement with online literature. Geographically and culturally, they are located in distant places and the education level, gross domestic product (GDP), freedom of expression, and demography vary tremendously. These distinctions affect the use of the internet. While the education levels in Lebanon and the Gulf are relatively high, literacy in Egypt is only 76 percent[20] with younger people being more literate than the rest. Economically, the Gulf countries are better off than Egypt and Lebanon that influences the internet penetration rate as well as how much time one has at his or her disposal to produce digital content. The internet penetration rate is over 90 percent in Bahrain, Qatar, and the UAE, in Kuwait, and Lebanon it is in the mid-70s percentage-wise; in Oman and Saudi Arabia it is in its 60s. Only in Egypt, the penetration rate reaches 36 percent.[21] However, factors such as shared internet access in cafes and other institutions (Egypt and Lebanon) influence the numbers in the same way that in the various GCC states a high number of expats impact the internet penetration rate.

Politically, all of the locations studied are very different. While Egypt had had the same leadership for decades and has subsequently gone through years of political turmoil, foreign intervention, and internal struggles, many of the Gulf countries did not experience the same events.

---

[20] According to the World Bank.
[21] According to the internet world stats.

Lebanon lives through constant stages of change, wars, and political unrest. From a publications perspective it is the freest country of the countries I study. Kuwait also rates as a country where freedom of speech is comparatively high.[22] Deborah Wheeler provides continues insights on the internet usage in Kuwait from its early stages onwards.[23] The political systems in each Gulf country is unlike another. Similarities can be found in having a ruling royal family and some form of council or parliament. Kuwait shows a lot of political engagement where debates are widely joined. Oman, Saudi Arabia, Bahrain, and the UAE do not rate as countries with freedom of speech, which also changes the political dimension and impact of online media. More on that is detailed in the chapter on censorship. In general, it can be said that there is more regular political activism online in Egypt, Kuwait, and Lebanon. Nevertheless, in Saudi Arabia and in Bahrain, literary forms of cultural production and other forms of activism are part of the expression of ideas and political views.

In the past few years, the significance of political activism has been disseminated globally in mainstream media. Riegert clarifies that all bloggers she interviewed in Kuwait, Egypt, and Lebanon found blogging ideal for discussions on politics, culture, and societal issues.[24] However, she also found that Lebanese bloggers did not identify themselves as activists, but only the audience would identify themselves as such.[25]

Users used to share content and narrate it through online tools such as forums, blogs, social media, and micro-blogging. In Egypt, political activism was already important before the Arab Uprisings. Since the Kefaya movement in Egypt and the broader availability of online media all over the Arab world, social media and other Web 2.0 services[26] served as an additional outlet for political dissent and social and cultural developments. The Egyptian Movement of Change (الحركة المصرية من أجل التغيير) was a grassroots movement protesting Mubarak, founded in 2004. It gained more profile during the 2005 constitutional referendum. Activists also reached

---

[22] According to a Freedom House report by 2016.

[23] Deborah Wheeler. *The Internet in the Middle East. Global Expectations and Local Imaginations in Kuwait.* 2005. New York.

[24] Kristina Riegert, Understanding Popular Arab Bloggers: From Public Spheres to Cultural Citizens, International Journal of Communication 9(2015), p. 464.

[25] Ibid., p. 470.

[26] As will be discussed further in the chapter on participation culture, Web 2.0 is defined by the change from static web pages to user-generated content and the increase of social media.

out to people as well as documented events online. Sahar Khamis shares detailed findings about Egyptian political blogosphere since the uprisings in 2011.[27]

From a literary point of view, Egyptian writers have stated that personal and genuine views help one discern realities on the ground from misinformation and mistruths during political turmoil.[28] In the Gulf countries, online literary production started out socially in circles of bloggers and literature lovers. Later it became more popular with a broader audience—so much so that online literature now is supported by bigger institutions such as the Emirates Airlines Festival for Literature. Additionally, national prizes in Bahrain, the UAE, and Kuwait are being awarded to creative literary projects.

Economic Developments in Online Writing

While online writing was at first a more non-commercial and private way of publishing, parts of it developed into more commercial forms. Writers turned into authors for mainstream media or founders for non-profit organisations. Riegert shows that Lebanese bloggers who become popular and enjoy high readership are offered space in mainstream media. She mentions examples of bloggers turning to work for magazines, talk shows, and NGOs.[29]

The publishing industry has benefited from online literature as online writers who get published in print already come with their own audience. During its peak years in the mid-2000s, many of the Egyptian authors—but also authors of other countries—published their works in print. The peak of Arabic digital literature was before 2011 and declined after that. As the development of social media accelerates, new outlets encouraged producers of digital cultural literature to engage with mobile phone applications to tap into a wider tech-savvy audience.

As part of the background discussion, it will be interesting to elaborate on the writers' involvement in print literature as well as public readings and recitals. Pepe clarifies that publishing in print requires a budget in

---

[27] Sahar Khamis. *Egyptian Revolution 2.0: Political Blogging, Civic Engagement and Citizen Journalism.* 2013. New York.

[28] Teresa Pepe, "Improper Narratives: Egyptian personal blogs and the Arabic notion of *adab*", in *LEA—Lingue e Letterature d'Oriente e d'Occidente*, vol. 1, pp. 547–562, 2012, p. 552.

[29] Kristina Riegert, Understanding Popular Arab Bloggers: From Public Spheres to Cultural Citizens, International Journal of Communication 9(2015), p. 470.

Egypt, as authors often need to pay for the publication of their works.[30] In Egypt, novels based on blogs were published rather early in comparison to other countries. Two publishing houses encouraged the dissemination of digital works in print; 2008 was a busy year for publishing online novels in print publishing houses like Dar al-Shuruq. To market the blog novels, the publisher introduced the authors at the Cairo book fair in the year 2009.[31] El-Ariss also mentions Dar Merit as an Egyptian publisher that dives into the publications of online literary texts.[32] As an additional forum, its editor created a Salon space for discussion at the publishing house.

In all countries that this book discusses, motivation for writers is usually not financial in nature but rather, authors like to share their texts and reach out to a community, educate its readership, and engage in discussions. In the various Gulf countries, many initiatives are taken to support the arts scene and in the last decade or two, a lot has been done to support local writers. One example is the encouragement of digital writing at the Emirates Airlines Literature Festival in Dubai in 2017. Other countries organise poetry festivals or award prizes to encourage more local writing but also to preserve heritage and diversify cultural outlets. The same engagement is present though book fairs, poetry shows on TV, and in the case of Abu Dhabi, state-subsidised translations of local writers. Pepe states that in Egypt blogging has contributed greatly to the proliferation of literature.[33] At the same time, El-Ariss highlights that digital literature is threatening the literary establishment.[34] In accordance with current support of writers online, this threat can be countered with embracing developments and making them part of the canon.

---

[30] Teresa Pepe, "Improper Narratives: Egyptian personal blogs and the Arabic notion of *adab*", in *LEA—Lingue e Letterature d'Oriente e d'Occidente*, vol. 1, pp. 547–562, 2012, p. 549.

[31] Ibid., p. 550.

[32] Tarek El-Ariss, *Trials of Arab Modernity: Literary Affects and the New Political*, 2013, p. 148.

[33] Teresa Pepe, "Improper Narratives: Egyptian personal blogs and the Arabic notion of *adab*", in *LEA—Lingue e Letterature d'Oriente e d'Occidente*, vol. 1, pp. 547–562, 2012, p. 559.

[34] Tarek El-Ariss, *Trials of Arab Modernity: Literary Affects and the New Political*, 2013, p. 151.

Combing Elements

Both the outline of theoretical approaches and socio-political pointers help understand the framing of the following chapters. Chapter 2 provides a primer on choices of aesthetics and visual setup of the sources. A fundamental assessment of a decision between blogs and forums is made, relating to textual and visual differences in both. Nicola Mahne reads blogs as "Gesamttexte" which provides us with the essential point the chapter makes: digital literature needs to be read in its whole as a visual and textual creative product. The third part of the book provides an even deeper insight on socio-political expression through looking at the use of language and narration. Making use of Wodak's approach to CDA, this chapter shows how writing in dialect and MSA is practised as well as pointing to autofictional and dialogical elements of the sources. Participation culture is the focus of the fourth chapter, going into dynamics of public and private as well as the interpersonal experience of writing online. Working with research results by Warschauer and Grimes on interactive writing and discussing Gauntlet's points on motives for creating user-generated content, this chapter serves to highlight the defining features of interactivity in digital literature. The fifth chapter relates to how main characters are presented and what they stand for when reading texts in a socio-political context. A close reading of original sources in a combination of theoretical findings by Susanne Paasonen on identities online will assist the reading of identity representation. Chapter 6 is concerned with censorship and self-censorship as well as with the challenges of redistribution and remixing of digital cultural production. Combining these perspectives in the analysis of literature online creates a new way of framing of Arabic literary content production. The analysis provided is supposed to frame the sources in a way that highlights the technological advantages and disadvantages of the medium and at the same time it intends to show how these impact the socio-political ideas presented in the examined texts.

The theoretical frameworks on literature and digital culture are connected and built on each other. Some of the concepts in use such as autofiction and CDA can be applied to both printed and digital text as they help to measure and define specific aspects of these cultural products. Introducing the theoretical backbone to my study helps to understand the reading of the texts not within the West-East binaries but as growing and changing elements of digital cultural production. Establishing a set of pointers on the political-economy in the countries studied relates to the theory in ways that underline developments in both areas. As the infrastructure and political setting flourish, literary output may be impacted in a positive manner as well. Both parts, the theoretical and the practical part on the political-economy, prepare a ground for further analysis of literature online.

Going more into detail of the visual appearance and media make-up, the next chapter will provide insights that show defining features of digital texts. The chapter serves as a starting point for further discussions of specific characteristic of literature online.

CHAPTER 2

Style and Media Make-Up of Digital Literature

Digital literary text comes in many forms. Visual aesthetics in expression influence written and spoken words. This chapter looks at questions of layout and the use of multimedia elements. I will analyse the visual setup of online short stories, literary works on blogs and websites as well as on YouTube.

Visual Setup

Examining various aspects of blog posts and short stories published in forums highlights common characteristics among them. This lays the foundation for understanding specific features of the construction of these texts.

The visual features of texts are evidenced in their layout, narrative structure, as well as use of multimedia applications. The digital body of online literature differs from that of printed texts in that it provides more possibilities for expression, such as the digital genres that texts manifest. Digital texts also vary in terms of their actual textuality—which has evolved considerably from that of printed texts—since layouts are easier to manipulate, texts can be readily edited, and copying text and distribution can be made almost instantly.

This chapter begins with a description of the layouts of texts and the use of multimedia applications. The former examines the overall and distinctive appearance and structure of texts, such as how introductory phrases underline a reoccurring construction in forum texts; the latter refers to the utilisation of multimedia elements being audio files and images. Subsequently, this chapter explores part of the early visual digital literature for instance interactive novels and video poetry.

Form and Appearance: Text Layout and Multimedia Elements

Since the first manifestation of digital literature in Europe and the US in the 1960s, authors have frequently (re)designed textual forms.[1] The emergence of hypertext literature, as a genre of electronic literature, is one such example. Hypertext literature uses the computer screen, instead of printed pages, as a medium to convey non-linear narratives; it also taps into elements of the digital sphere, such as the linked World Wide Web pages (to provide additional context and user interaction), audio, and motion. The presence of multiple embedded hyperlinks or hypertext links enables reader interaction as readers select links that would lead them to sections that interest them, thereby allowing the creation of a plethora of narratives. This new form of literature has gained prominence and recognition with major newspapers awarding prizes for stellar literary works.[2] Theoretical frameworks for early digital text have mostly been offered by European scholars. Roberto Simanowski's research on digital literature identifies intermediality as a trademark of digital literature. As illustrated in the preceding paragraph, digital literature builds on traditional media by including texts, pictures, and music.[3] Since the 2000s, internet access has increased and Arabic digital literature has been published in forums, blogs, e-publishing houses, YouTube, and other social and micro-media sites. In the theorising of visual output, I consider the works of two scholars who have dealt with visual appearances of digital literature. Nicole Mahne

---

[1] Christopher Funkhouser, "Digital Poetry: A Look at Generative, Visual, and Interconnected Possibilities in its First Four Decades", in Ray Siemens and Susan Schreibman (eds.), *Companion to Digital Literary Studies*, Oxford 2008, http://www.digitalhumanities.org/companion/view?docId=blackwell/9781405148641/9781405148641.xml&chunk.id=ss1-5-11&toc.depth=1&toc.id=ss1-5-11&brand=9781405148641_brand, last accessed January 27, 2012.

[2] One example of such awards is the German "Pegasus" prize, awarded to Dirk Günther and Frank Klötgen for "Die Aaleskorte der Ölig" (1998 by the German weekly newspaper "Zeit", IBM, and a state-owned television channel (ARD). More information on the artwork as well as the prize can be found on the website http://www.aaleskorte.de/, last accessed December 26, 2011.

[3] Roberto Simanowski, *Interfictions*, Frankfurt am Main 2002, p. 18.

(2006) divides texts into two categories: texts that consist purely of words and "Gesamttexte" (overall texts) that use more than one medium.[4] In the later examples, both Gesamttexte and plain layout are present. David Crystal (2001) makes a similar point when emphasising that the mere possibilities offered by a new visual language does not mean that everyone is able to use them.[5] One could add that for aesthetic or other reasons not every author might want to use a multitude of visual elements even though others might feel inclined to use the full range.

Setup of Online Literary Texts on Blogs and Forums

This section deals with the setup and genre of online literary texts in forums and blogs. I will first describe features of blogs and then move on to outlining the benefits and distinctions of short stories and short texts through an example of a story which has been posted multiple times in many forums—this sheds light on the kind of texts that appear in forums. Finally, I compare blog posts and forum posts to visual digital novels and video poetry.

Carolyn R. Miller and Dawn Shepherd (2004) deal with the challenge of categorising blogs. Blogs are not a homogeneous form of text production. In fact, blogs can be concurrently private and public, addressed to everyone or simply no one. Blogs have multiple ancestors, such as reality TV, memoirs, political journalism, journals, and diaries. Many of my source blogs provide a variety of texts: criticisms of cultural products such as films, music, and events, rants about things that concern the author, literary texts, or political views. It is rare that a personal blog presents only one genre of texts or addresses only one subject. My research focuses on literary texts and ignores other published texts such as writings by political activists or business ventures. Fortunately, Gail Ramsay and Jon Nordenson research political activism in the Arab world of online culture since many years.

In blogs, the reader usually does not find complete stories with a beginning and an end; rather they tend to resemble more of a column or a short essay. Typical blog texts take the form of self-expression and consist of informal descriptions of thoughts or events and do not have a thoroughly planned plot. Common elements that loosely structure blogs are its

---

[4] Nicole Mahne, *Mediale Bedingungen des Erzählens im digitalen Raum*, Frankfurt am Main 2006, p. 43.

[5] David Crystal, *Language and the Internet*, Cambridge 2001, p. 35.

chronology, personal commentary, and hyperlinks. As a defining conclusion, Miller and Shepherd state:

> We see the blog, then, as a genre that addresses a timeless rhetorical exigence in ways that are specific to its time. In the blog, the potentialities of technology, a set of cultural patterns, rhetorical conventions available in antecedent genres, and the history of the subject have combined to produce a recurrent rhetorical motive that has found a conventional mode of expression. Bloggers acknowledge that motive in each other and continue enacting it for themselves. The blog-as-genre is a contemporary contribution to the art of the self.[6]

This statement demonstrates what uniquely characterises blogs and at the same time takes up the notion of the "art of the self", the latter which will later be discussed in connection with autofictional aspects and in the chapters *Participatory Culture* and *Portrayals of Heroes*.

Multimedia Elements

There are three major multimedia elements often appearing in digital texts in the Arab world, especially in forums and blogs: images, videos, and audio files. Most common is the integration of images into the texts.

Images underline the message of a story. A good example of this is the story "How was she killed? The complete story of an Emirati woman who was found dead in a well" that was published in different forums in the United Arab Emirates and other GCC countries.[7] This crime fiction appeared in more than 50 forums and is commented on by many readers.[8] In its introductory text, it was claimed that the story was in fact non-fiction. A true story may appeal more to an audience's voyeurism than would a story explicitly described as fiction. The pictures in the story are watermarked and appear in a separate photobucket[9] account to share the pictures. The truth or fictitiousness of the story is irrelevant to the analysis

---

[6] Carolyn R. Miller and Dawn Shepherd, Blogging as Social Action: A Genre Analysis of the Weblog, 2004, http://blog.lib.umn.edu/blogosphere/blogging_as_social_action_a_genre_analysis_of_the_weblog.html, last accessed December 26, 2011.

[7] كيف قتلت؟/القصة الكاملة للفتاة الاماراتية التى عثر عليها في بئر مقتولة forum.uaewomen.net/showthread.php?t=476260, last accessed January 30, 2012.

[8] The story is also part of the analysis of participatory culture in Chap. 2.

[9] A photobucket is a website that offers image hosting. Pictures can be stored and shared on this website.

of the story. Depending on how the story is reposted, the layout, title, pictures, and content differ slightly. These changes to the story will be discussed in the chapter *Participatory Culture*. The chapter on *portrayals of heroes* gives a more detailed summary of this story. Here it is sufficient to note that the story, narrated in the third person, tells of a young Emirati woman who is tortured and finally killed by her husband. An important element of the story is the use of photographs to describe the crime scene. These photographs vary in their many repostings, but a lot of them show the same scene: a close-up of the well with an arrow pointing to a stain which is purported to be the victim's blood.[10]

Surprisingly, in the first few repostings of the story, pictures were not attached. Not until four days after the first distribution of the story did repostings with pictures surface. This development demonstrates how digital platforms offer a space for user interaction and creativity. In a subsequent repost, a user had modified the story by adding multiple images to it—this, however, is the only version which was not reposted by other users. In fact, the version most subscribed to and republished was the one described above. Later repostings then disposed of photographs—users instead changed colours of the font in order to highlight what they considered to be important. The multiple pictures used serve different functions. Primarily, they describe the setting. It is in the nature of short stories not to be very detailed in a description of set and characters, leaving scope for the reader's imagination, so pictures might supplement details left out in textual description. These detailed descriptions and the amount of work that was put into authentifying the text makes it very clear that the "realness" is an important element of the circulated stories. In the chapter on *narration and the socio-political implications*, I go deeper into questions of autofictionality and authenticity. Stylistically, these stories are condensed, and the anthropologist Rebecca L. Torstick states, "Such pieces require their reader to fill in the gaps and insert the required meanings as they move from sentence to sentence in the piece."[11] The example above illustrates the utility of photographs in forums. In the following example, I highlight a different way of including medial elements in blogs. Concerning incorporating media, blogs differ from forums because they provide many more possibilities of individualising and adjusting design and layout. This

---

[10] http://www.adbuae.com/vb/archive/index.php/t-4491.html, January 2, 2012.
[11] Rebecca L. Torstrick and Elizabeth Faier (eds.), *Culture and Customs of the Arab Gulf States*, Westport 2009, p. 46.

is because the layout of forums is predetermined and not many individualising changes can be made. By contrast, blogs permit a variety of adjustments. With the applications provided by Web 2.0,[12] the average user no longer needs to write computer code. Web 2.0 also allows users to copy designs and layouts with the help of toolbox systems.

To illustrate the points stipulated above, I shall use the blog "From the Stories of Alzain".[13] The first visual aspect of the blog is its header, which consists of three pictures seemingly taken from a fashion magazine, and which features women that seem to be in dancer's poses. Beneath the header lies a disclaimer which states that the blog's texts are not allowed to be redistributed without reference to the original author. This stands in contrast to what happens in forums, where content is freely modified and reposted without explicit reference to the author, and therefore highlights a participatory culture among forum users. Another visual element on this blog is its list of "followers",[14] indicated by a cluster of BlogSpot followers in the right-hand column of the blog. This is followed by a quote by Eleanor Roosevelt. The quote is considered a visual element as it stands out from other texts in that section; statements like Roosevelt's quote reflect the author's identity, ideas, and attitudes. Located below the quote is the blog's archive and blogroll[15] which indicate that Alzain has been blogging since May 2007. The blogger gets to design the layout of his or her blog by easily manipulating various elements of the blog using Web 2.0. Three additional elements on the website inform the user about visitors to his or her blog: these are widgets that describe countries where readers come from,[16] a live traffic feed,[17] and a *radarurl* that measures the number of visitors to the blog.[18] This is especially useful in helping the blogger monitor and subsequently expand his readership. These three elements are visible to visitors of the blog, and they help highlight the popularity and international outreach of the blog. Further, the ability to manipulate and integrate these various elements into one's blog highlights

---

[12] This term is explained in the chapter that deals with participatory culture.

[13] http://al-zain.blogspot.com/, last accessed December 26, 2011.

[14] Followers in social media such as blogs and Twitter are other users who subscribe to the cultural product offered by one user.

[15] A list of links to other blogs that she supports to be read.

[16] A *widget* counts the number of visitors to websites.

[17] A live traffic feed shows the number of users visiting the website from different locations in real time.

[18] *Radarurl* is another tool that measures the number of visitors to a website.

the blogger's tech-savviness. As an additional multimedia element, Alzain's blog is underlain with music: when users open the page, a *mix pod* starts and plays a variety of songs chosen by the blogger: soft, classical guitar tunes by the Turkish composer Melih Kibar.[19] In contrast to the transparency of the statistics and readership, the blogger does not explicitly reveal much about himself/herself. Multimedia applications are used to underline messages in blog posts and therefore function as tools of self-representation. Pictures and music help catch the reader's attention. Multimedia elements thereby engage reader's participation in more than one sense. Keeping Mahne and Crystal in mind, this kind of blog thus constitutes a Gesamttexte because it includes a variety of media in one outlet. In another example, Omani blogger Muawiyah's blog displays a more conservative approach to online literature. The blog is kept very simple in layout, with two columns and a *Blogger* theme design.[20] No multimedia elements are added to the text—not even emoticons. It could just as well be a story published in print. According to Mahne, this blog would not be considered as a "Gesamttexte".The many elements of blogs and forums have also been utilised by authors of digital literature in Arab countries to contextualise narratives and to highlight peculiar subjectivities. In various combinations, videos and poetry have been overlain or embedded with images, songs, and poetry in order to effuse particular moods and atmosphere.

While the use of videos was uncommon in the years under consideration—the early 2000s up till 2011—visual artworks have nonetheless been produced. One example of this is "Hicham" from Morocco, who makes videos with poetry.[21] A number of examples of creative exceptions in digital literature from Arab countries put the mainstream use of media tools in blogs and forums in context. In some cases, videos, for example with songs or poetry, support the mood of the story. Poetry might be displayed overlaying a picture, accompanied by music or a reading of the text. The use of videos is rare in the years under consideration—the early 2000s until 2011. Still, users create visual art works, for example "Hicham" from Morocco, who makes videos with poetry. Hicham produces visuals for his works and

---

[19] *Mixpod* is a tool that allows users to create their own mixed tapes and embed them in websites http://www.mixpod.com/.

[20] A *Blogger* theme is a layout for blogs that is offered by the blog host Blogger.com. These layouts come in many forms and are free to use for every subscriber to the platform.

[21] Hicham distributes his works on World TV, which is hosted by YouTube, http://worldtv.com/hicham_tv, last accessed December 26, 2011.

posts them on YouTube.[22] Visuals are in the background of the videos, and the foreground is a canvas for literary texts; music is also played in the background. Another example of multimedia application use is the interactive online novel. Especially during the Arab Uprisings video poetry increased and some of it went viral. Eman Younis shows several examples from the Palestinian Territories in her work on "Video Clip Poems".[23] Additionally, a poem that went viral internationally was recited by the Egyptian activist named Dania first in Arabic[24] and then in English language.[25] The poet creates awareness of "Virginity tests"[26] that were conducted by the Egyptian military on March 9, 2011. In the video, the poet faces the camera and recites her lines. The picture is in black and white.

Unique among digital poetry and literature is the electronic novel, *Chat*. The Jordanian writer Mohamad Sanajleh produced the novel "shāt" (chat), which is integrated in a flash animation and hosted on the website of the "Arab E-Writers Union".[27] *Chat* is an interactive novel that engages with political subjects and makes references to a variety of Arab poets and thinkers. It was first produced in 2001. *Chat* leads the user through its story by encouraging him or her to click on each new text bit, offering extra text pieces in pop-up windows that simulate IM (instant messenger) conversations.[28] This interactivity allows the reader to travel actively through the story and partake in constructing his or her very own storyline.

---

[22] YouTube is a website that allows users to distribute videos.

[23] Examples of Arab Spring poems that turned into You Tube video clips are the Iraqi poet Ahmad Matar's poem "Fighter and Chatter"; 11 the Palestinian poet Tamim al-Barghuthi's "Oh People of Egypt"; 12 Abdul Aziz al-Jami'an's "Damascus and the Caliphate State"; 13 the Palestinian poet Basam al-Ashram's "Bu Azizi"; 14 and many others' Journalism and Mass Communication, Manifestations of the Arab Spring in Literature: "Video Clip Poems" on You Tube as a Model. Eman Younis, *Transcontinental Texts: Reality or Fantasy? Muhammad Sanajilah's Novel Chat as a Sample*, Hyperrhiz 16: Essays, Spring 2017, http://hyperrhiz.io/hyperrhiz16/essays/5-younis-transcontinental-texts.html, last accessed December 29, 2017, p. 36.

[24] https://www.youtube.com/watch?v=HU31hvjF1xA&context=C43ce1beADvjVQa1PpcFNv1b35puAIpq2-CmH8GwENT3OCM5WnUZg.

[25] http://yfa.awid.org/2012/03/young-woman-recites-poem-in-solidarity-with-egyptian-women-who-underwent-virginity-tests/.

[26] These tests were sexual abuse conducted by the military and did not serve to secure stability.

[27] http://www.arab-ewriters.com/chat/, last accessed December 30, 2011.

[28] Instant Messaging is a form of text-based communication carried out online in real time.

Sanajleh's first interactive novel is from 2001 and all together he managed to create four by 2016.[29] This form of interactive literature is rare in the Arabic-speaking world at the time of study.

Video poetry and the interactive novel with multimedia applications are two different genres of visual digital literature. Posting on *YouTube* is similar to self-publishing in that the author is responsible for generating his or her own readership. In contrast, distributing on the E-Writers site is more institutionalised. It is an official union site with members and an accompanying, established base of audience. Both projects are exceptions among Arabic online literary works.

Online digital text needs to be divided in its analysis according to the platform it is published in. A variety of genres are distributed in a multitude of outlets. In many literary forums, the text remains relatively static. Instead of using visuals, text colour can change and pictures, sound layers, and emoticons can be included. In contrast, design and layout are much simpler in blogs. The layout of Arabic online literary texts is usually very basic compared with possibilities that the medium offers. It is modest even in comparison with ready-made solutions like the themes that can be chosen on blog hosts such as Wordpress or BlogSpot.[30] This is often a conscious decision and the simplicity is a question of taste, rather than of skills in using online media. However, it is still a big change compared with its printed predecessor.

The chapter highlighted how design is implemented and relevant for online literature. In blogs design can be adjusted according to the authors wished within the boundaries of the blogging platform. In forums the choices in layout for the authors are limited. Digital novels that are programmed have the most freedom when it comes to making choices about the visual appearance of the text. Layout and design are an additional part of antithetical expression of online literary text.

The way the outer shell of the text is designed can also be reflected in the writing. Socio-political expressions in the visual are therefore connected to the same in language and narration which will be part of the discussion in the next chapter.

---

[29] *Zilal al-Wahed* (*One's Own Shadows*) 2001, *Chat* (2003), *Saqi'* (*Frost*), and *Zilal al-Ashiq* (*Shadows of the Lover*) 2016. Eman Younis, *Transcontinental Texts: Reality or Fantasy? Muhammad Sanajilah's Novel Chat as a Sample*, Hyperrhiz 16: Essays, Spring 2017, http://hyperrhiz.io/hyperrhiz16/essays/5-younis-transcontinental-texts.html, last accessed December 29, 2017, p. 2.

[30] Both blog hosts provide personal publishing tools for online use.

CHAPTER 3

Socio-Political Expressions Through Language and Narration

This chapter examines a variety of literary texts in order to elicit nuances in narration, language, and style—these are important in identifying connections with forms of socio-political expressions as well as the broader phenomenon of globalisation. In the original material, linguistic aspects of short stories and blog posts are as important as looking at the purpose and functions of dialogue, which are vital to stories distributed in forums. As the style of writing is also politically coloured, it goes hand in hand with a connection to socio-political developments. The chapter is divided in two parts. The first part examines narration and the second looks at the use of language, including dialogues and dialect. I will start this chapter with introducing an example from a blog post that shows a range of styles in writing and content; I will then discuss various features of stories posted in forums, and end with a general analysis of the use of language and dialect. Language and narration frame discourses and their representation. The position of narrators and the writer's point of view can be expressed through involvement and distance. In Wodak's critical discourse analysis, devices for these expressions include direct and indirect speeches, quotation marks and discourse marks, as well as metaphors. To intensify the message, vague expression, tag questions, hyperboles, verbs of saying, feeling, and thinking are all useful. Predictions can be made by evaluating attributions, collaborations, explicit comparisons, implications, and topoi.[1]

---

[1] Methods of Critical Discourse Studies, edited by Ruth Wodak, Michael Meyer, third edition, 2016, p. 33.

Most of the literary blog segments that I analyse are prose and can include dialogues, pictures, or videos. Arabic blogs often deal with everyday events and sometimes include criticisms of individuals or society. These kinds of texts are very typical of blogs and Tumblrs,[2] but can be found in newspaper columns offline too.

The following blog post displays the use of a diversity of writing styles in a single post—something that is not very common in single postings. This text was posted on Alzain's blog on February 14, 2011—the layout of the post is discussed in the chapter on media make-up. The blog post is titled "Love in a Loveless Age" and it illustrates the variety styles of literary texts distributed in blogs. The blog post comes in six parts with the first and last parts being more political.

عندما طغت السياسة في زمن الثورات على كل اللحظات المباحة للحب .. توارى ذلك المسكين خلف ستائر المساء .. وبات يرتشف من العتمة لونا بعيدا عن الأحمر .. ينزوي خجلا في زاوية من التأجيل المستمر .. ويموت مللا على رفوف الأخبار الطارئة .. والحكومات المنحرفة .. والتغيير القادم .. ويغني كمدا على حاله .. الثعلب فات فات بيدينه سبع لفات ..
وفي زوايا الانتظار خلعت سندريلا حذاءها لأنه ضاق ذرعا بقدميها .. وفضل الجلوس على اعتاب سجادة فارسية تزخر بكل الزخارف المتوارثة من عهد النار الى جمهورية الدين وزمن الثوار .. وأجلت الدعوة لحضور حفل اختيار الزوجات الموعودات وفضلت الاسترخاء امام شاشة التلفاز ومتابعة اخبار ثورة الخامس والعشرون من يناير ..[3]

When politics prevailed in the times of revolutions over all moments that were sanctioned for love ... that poor one hid behind the curtains of the evening ... and began to sip on the darkness of a colour that is far from red ... It hides in shyness in a corner of continuous deferment ... and dies out of boredom on the shelves of breaking news ... and the deviant governments ... and the coming change ... and wistfully laments its own condition ... the fox has passed with seven rolls in its hands...

In the corners of waiting, Cinderella took off her shoe because it grew tight on her foot ... and the shoe opted to sit on the edges of a Persian carpet decorated with designs passed down from the era of fire to the republic of theocracy and the era of revolutionaries ... and it deferred the invitation to attend the party for the selection of the betrothed wives, and opted instead to relax in front of the television screen and follow the news of the January 25 revolution...

Alzain, being only a spectator, tells us about the Egyptian uprisings in metaphorical anecdotes. The second part is written in a lyrical style with pictures added underneath every paragraph.

[2] Tumblr is a social media and blogging tool that lets users post and share images and text.
[3] These and the following translations are my own. http://al-zain.blogspot.com/2011_02_01_archive.html, last accessed December 26, 2011.

عندما خلعت ليلى رداءها الأحمر .. لأنهم او هموها انه يمثل الغواية المطلقة لذلك الذئب المترصد بكل خطواتها البريئة .. واختلفت الأهداف وتأولت المقاصد .. فهي تعلم انها تبحث عن الحب والاحتواء .. وهو يعلم انه يبحث عن المتعة وتجارة الغواني والبغاء ..
أبلغت ليلى ان عليها ارتداء العباءة .. واسدال الخمار .. وتحجيم المساحات المستحقة لها للتعبير عن ما ترنو اليه .. وانتهاج التنسك .. لأنها نوع من انواع الفتنه .. وكل فتنة ضلاله وكل ضلالة بالنار ..[4]

When Little Red Riding Hood took off her cape/cloak, because they made her believe that it embodies absolute seduction by that fox watching each and every innocent step she takes ... and the objectives changed and the intentions were misinterpreted ... for she knows that she is looking for love and shelter ... and the fox knows that it is looking for pleasure and prostitution...

When Little Red Riding Hood was told that she has to wear the cloak ... and cover with the veil ... and limit the space given to her to express her desires ... and that she has to be a monk ... because she is a form of seduction ... and that any seduction is a stray act and any stray act leads to hell...

The above is a prose which references the fable "Little Red Riding Hood" and which puts forth questions related to gender roles and sexuality. The fox is already mentioned above, but it occupies a different role in the second part of the post. The text establishes feminist ideas and articulates issues one encounters when growing up oppressed and sexualised—with an emphasis on the notions of purity and virginity. The third part is written as a poem and is followed by a reply in the same form from a reader, which I will discuss in the chapter on participatory culture.

كوني جميله ليحبك
كوني رقيقه القلب هينة المعشر ليحبك
كوني ربة منزل وطباخه ماهره يشهد لك بالبنان ليحبك
كوني مدبرة لأموره اليومية والمعيشيه والماديه ليحبك
كوني ام حنون وزوجة رؤوم .... ليحبك
كوني سخيه معه واحظي ماله وعرضه وبيته في غيابه ليحبك
ظلمك التاريخ يا حواء .. وباع لك سيرة الجواري بقليل من الحب
سؤال على هامش اللائحة التي قد تطول
اين النصائح المقدمة له!![5]

Be beautiful so that he will love you
Be gentle-hearted and easy to live with so that he will love you

---

[4] http://al-zain.blogspot.com/2011_02_01_archive.html, last accessed December 26, 2011.
[5] http://al-zain.blogspot.com/2011_02_01_archive.html, last accessed December 26, 2011.

Be an excellent housewife and cook [...] so that he will love you
Be a manager of his daily living and financial affairs so that he will love you
Be a loving mother and a forgiving wife ... so that he will love you
Be generous with him and protect his wealth and honour his house/family in his absence so that he will love you
History has not been just to you, O Eve ... and it sold you the stories of female slaves in return for a little love
A question on the margins of the list that might be too long
Where are the advice given to him!![6]

Here again gender identity is the topic of the text. Instead of describing the narrator's appearance, the poem lists mannerisms and personality traits that women ought to display or possess to be desirable to their male counterparts. The fourth part is a dialogue written in dialect. In it, two people are speaking to each other and each person's speech is marked by different colours of red or grey. White is chosen as a colour for stage directions.

سؤال وجه لي اليوم وجعلني اصمت لبرهة
" شنو البس له اليوم؟؟"
"مدري .. مو المفروض تلبسين له احمر !!"
"واذا فيه عمى الوان !!"
"هاااا .. شلون يعني ؟؟"
"ما يشوف اللون الأحمر "
صمت .. صمت ... صمت
"عيل شلون يشوف اللون الأحمر اصلاً؟"
" يقول ان يشوفه رمادي "
" .. اها!"
.. صمت
"لبسي رمادي عيل"
تفكر
"صاجه .. ما فرقت .. ويقول له لابسه احمر ."[7]

---

[6] A reply to this poem can be found in the comment section. The content of this literary piece is worth discussing. The language is very refined compared to writings in forums. The political message is transformed into a personal narrative and first-hand encounter. Of interest here is the fact that the commentator has chosen to respond through poetry. In the chapter on participation culture, more on interaction in online writing is discussed.

[7] http://al-zain.blogspot.com/2011_02_01_archive.html, last accessed December 26, 2011.

A question that was posed to me today and made me quiet for a bit:
"What should I wear for him today?"
"I don't know ... aren't you supposed to wear red for him!!"
"What if he is colour blind!!"
"Ha!! What does that mean??"
"He does not see the colour red"
Silence ... silence ... silence
"How does he then see the colour red?"
"He says he sees it as grey."
"Ha! ..."
Silence ...
"So, put on grey then, kid!"
She is thinking.
"True ... It doesn't matter ... I will tell him I am wearing red."

This section is presented as a dialogue using internal thoughts, rhetorical questions, and metaphors related to the language of love. While the last two parts of the blog post deal with how society perceives women and how women are expected to act, this part occurs between two protagonists and shows two things: that while the woman has internalised society's expectations, she has also exercised agency to emancipate herself from these very expectations.

The fifth part shows separate lines in staccato form and resembles a prose poem.

تويتر
مسج منك ..
مكالمة هاتفية ..
نقاش مثري ..
نقاش آخر عقيم ..
اوراق ..
استلام وارد .. توزيع صادر
كتاب موجه للوزير ..
مواعيد مؤجله
لقاءات بعيده .[8]

Twitter...
A message from you...
A telephone call...

[8] http://al-zain.blogspot.com/2011_02_01_archive.html, last accessed December 26, 2011.

An enriching discussion…
Another futile discussion…

Papers…
Incoming received … outgoing distributed
A letter addressed to the minister…
Postponed appointments…
Long-term meetings

This prose poem is narrated in the first person, reads like a list of things to do, and stands as a reminder of passing time.
The sixth part directly addresses the readers.

كنت اتمنى اكتب شيئا قريبا من رومانسيتي .. تشبهها نوعا ما ..
شيئا غارقا بالعشق .. يحكي سيرة الحب .. ويتغنى مع ام كلثوم بألف ليلة وليلة .. وانت عمري .. وربما بعيد عنك
ولكن .. يا اصدقائي ..
اكتشفت انني في عهد الثورات .. والحراك السياسي اليومي ..
قد شحت انسكابات قلبي .. واضحت مشاعري عنيده
تبا لهذا العصر المتعب ..
وتبا لوعود اللقاءات التي لن تتحقق .[9]

I wished I could write something that would come close to my romanticism … that would be like it to some extent…
Something drowned in love … that would tell the story of love … and sing to Umm Kulthoum "Alf Laila wal Laila" and "Inta Umri" and maybe "Ba'eed Annak"
But … my friends
I discovered that in the age of revolutions … and the daily political turmoil
My heart's outpourings have become scarce … and my feelings have become stubborn
God damn this tiring age…
and God damn the promises of meeting that will not materialize.

This paragraph references a cultural cannon by reciting songs that stand for desire and longing. The author frames her romantic text in the political and historic context of the Egyptian uprisings of 2011. Many topics are

---

[9] http://al-zain.blogspot.com/2011_02_01_archive.html, last accessed December 26, 2011.

addressed in one blog post; political and romantic context are part of a deeper discussion of the writer's perspectives and emotions. The text is followed by a comment section with 45 comments. About half of the comments are from readers and the other half are replies from the author. Many of the commentators have their own blogs, as can be seen in the links connected to the commentators' names. Comments by readers vary in nature; most creative are the replies to the poem that mimic its poetic form; the variety of styles and topics shows a level of sophistication in thought and writing.

While the above example is a great source for the analysis of narration in Arabic literary blogs, a theoretical framework will lead to a better understanding of the use of narrative styles and language in forums. To analyse narration in this blog post, I apply Gerad Genette's theoretical framework. Especially important for literary online texts are his identification of a narrative instance (which refers to the actual moment and context of narration) and narrative levels (which looks at both the acts narrated as well as the act of narration itself). Within his work the text is seen as part of a larger structure of the blog. When we look at the narrative instance, the actual moment, and context of the narration, we can see that the temporal setting is around the time of the uprisings in Egypt in 2011/12. It is crucial to keep the time frame in mind for reading the piece in its entirety. The narrative time is set in the present for most parts of the writing, except for descriptions of the uprising from behind the curtain. With respect to narrative levels, we can locate several levels within this one blog post, for example from the setting of the text to internal dialogues. The sequence of events is unclear as there is movement within narrative levels. Further, we also see intertextuality present through the reference made to a popular song. When comparing the blog post with earlier printed literature, differences in style can be seen.

Sabry Hafez describes the language used in Egyptian literature of the 1990s as fragmented and fractured. New narratives are used and epistemological mazes are part of the text.[10] This is in stark contrast to online contemporary literary text. In these newly distributed texts, narration is rather straightforward (either first- or third-person) and plots are mostly linear.

---

[10] Sabry Hafez, "The Aesthetics of the Closed Horizon. The Transformation of the City and the Novel in Egypt Since 1990", in Stephan Guth and Gail Ramsay (eds.) *From New Values to New Aesthetics Turning Points in Modern Arabic Literature, 2. Postmodernism and Thereafter*, Wiesbaden 2011, pp. 109–138, p. 18.

Text in Context: Forums, Short Stories, and Storytelling

Works by other researchers on narration in digital literature have been instrumental to examining the style of writing and narration in the above-mentioned sample texts. Beyond the facets explored above, aspects of self-referentiality and autofiction as well as the contrast of online literature with literature from the 1990s also add much-needed rigour to our analysis. N. Kathrine Hayles (2008) puts things into perspective by noting that printed literature also has a basis in electronic files, since it is first typed on computers. Accordingly, it is not entirely different from digital text.[11] Loss Pequeño Glazier (2002) points out that literary practice in digital poetry is often not ground-breaking, but is still oriented towards techniques in use before the emergence of the World Wide Web.[12] This appears to be particularly true for Arabic online literature, where digital narration is similar to printed literature. What *is* different is digital text's personal approach, self-referentiality, and use of language, which is discussed in the subsequent paragraphs in connection with the autofictional character of stories. The interactive and communicative quality of narration in online literature forums is a continuation of practices in earlier works.[13]

When differentiating between forums and blogs, it can be said that in forums it is much more common to post traditionally structured short stories in a variety of styles. Online readers are used to reading short texts which are structured in a few paragraphs.[14] Therefore, the internet is particularly conducive for literary production of this kind and it is only natural that stories are produced and structured according to the nature of their medium. Short stories in forums are often organised in a similar structure: an initial incident occurs, the setting and characters are briefly described, complications arise, a climax is reached, and the initial problem is finally resolved.

---

[11] N. Katherine Hayles, *Electronic Literature: New Horizons for the Literary*, Notre Dame 2008.
[12] Loss Pequeno Glazier, *Digital poetics*, Tuscaloosa 2002.
[13] Interactive means here the users' ability to participate in reading the texts through clicking on pictures and links. Communicative means that the readers can be in a dialogue about the texts and have a discussion in the comment section.
[14] Cf. Tom Johnson, "Less Text, Please: Contemporary Reading Behaviors and Short Formats", January 21, 2011. http://idratherbewriting.com/2011/01/21/contemporary-reading-behaviors-favor-short-formats/, last accessed January 2, 2012.

The distribution of stories in forums seems to have become more popular from the end of 2004 onwards.[15] Differing from their printed predecessors, the interactive part of stories as well as the "storytelling" character add a new dimension to conventional storytelling. The composition and narration, in particular, are often close to oral traditions or even to performances of a basic plot on stage.[16] Storytelling is a great art form and an essential part of culture, carried out by experienced and accomplished storytellers—it is thus interesting to look at forum literature as a digital adaptation of storytelling. This form of storytelling can be found in online literature from other countries, but the sample texts selected here can be interpreted to continue traditional forms of storytelling that have been performed for centuries in all Arabic-speaking countries. Tarek El-Ariss points out that "current literary practices generate new meaning but also identify hitherto unexplored intertextual trajectories that reflect and mediate our return to the past".[17] Digital storytelling can be seen as one such development moving forward in its intertextuality while not losing touch with earlier works.

Knut Lundby edited a volume on the subject of digital storytelling in 2008.[18] The collection deals with various aspects of digital storytelling such as narrative, authorship, and authority, and views on authenticity: these aspects apply across socio-cultural contexts form in the Arab-speaking world, and are therefore part of my analysis. Birgit Hertberg Kaare and Lundby (2008) make clear that digital storytelling should not be seen as equivalent to oral storytelling or written narratives—this is also in line with my finding that storytelling in the Gulf may be inspired by oral

---

[15] Many of the various forums seem to present more literary production from 2004/5 on.

[16] Online literature resembles the "storytelling" of oral tradition in that stories are sometimes changed a little when retold on different platforms. When I asked online writers during my research whether they see themselves in the tradition of storytellers, they all rejected the idea and explained that there is no connection between traditional storytelling at the tea house and what they are doing. This contrasts with the self-perception of poetry websites and poetry TV shows that always present a connection with the past. Examples for that can be the TV show "Prince of Poets) that is produced in Abu Dhabi www.princeofpoets.com.

[17] Tarek El-Ariss, *Trials of Arab Modernity: Literary Affects and the New Political*, 2013, p. 179.

[18] Knute Lundby, Digital Storytelling, Mediatized Stories. Self-representation in New Media, New York 2008.

storytelling, but cannot be seen as identical to traditional forms of storytelling in the region.[19]

Simon Jargy describes a variety of oral poetry in the Gulf region and shows that even if there are fixed rules there is room for improvisation.[20] Still, the particular use of this technique indicates a connection between the act of performance in an offline context and its re-application in online media. What is new in digital media is enhancement through the use of multimedia elements such as pictures and audio files and interactions with the audience across physical space. Eman Younis works on YouTube poetry and highlights "the role of cheerleader" in the relationship between the Arab Uprisings and video clip poetry.[21] In her work she describes the use of a large variety of visual elements that contribute to underlining the messages of the poets.

An emerging trend of Arabic online literature in forums in the Gulf is the "travelling" story. This means that users post their favourite stories on many forums. As a result, these stories appear in multiple places and are circulated at different times all over the Arabic-speaking world. This also resembles traditional oral stories, since these online stories are transmitted from one (virtual) place to another. In the chapters *Participatory Culture* and *Challenges of Online Distribution*, I will use tables to illustrate these repostings. The texts published interact not only with print literature, but also with a local literary category, *nabaṭī* poetry, which is spreading in the region (on this genre, cf., among others, Saad Abdullah Sowayan, *Nabati Poetry: The Oral Poetry of Arabia*, 1985). This poetry in colloquial language has a great tradition in the region. It is generally accepted as a form of art and presented in front of a live audience, on the radio and televisions shows, as well as online and in printed books. Here, the use of colloquial language is a return to traditional local culture, and is therefore not an innovation but a kind of renaissance.[22] Certainly, these stories transmit messages either purely for entertainment, they can

---

[19] Birgit Hertberg Kaare and Knut Lundby, "Mediatized lives. Autobiography and assumed authenticity in digital storytelling", in Knut Lundby (ed.), *Digital Storytelling, Mediatized Stories. Self-representation in New Media*, New York 2008, pp. 105–122, p. 107.

[20] Simon Jargy, "Sung Poetry in the Oral Tradition of the Gulf Region and the Arabian Peninsula", in *Oral Tradition*, 4/1–2, Columbia 1989, pp. 174–188.

[21] Eman Younis. Manifestations of the Arab Spring in Literature: "Video Clip Poems" on YouTube as a Model. *Journalism and Mass Communication*, 6, 33–42. https://doi.org/10.17265/2160-6579/2016.01.005, p. 35.

[22] P.G. Emery, "Nabaṭī", in *Encyclopaedia of Islam*, 2nd ed., vol. 7, 1993, p. 838.

have educational elements in them or transport political messages. All of them are embedded in a socio-cultural context wherein the message stands within or against social norms and traditions.

Style of Writing and Narration

One example of a literary genre that was distributed in print shortly before the internet became prevalent and more accessible is Egyptian literature of the new generation of the 1990s. Christian Junge examines aspects of self-referentiality within this literary category, comparing online literature to earlier genres, and looking at autofictional characteristics in novels.[23] The same can be found in some of the literary texts in forums and blogs. In blogs, the boundary between fiction and fact is blurred as authors mix political thoughts with literary texts; here, readers might have difficulties distinguishing fiction from other forms of texts. Autofictionality should be studied in relation to authenticity. In forums, an autofictional touch sometimes gives the story a more authentic feel. Related to Junge's findings in print, Teresa Pepe works on autofictionality in Egyptian blogs, and identifies three characteristics of narration styles within her sources: authors that publish with pseudonyms, the self-conscious narrator, and hoaxes.[24]

Kaare and Lundby (2008) studied "assumed authenticity in digital storytelling".[25] They make clear that autobiographical writing is narrated based on circumstances.[26] They conclude that there is no guarantee for authenticity in digital narrations as well as "disparate types of expressions and reflections".[27] In my examination of sources I came to the same result of a variety of online literary texts. The question of authenticity is important to scholars and readers alike and is expressed in autofictional characteristics that I discuss below. As we will see in the example discussing *layout*

---

[23] Christian Junge, "I Write, Therefore I Am. Metafiction as Self-Assertion in Mustafa Dhikri's 'Much Ado About a Gothic Labyrinth'", in Angelika Neuwirth, Andreas Pflitsch, and Barbara Winckler (eds.), *Arabic Literature: Postmodern Perspectives*, London 2010, pp. 444–460.

[24] Teresa Pepe, "When Writers Activate Readers. How the autofictional blog transforms Arabic literature", *Journal of Arabic and Islamic Studies* 15 (2015): 73–91, p. 84.

[25] Birgit Hertberg Kaare and Knut Lundby, "Mediatized lives. Autobiography and assumed authenticity in digital storytelling", in Knut Lundby (ed.), *Digital Storytelling, Mediatized Stories. Self-representation in New Media*, New York 2008, pp. 105–122.

[26] Ibid., p. 109.

[27] Ibid., p. 120.

and style, authenticity plays a vital role in forums too—in some cases, the authenticity of forum posts needs to be proven by photographic evidence.

When it comes to the original sources that I study, autofictional elements can be seen in the introduction of forum short stories. Frequently, they start out with an introductory statement in which the narrator explains that he or she has heard the story somewhere and felt the need to share it because it was interesting or entertaining. I chose the story "How was she killed?" as being representative of stories posted in forums because it received a lot of feedback and reposting. It exemplifies how texts are changed by various users and are transmitted through forums. It also provides an example of the intertextual practice of using pictures. The story is supposed to be based on an actual event, but for literary purposes it is altered. Ultimately, it does not matter whether it is fictional. The introduction is already enough to capture the reader's attention and satisfy his or her voyeuristic desires. The first time the story was posted it was prefaced with an introduction that explains how the narrator got to know about the story, making clear that there is a personal connection to the described events. For the narrator it is important to stress that the story is 100 percent true and genuine—however, because it is narrated differently, the story might turn out to be 99 percent factual as certain facts might have been altered.[28]

Examples of simple narration can be found in stories published in forums. In the section that dealt with the story "Love in a Loveless Age" an example of a simple narration is represented in the first and last sections. The last paragraph is also particularly directed at the reader and establishes a connection. In style and narration, forums posts are much simpler and linear than preceding printed texts from the 1990s as described in Junge's and Hafez's articles. Varieties are present in forums and blogs, and blog texts often offer more literary depth that reminds the reader of earlier printed stories.

Stories in forums, in particular, tend to show a relatively homogeneous style of narration. Narrators are mostly omniscient and adopt the first-person or third-person voice; time is arranged chronologically. The comment function makes narration much more interactive and instantly more personal. In blogs this may also be important as it is apparent in the example where Alzain and the commentator communicate. The aspect of communication will be picked up again in *Participatory Culture*. As a stylistic

---

[28] http://www.adbuae.com/vb/archive/index.php/t-4491.html, last accessed December 30, 2011.

choice, this particular example is told in questions. The narrator asks in an accusatory tone why and how the villain was able to commit the crime. In later repostings the introduction was dropped and the story moved directly into the action. I have not been able to determine with certainty why the introduction was later dismissed, but pictures added in repostings may replace the introduction as "proof" of authenticity. When Pepe writes about narrators in blogs from Egypt, she highlights the pseudonym and the self-conscious author which are also represented in the kind of literary texts from the Gulf and other Arabic-speaking countries. In my sources the pseudonym is more common in forums than in blogs, but can be found across all digital literary texts.

Looking at Language and Dialect

The range of formal and colloquial language in my samples highlights the variety of language used in online literary texts. I demonstrate global impacts on online literary text and describe the discussions around the question of the quality of literary language in recent literature from Arab countries, part of which is the MSA/fuṣḥā versus dialect issue. Traditionally, the language used for literary writing in Arabic is either classical Arabic or Modern Standard Arabic (MSA), while much of the online texts are written in less formal varieties of the language.

MSA and Colloquial Arabic in Forums and Blogs

In the dialectical-relational approach by Norman Fairclough, it is established that language is shaped by its social functions. The theory looks at the relationship between elements of social practices and dialect.[29] As far as language use goes there are three dominant ways to write online. Language in online literary texts divides authors into those who use colloquial, those who stick to MSA, and those who use a hybrid of the two. Three major groups can be differentiated: (a) blogs that are written in MSA, (b) literary texts that are mostly in MSA but with dialogues in dialect, and (c) stories—posted mostly in forums—that are written completely in dialect. The use of foreign words in Arabic script is also increasing in literary language online.

---

[29] Norman Fairclough, Methods of Critical Discourse Analysis, second edition, edited by Ruth Wodak, Michael Meyer, 2009, p. 27.

Literature, newspapers, TV, and official occasions are the only places/instances where formal Arabic (MSA or Classical Arabic) is used. "Correct/eloquent" (*faṣīḥ*) Arabic is highly valued and of great importance for literary scholars and academics. However, colloquial language has been present in literary texts for more than a century[30] and is increasingly in use when narrating dialogues. For example, Rajāʾ ʿA. al-Ṣāniʿ, in her bestselling novel *Banāt al-Riyāḍ* (The Girls of Riyadh, 2006), uses colloquial language to make her dialogues sound more natural. Naguib Mahfouz used the same stylistic element throughout his novels. Many literary texts in online media are partially or completely written in dialect,[31] much to the disapproval of conservative critics. In public discussions, the subject of using dialect appears frequently. Alireza Doostdar emphasises, "The main critics of 'vulgar' language and culture in *weblogestan* have been journalists, writers, and literary critics (…)."[32] But the audience do not seem to agree with these critics; blog literature and other online literary products are still widely read. Colloquial language is especially prevalent in forums where correct spelling is, from the outset, considered unimportant. Creating a specific atmosphere and conveying a distinct message are the goals of stories in forums. Internet language is less formal than language used in printed literature. Without an editor or copy-editor, every writer decides individually which variety of language to use and how important it is to stick to conventions of grammar, spelling, and diction. Often, even reposted stories are left uncorrected in spelling and grammar, whether because the reposters do not care about these aspects or because they accept them as a stylistic means that creates an impression of immediacy and urgency. For Egyptian blog literature it is the same as in the Gulf: mistakes in grammar and spelling are common and stand for spontaneity

---

[30] The use of dialect has also been present in literature before internet was part of mainstream culture. In theatre plays this was observable already more than 100 years ago. More on that can be read in the collection *The Performance of the Comic in Arabic Theatre Cultural Heritage, Western Models and Postcolonial Hybridity*, edited by Mieke Kolk, and Freddy Decreus (co-editor) 2005. www.artsafrica.org/archive/documents/docu-01/002_comic.pdf, last accessed January 3, 2012.

[31] Ivan Panovic writes more about dialect and the internet in Egypt in his analysis "Arabic in a Time of Revolution: sociolinguistic notes from Egypt" in *Media in the Middle East: Activism, Politics, and Culture* (2017) edited by Nele lenze, Charlotte Schriwer and Zubaidah Abdul Jalil, 2017.

[32] This example is from Iran but can also be applied to my field. Alireza Doostdar, "The Vulgar Spirit of Blogging: On Language, Culture, and Power in Persian Weblogestan", in *American Anthropologist 106*, no. 4, 2004, pp. 651–662, p. 658.

in works.[33] Culturally, the Gulf is influenced not only by its immediate neighbours, but also by European and American culture on the one hand, and South East Asian, Korean, and Japanese culture on the other. Lebanon and Egypt are also impacted by other languages. In Lebanon, it would be French and English and in Egypt it would be mainly English. People from all over the world come to work in the Gulf countries. Their presence influences the use of language in everyday life as well as in literature. The influence of Indian languages dates back long before the discovery of oil and the huge waves of immigration to the Gulf that accompanied increasing construction and wealth. Hindi began entering the language with the rise of seagoing trade centuries ago. Clive Holes emphasises that the long-standing contact between India and the Gulf region has influenced the Gulf Arabic dialect. In addition to Hindi and Urdu, other languages such as Persian and English have an impact on the language used in everyday life.[34] It still needs to be studied how much influence Tagalog has on the current language, given that a lot of the domestic workers and child caregivers are from the Philippines.

Digital literature has had a global flavour from its beginning, as Funkhouser states: "Digital poetry has always been a multi-continental, decentralized practice. Works have been created in many languages."[35] Using different styles of language as well as foreign words is thus a common element. As a manifestation of global influence on Gulf society—and the Arabic-speaking world in general, many stories in forums are coloured with English phrases. In all the stories I examine, such English phrases are written in Arabic characters.[36] That English is written with Arabic letters is interesting because in chat-room Arabic it is the other way around: Arabic

---

[33] Teresa Pepe, "When Writers Activate Readers. How the autofictional blog transforms Arabic literature", Journal of Arabic and Islamic Studies 15 (2015): 73–91, p. 87.
[34] Clive Holes "Gulf States", in Versteegh, K., Woidich M., and Zaborski, A. (eds.), *Encyclopaedia of Arabic Language and Linguistics Vols 1: A-ED*, Leiden, Boston and Cologne 2006, pp. 210–216.
[35] Christopher Funkhouser, "Digital Poetry: A Look at Generative, Visual, and Interconnected Possibilities in its First Four Decades", in Ray Siemens and Susan Schreibman (eds.), *Companion to Digital Literary Studies*, Oxford 2008, http://www.digitalhumanities.org/companion/view?docId=blackwell/9781405148641/9781405148641.xml&chunk.id=ss1-5-11&toc.depth=1&toc.id=ss1-5-11&brand=9781405148641_brand, last accessed January 27, 2012.
[36] "Ḥiṣṣa and the Taxi Driver" is also examined in Chap. 4, *Who are the Actors?* http://www.alghat.com/archive/index.php/t-614.html, last accessed December 30, 2011.

is transcribed into Latin letters.[37] Other languages and dialects are also used in the stories. Often, a character's use of a sociolect or dialect marks his cultural background. Later in this chapter the story of "Ḥiṣṣa and the Taxi Driver", is examined in more detail—for now it serves as an example of a protagonist using language specific to migrant workers in the Gulf. For example, the driver calls the young women "mama".

مريم : رفيق سير قاعة الأعراس الفلانيه.
حميد مستغرب وحاير ويكلم نفسه شو اسوي شو هالورطه والله فشله, صرنا رفيق بعد, يالله مشي.
حميد: زين ماما.
مريم : وهي محرجه أنا مب أمك.[38]

> Mariam: *Rafiq*,[39] drive to such and such wedding hall
> Hameed finds it strange and is perplexed and asks himself 'what do I do?' 'what is this situation?' Surely he is embarrassed, started to be a 'Rafiq' after all. Let's go, it's O.K.
> Hameed: Ok, mama
> Mariam: And it is embarrassing. I am not your mother.

Here, language is used to define the character's status in society and ethnic background. The stereotype is that most taxi drivers in the Gulf are from South Asia and this is mirrored in the language used here. In blogs, it is more common to find texts written in a mixture of colloquial and MSA or entirely in MSA. Writing in dialects leads to a regionalisation of literature, rather than making thoughts and feelings accessible to a bigger audience. This is due to the fact that not everyone understands all Arabic dialects in comparison to a general comprehension of formal language. However, due to the extensive movie production, Egyptian dialect is widely understood in most countries. Using dialect underlines the personal side of online literature and contradicts the assumption that the internet is encouraging the spread of cultural goods to a worldwide audience. Gail Ramsay argues that Egyptian bloggers in particular are making

---

[37] More on the phenomenon of using English letters or words in Arabic can be found on the blog http://arabizi.wordpress.com/, last accessed January 17, 2012.
[38] http://www.alghat.com/archive/index.php/t-614.html, last accessed December 30, 2011.
[39] Rafiq means buddy or friend and is a way to address an unknown male.

deliberate choices when choosing between writing in dialect and MSA.[40] Still, blogospheres in both the Arab world and elsewhere serve a limited region or subject and tends to be limited to a more or less isoglossic region. It is difficult to generalise whether the literary quality of language is poorer or richer in blogs and forums than it is in print, because the styles are individual and quite varied. Blog posts on "Muawiyah"[41] are often linguistically more elaborate than, for instance, *Banāt al-Riyāḍ*. Posts published in forums differ greatly in language and style between "Muawiya" or Zain compared to *Banāt al-Riyāḍ*.[42] One of the major issues here is that readers of digital works approach electronic literature with expectations that were formed by print media, and thus readers try to impose certain criteria of forms, conventions, and modes on electronic literature.[43] Language and style are individually chosen in both printed and online literature. There is not *one* definition of what constitutes good literature, and the classification of high literature or trivial literature is often debatable. As Reuven Snir puts it:

> A literary text may be defined as any text that in a given community has been imbued with cultural value and that allows for high levels of complexity and significance in the way it is constructed (…) text perceived as literary by one

---

[40] Gail Ramsay. (2013). What kind of Arabic and why? Language in Egyptian blogs. Orientalia Suecana, Uppsala. 61(Supplement): 49–87, p. 50.

[41] http://www.muawiyah.com/—the last time the blog was updated was in October 2011 and after that it was taken offline.

[42] *Banāt al-Riyāḍ* was one inspiration for conducting research on online literature. It was written by young female Saudi author Rajāʾ ʿAbdallāh al-Ṣāniʿ and reached great popularity in the Middle East as well as in many other countries as it was translated into more than 18 languages. A change in printed literary production could be observed after the publication of *Banāt al-Riyāḍ* (Girls of Riyadh) in 2006. The novel mirrors the openness of the web as chapters were arranged appearing to be emails, sent through a yahoo news group to all Saudi users. After its publication the number of printed literature increased to the double of what was there before. This is also due to the fact that writers could actually see that Rajāʾ ʿAbdallāh al-Ṣāniʿ was not penalised for her publication. Possibly, *Banāt al-Riyāḍ* marks a transition of literary style in the Gulf. Making the style of online literary texts more popular within a broader readership in print. Also introducing it to an audience outside the Gulf, even outside the Middle East, and outside the internet.

[43] N. Katherine Hayles, *Electronic Literature: New Horizons for the Literary*, Notre Dame 2008, p. 4.

culture or community are seen as non-literary by another, and one and the same text may also change from the former category to the latter an vice versa.[44]

When looking at the literary quality of digital stories, Friedlander argues that the global phenomenon of digital stories is "not so much 'bad' stories as new stories suited to new kinds of times".[45]

From the examples that I studied, it appears that dialect is used more often in literary texts in forums than in literary texts in blogs. The use of dialect is one aspect of literality that it is often discussed by critics. In blogs and forums a variety of language usage is observable. Colloquial and vernacular language is used in written form in complete texts or just in dialogues in order to underline social settings. The particular function of dialogues will be highlighted in the following because they are often incorporated in stories and blog posts.

Dialogues in Online Short Stories

The use of dialogue is a feature even more common, space consuming and impactful in stories posted in forums than in texts in blogs or in print. The story "Ḥiṣṣa and the Taxi Driver" that was briefly mentioned earlier makes use of much dialogue.[46] Dialogue performs a number of functions in stories. It enhances the setting, creates the mood, helps to set the tone, and develops the characters by revealing their desires and motivations. Dialogues are thus intensifying elements that bring the story to life and make it appear more "real". Dialogue is essential in reflecting the general

---

[44] Reuven Snir, *Modern Arabic Literature. A Theoretical Framework*, Edinburgh University press, 2017. p. 8.

[45] Larry Friedlander, "Narrative strategies in a digital age. Authorship and authority", in Knut Lundby (ed.), *Digital Storytelling, Mediatized Stories. Self-representation in New Media*, New York 2008, pp. 177–196, p. 181.

[46] But also other short stories in forums can serve as examples: قصه مؤثره لفتاة على الانترنت
السر المـخفي؟ http://www.hbktmlkni.com/vb/archive/index.php/t-2855.html.
أوطـــانك غربتي http://www.alamuae.com/story/showthread.php?t=385 D
http://www.alamuae.com/story/showthread.php?t=396
حب في الــــيونان http://www.alamuae.com/story/showthread.php?t=391
ليه عمري مالقى ليبرده دفى الا دفاكي؟ http://www.alamuae.com/story/showthread.php?t=395
نار الغيرة تحرق رجلا http://www.alamuae.com/story/showthread.php?t=394

All stories were last accessed December 15, 2009. These links just serve as examples, there is an infinite number of short stories in colloquial language that make use of dialogues in forums from the Gulf.

mood of the youth and in conveying characters' social status and the values of society. These numerous dialogues also include humour and word play. Additionally, language in dialogues is typically vernacular language. The witty and humorous character of dialogue is exemplified in the final part of "Our supermarket is closed". This is a short story written on the Kuwaiti blog *t7l6m.com* in 2011. It intends to contrast the ignorance of wealthy locals and the gratitude of refugees using the phrase "It doesn't carry brioche (pastry)?", as will be shown in more detail in the following. Socio-political elements take a great part in this blog post and they serve to educate the readership by raising awareness of privilege.

The story "Our supermarket is closed" displays the use of dialogue as well as colloquial Arabic and MSA.[47] It is narrated in the first person. A male protagonist intends to go to the supermarket, but finds it closed. Inquiring why it is closed, he learns that the supermarket is hosting Somalis who found refuge in it. The narrator describes in detail men, women, and children feasting on the food offered to them and expressing joy over what they eat. Talking with one of the Somali men, he learns that for poor people, his country is paradise because one can afford to eat and shop. The narrator answers that this is truly great and that he thanks God for the circumstances he lives in. After leaving the mosque, he meets locals outside, who indicate that despite all the luxury, they are still not satisfied. He is disappointed by their ingratitude. The story and all its dialogues are written in MSA except for the last dialogue with the locals, which is written in Kuwaiti dialect. The text is followed by 12 comments, half of which are the author's replies to the audience.

قال:"أنت من أهل هذه الجنة"

أجبت "بل من أهل هذا البلد"

قال:"اعلم إننا محظوظون فلا نزال أحياء في هذه الدنيا ولم نموتْ/نهلكْ كما هلك جوعا آلاف من شعبنا ولكن بلدكم جنة ويكفي سوقكم هذا ففيه سلع لم نراها من قبل ,ولم نسمع بها, بل ولم يخطر في بالنا وجودها في الدنيا فهنيئا لكم بلدكم"

قلت:الحمدلله فنحن في خير غامر , ... السلبيات ,وأدعو الله أن نحمده على هذه النعمة ونحن ننعم بها لا أن نقدرها بعد أن نفقدها.[48]

---

[47] http://t7l6m.com/category/%D9%82%D8%B5%D8%B5/, last accessed December 30, 2011.

[48] http://t7l6m.com/2011/08/08/%D8%AC%D9%85%D8%B9%D9%8A%D8%AA%D9%86%D8%A7-%D9%85%D8%BA%D9%84%D9%82%D8%A9/, last accessed December 26, 2011. Text part seems to be missing in the last two lines of the original source.

He said, "Are you a resident of this paradise?"
[I replied,] "Rather, I am a resident of this country"
[He said, "You should know] we are lucky, for we are still alive in this world and did not die like thousands of our people who starved to death. Your country is paradise and this market of yours is the best proof, for it has goods we have never seen; we may have heard of them before (but) it never crossed our minds that they might exist in this world. Congratulations to your country."
[I said,] "Thank God, we live in prosperity, in spite of all the negativities. And I pray to God to thank Him for this blessing as we are enjoying it, rather than to appreciate it after we lose it."

In this first paragraph, the narrator is in a dialogue with a Somali man and uses MSA. Political refugees are introduced to the story and showed gratefulness and local hospitality. The wealth of Kuwait is set in contrast to the poor living conditions in Somali, making the reader aware of social and political injustice.

خرجت ... من الجمعية فإذا المواقف ملينة بالسيارات,والناس تخرج من البوابة الأخري يتبعهم عمال يدفعون عربات ملينة بالأكياس ... لم أصدق عينيّ فعدت مرة أخرى إلى الداخل.فوجئت ... برجل بملابس رياضية ينهر موظف الجمعية "شالسالفه كل الحليب بتاريخ أمس" .... تبعته إمرأة مواصلة النقد والتذمر "شنو هالجمعيه ما فيها بريوش" ....
وقفت في منتصف الجمعية وصرخت"يا ناس حرام عليكم.حمدوا ... ربكم ترى النعمة زوّاله"[49]

I left the cooperative to find the parking lot bustling with cars, as people left from the other gate followed by workers pushing carts filled with bags. I could not believe my eyes, so I went back inside again. (…) a man wearing gym clothes scolding the supermarket worker, "All the milk expired yesterday!" A woman followed suit, criticizing and complaining, "What kind of supermarket is this? It doesn't carry brioche?"
I stood in the middle of the supermarket and yelled out loud, "O people, (…) thank God, for this blessing may disappear."

In this second paragraph, the narrator turns away from his conversation with the Somali refugee and speaks in the vernacular to local visitors outside of the supermarket. Here, the dialogue shows a number of uses of language in order to present different forms of communication. The first dialogue is written in MSA and both parties in the conversation speak about a serious subject in a formal language. The second part shows a conversation in colloquial language. Here, a mood is created through the choice of words. The use of language and content of dialogue represents class difference and

[49] Ibid.

understandings of political difference. These dialogues offer perspectives of the narrator and represent the discourse. The story takes on a humorous twist by displaying the ingratitude of the narrators' fellow locals. This later dialogue mirrors a disposition in society. The content of story serves as an educational piece and is supposed to encourage more gratitude. The direct speech emphasises the writer's point of view and expresses involvement—this bridges the distance between the reader and the narrator. Both parts, on narration and on language carry implications that represent discourse in society. The examples show that migration, class, politics, and identity representation are all expressed in the way texts are composed. Dialects, dialogues, and the general framing through narration offer essential information to the reader that is additional to the content. Both are necessary to transport socio-political and cultural notions to the reader.

From the above observations, it is evident that blog literature differs from forum literature. While blog literature often seems carefully composed with language playing an important part, in forums it appears that the intended message is considered more important than literary style as measured by the aesthetic standards of earlier printed texts. Blog literature might not differ greatly from printed literature in the structure of its plots and style of narration, but its interactivity and communicative function are new, as discussed in *Participatory Culture* and *Challenges of Online Distribution*.

Academics have been debating the quality of recently published Arabic novels such as *Banāt al-Riyāḍ* and *ʿImārat Yaʿqūbiyān*. At the 2010 EURAMAL conference, it was debated whether works such as *Banāt al-Riyāḍ* are even worth translating.[50] These novels' language and plots differ from those in "high literature". Some literary products that are not accepted as literature by more conservative critics might fall into the category of popular literature, which reaches a broader audience than its postmodern predecessors/cousins. Holes points out that there are "whole genres of popular literature" that are composed and distributed in Gulf dialect. He continues, "This kind of language is sometimes frowned upon by language purists, but is very popular among ordinary people nonetheless."[51] When it comes to Egyptian and Lebanese dialect the same

---

[50] At the 2010 EURAMAL conference in Rome, recent developments in Arabic literature came up for discussion. A senior male academic said he refused to translate *Banāt al-Riyāḍ* because he did not find its literary quality worthy of translation.

[51] Clive Holes "Gulf States", in Versteegh, K., Woidich M., and Zaborski, A. (eds.), *Encyclopaedia of Arabic Language and Linguistics Vols 1: A-ED*, Leiden, Boston and Cologne 2006, pp. 210–216, p. 214.

criticism is raised. While Egyptian blogs are questioned to have literary value and should be adopted in the literary canon, some of the Egyptian bloggers do not even want to be seen as *literatis*.[52]

A variety of texts and genres are present in blogs. In forums, short stories are popular. Short stories in forums bear resemblances to oral storytelling, since stories are retold and redistributed. The style of writing and narration in online texts does not differ much from printed texts, but other aspects are different. Autofictionality is found in both earlier printed texts and online texts. Simple narration and linear story line are more common in online texts than in printed literary texts from the 1990s or postmodern texts. Online literature makes use of both colloquial and MSA. The literary quality of recent literary texts online and offline is an aspect of a broader academic debate on the use of language. Dialogues are an essential part of short stories in forums. Often they are tinged with humour and function to effuse a particular mood, while their sociolects accentuate the protagonists' backgrounds. Structure, narration, and choice of language are important features of online literature everywhere, and not just in the Gulf region. A distinct style of language is typical of online cultural production, and not only in the region. It will be interesting to see how the use of language in a local and global context and the use of hardware and software will continue to change literary production but also general societal development. To contextualise the emerging literary phenomenon this chapter introduced an impression of language and narration. The above examination presents an initial observation.

---

[52] Teres Pepe Adab-icty 552.

CHAPTER 4

Participatory Culture

The connection among authors, readers, and critics is part of the analysis of this chapter. It first discusses cultural production in Web 2.0 and user-generated text and the benefits of online writing. This serves as a basis to understand the role of writers in online literature in connecting the public and the private. Second, the chapter elaborates on the interpersonal experience of readers who participate in the reposting and remixing of cultural goods. This highlights the importance of "sharing" in online interaction and cultural production; such a practice includes the circulation and redistribution of text, Web 2.0 studies, interactivity, communication, and authorship. Many of these subjects are inherent to online media, and stand in contrast to the static form of printed works.

Participatory Culture, Interaction, and Web 2.0

The possibility of participation distinguishes online literature from print. Examining the role of participatory culture embeds literary texts in a broader context of online content production. The role of the author changes with new tasks that arise. These tasks include designing layout and publicising their own works. This role is closely connected to the dynamics of the public and private spheres that can be contextualised within the newly gained privileges that online media offer. For instance, the audience influences decisions on publicness, which also affects the writing of literary texts.

Participatory Culture

Participatory culture connotes cultural production in which the audience not only consumes a product, but also interacts with the producer. Both the reader and writer can be considered users of the medium. The term "user" may sound passive, but the opposite is true: the act of interaction means that at least two individuals actively contribute to the formation of a newer cultural product. Unlike earlier forms of distribution, these online literary platforms offer a decentralised and less hierarchical platform for interaction. This new liberty easily leads to the assumption that "Web 2.0 is user-controlled".[1] This assumption is debatable, because the fact is that the medium is not completely free of power structures—almost all commonly used applications (*Blogger*, *Twitter*, forums) are owned by corporations. But digital media are much more user-controlled than any other medium before.

As a basis for taking part in online participatory culture, certain preconditions need to be fulfilled. Cultural production online is closely dependent on access to facilities as well as on knowledge of how to use those facilities. Not only is it necessary that the technical utilities are accessible, the user also needs to have enough spare time to create such works.[2] As a consequence, producers of artistic works usually belong to an educated social class that is privileged when it comes to free time. The facilities to participate in user-generated content are well established in the Gulf region, since it is one of the richest regions in the world with a high gross domestic product (GDP) and a young population, giving people more possibilities to create and distribute creative pieces than in poorer countries (e.g. in nearby Yemen). As discussed in the introduction, internet access varies across Arabic-speaking countries, but is sufficient to make users distribute cultural products. Online participatory culture is a global phenomenon, but media usage and media coverage exhibit regional characteristics. This is also true for literature; as Nils Erik Enkvist (1985) underlines, literature has to be viewed against "a situational background". He emphasises that communication as well as "the subject, the occasion, and the relevant cul-

---

[1] Louis Leung, "User-generated content on the Internet: An Examination of Gratifications, Civic Engagement and Psychological Empowerment", *New Media & Society*, 2009, pp. 1327–1347, p. 1329.

[2] Mark Warschauer and Douglas Grimes, "Audience, Authorship, and Artifact: The Emergent Semiotics of Web 2.0", in *Annual Review of Applied Linguistics*, 27, no. 1, 2007, pp. 1–23, p. 15.

tural traditions, fashions as well as taboos"[3] should be considered when dealing with texts. Thus, within my analysis I consider conditions related to the digital divide as well as censorship. Access to a variety of information forces users to make many choices in selecting their sources. Since online media developed rapidly in the last 20 years, users are exposed to constant changes; these include new additions to sources of information as well as the use of applications to work with these media. A generation that grew up with technology and intuitively knows how to deal with it is called *digital natives*.[4] In most of the developed world people grew up as digital natives in the last two decades. Digital natives have an intuitive media usage behaviour compared to their parents' generation, and they integrate contemporary technology in most aspects of everyday life. Hence, internet and mobile phones are catalysts of this new meaning of information for the new generation.[5]

Interactivity in Online Literary Texts

Web 2.0 enables people to distribute works quickly and to interact with other writers and the audience. Warschauer and Grimes underline this, stating that authorship is an increasingly interactive task. They assume that the author has to interact with and join the audience to practice their norms and achieve discursive competence.[6]

Alan Kirby documents another form of interactivity. He makes clear that online media are interactive because of the way users move in the medium. A user navigates through the internet individually, thereby deciding which sites to use, depending on his or her interests: watching videos, listening to music, reading, or participating in a social network. In online

---

[3] Nils Erik Enkvist, "Text and Discourse Linguistics, Rhetoric, and Stylistics", in Teun Adrianus van Dijk, *Discourse and literature*, Amsterdam 1985, p. 16.

[4] More on this in: John Palfrey and Urs Gasser, *Born Digital: Understanding the First Generation of Digital Natives*, New York, 2008.

[5] Nada Mourtada-Sabbah, Mohammed al-Mutawa, John W. Fox and Tim Walters, "Media as Social Matrix in the United Arab Emirates", in Alanoud Alsharekh, Robert Springborg and Sarah Stewart (eds.), *Popular Culture and Political Identity in the Arab Gulf States*, London 2008, pp. 121–142, p. 127.

[6] "Authorship involves not only writing for an audience but also, in essence, joining an audience by entering into a community of practice and acquiring its norms of discourse competence." (Bizzel, 1992) Mark Warschauer and Douglas Grimes, "Audience, Authorship, and Artifact: The Emergent Semiotics of Web 2.0", in *Annual Review of Applied Linguistics* 27, no. 1, 2007, pp. 1–23, p. 4.

literary texts, users have a choice between following links or reading texts chronologically or in some other order. Kirby states that this participation is a cultural process and is "far more intense" than in any medium before.[7] "You click, you punch the keys, you are 'involved', engulfed, deciding." This gives readers a wider choice and also a greater responsibility in selecting what and how to read. Readers do not need to follow pages in sequence, but can instead pick and choose their own way through texts. Due to this freedom of choice and interaction, Kirby assumes that everyone is now part of the literary work and concludes: "You are the text."[8] In its changeability and its independence of institutions, online text is freer than print, but it is still bound to a context of societal norms and cultural standards. These can differ from those in the world outside the internet, but social rules also apply online. Users do not have unlimited freedom in their choice of actions on blogs. Influencing a text is restricted to the administrative rights or possibilities the original writer offers, and consists mostly of a rating button or the comment function. In contrast, texts published on forums are copied, rewritten, or remixed on other platforms. Interaction has broader or narrower limits, depending on the platform approached.

Introduction to and Benefits of Web 2.0

Writing in Web 2.0 is easy, helps to spread texts fast, and is free and open to a variety of cultural products. Participatory culture and user-generated content online have rapidly increased as internet access for average households has gone up. The term Web 2.0 was coined by Tim O'Reilly, who organised a conference on it in 2004.[9] In 2009, the media researcher Louis W. Leung came up with a concise definition:

> Within Web 2.0, the web is seen as a platform for service delivery which emphasizes user control, participation and emergent behaviour and can be defined as a way of creating pages focusing on microcontent and social connections between people.[10]

---

[7] Alan Kirby, "The Death of Postmodernism and Beyond", *Philosophy Now* 58, 2006, http://www.philosophynow.org/issue58/58kirby.htm, accessed November 11, 2011.

[8] Ibid.

[9] Paul Graham, "Web 2.0", November 2005. http://www.paulgraham.com/web20.html, accessed November 11, 2011.

[10] Louis Leung, "User-generated content on the Internet: An Examination of Gratifications, Civic Engagement and Psychological Empowerment", in *New Media & Society*, 2009, pp. 1327–1347, p. 1329.

In his own definition of Web 2.0, O'Reilly emphasises, "Web 2.0 doesn't have a hard boundary, but rather, a gravitational core." It is difficult to pin this term down to one clear description. As O'Reilly explains, it is "a set of principles and practices" that unites various Web 2.0 tools. Blogging can serve as an illustration of these principles. Blogging is usually conducted through a "platform for service delivery", for example a blog host that provides the coded background to blogs. The participation of bloggers and audience make it user-controlled, and it facilitates establishing social connections between people. These aspects of Web 2.0 are also found in other tools such as *Twitter, Instagram, Snapchat,* or *Tumblr,* as in O'Reilly's description of a loosely organised set of practices and principles. All of these platforms share the goal of enabling users to easily and quickly distribute content such as films, audio files, pictures, and texts. They all make it almost effortless for all participants to interact.

Web 2.0 has led to a big leap in online cultural production because it offers easy access to ready-made solutions for distribution. It has not only increased user-generated content, but it has also taken this content a step further by influencing traditional media. It is more conducive than corporate-owned media to the distribution of independent views. However, as we have seen in the 2016 US elections, it can also be manipulated. It influences print media by encouraging cooperation among lay journalists and it increases interactivity in the form of comments and polls. Additionally, most of the traditional media now have a representation online.[11] Critics of Web 2.0, for example Andrew Keen (2008), emphasise that Web 2.0 created a cult of amateurism and encourages narcissism in the digital media.[12] He states that it is a misguided assumption that all user-generated content is equally relevant. As explained in the introductory chapter, I was selective about the sources for my analysis, because for this research not all distributed literature is equally relevant. Since the introduction of Web 2.0 in the mid-2000s, it has become much easier for people with limited knowledge of coding or other relevant skills to distribute cultural elements such as audio files, films, and texts online. Web 2.0 applications provide a possibility to adjust visual elements and personalise the

---

[11] Louis Leung, "User-generated content on the Internet: An Examination of Gratifications, Civic Engagement and Psychological Empowerment", in *New Media & Society*, 2009, pp. 1327–1347, p. 1329.

[12] Andrew Keen, *The Cult of the Amateur: How blogs, MySpace, YouTube, and the rest of today's user-generated media are destroying our economy, our culture, and our values*, Random House 2008.

individual online representation. A variety of themes[13] or layouts and other applications are offered to customise personal representations of cultural production. Additionally, publishing is much faster than in print—these works of art are instantly public. Another difference from print media is that Web 2.0 offers the possibility of intermediality through the use of multimedia applications.

In the countries analysed in this book, the most frequently used tools (at the time of research) for spreading user-generated content are forums and blog hosts such as *Windowslive*, *Maktoob*, *Wordpress*, and *Blogger*. Additionally, writers post their works on *Twitter* and *Tumblr*. Another mode of distribution, but much less frequently used, are facilities such as those provided by the e-publisher *Nashiri.net* in Kuwait and literary criticism on Goodreads.[14] All of these platforms except *Nashiri* and *Maktoob* are intended to serve a worldwide audience. *Maktoob* is owned by *Yahoo!* and was explicitly designed to serve an Arabic writing and reading audience. Furthermore, online publishing is usually[15] free of charge for both author and audience and therefore enables the distribution of cultural products that might not have found a way into print or other forms of distribution because they are deemed unprofitable. Carolyn Guertin, a researcher on culture and technology, examines online distribution from a historical perspective. The phenomenon of easy distribution of thoughts is not new and cannot be solely credited to online media. She points out that the movement of "interactive authorship and personal publishing" started in the 1940s with Xerox machines.[16] It can be argued that interactive writing has happened even before. For instance, in the Dada movement and also within Surrealist circles, as Peter Gendolla and Jörgen Schäfer (2004) clarify.[17] Even if this is a valid point, Xerox publishing was not a

---

[13] A theme is a visual frame for blogs that is provided by the blog host of the platform.

[14] Goodreads is a Web 2.0 application that enables readers of printed literature to share their thoughts on what they just enjoyed reading.

[15] When texts are not published in open media, non-profit, or other free Web 2.0 applications, audiences sometimes have to pay for e-books provided by corporate or other for-profit publishers.

[16] Carolyn Guertin, "Handholding, Remixing, and the Instant Replay: New Narratives in a Postnarrative World", in Ray Siemens and Susan Schreibman (eds.), *Companion to Digital Literary Studies*, Oxford 2008, http://www.digitalhumanities.org/companion/view?docId =blackwell/9781405148641/9781405148641.xml&chunk.id=ss1-5-6, last accessed January 27, 2012.

[17] Peter Gendolla and Jörgen Schäfer, "Auf Spurensuche: Literatur im Netz, Netzliteratur und ihre Vorgeschichte(n)", in *Dichtung Digital*, 2002, http://www.brown.edu/Research/

widespread or mainstream movement. If this was a starting point, it was only with the introduction of the internet and, even more, with the introduction of Web 2.0. that a broader movement in this direction started. Compared with "Xeroxing", online distribution is a mainstream, worldwide phenomenon. As can be observed, distribution of texts without a traditional publisher is not a feature that can be uniquely attributed to online writing platforms, but in contemporary times, similar processes of online writing spread widely all over the world through the net.

USER-GENERATED CONTENT: EXAMPLES FROM KUWAIT

User-generated content is beneficial to producers as well as to users. The distribution of creative products is beneficial on several levels. On the one hand, it can be a stimulus to users and promote a wider debate or simply entertain. On the other hand, the production of user-generated content empowers its producers because they receive feedback in various forms. Interestingly, many user-generated cultural products are made without economic motives, as David Gauntlett points out.[18] Individuals pool their time in order to create something new.[19] One example of this is the non-profit publisher *Nashiri.net*, the first online publishing house in the Gulf, physically located in Kuwait and launched by Hayat Alyaqout, a Kuwaiti freelance writer. "Dār al-Nāshirī" was founded in 2003 and has published more than 120 e-books by about 100 writers. As a non-profit e-publisher, financial benefits are not part of the reward system for either writers or producers.[20] If money is not the source of motivation for online writers, what is? Little is known on this question—especially for online writers of the Arabic-speaking world. For Polish bloggers, the following motivations were found: first, self-expression was relevant[21]; second, social interaction

---

dichtung-digital/2002/05/08-Gendolla-Schaefer/index.htm, last accessed January 3, 2012.

[18] David Gauntlett, *Transforming Audiences 3—introduction by David Gauntlett (Sept 2011)*, August 22, 2011. http://www.youtube.com/watch?v=VQp3q_z47ys, last accessed January 3, 2012.

[19] Yochai Benkler, *The Wealth of Networks: How Social Production Transforms Markets and Freedom*, New Haven 2006, p. 81.

[20] Benkler states that money is typically absent of the majority of projects. Ibid., p. 82.

[21] Trammell, K.D., A. Tarkowski and J. Hofmokl (2004, June) "Rzeczpospolita blogów" "Republic of Blog"], paper presented at the 5th Annual Meeting of the Association of Internet Researchers, Brighton, September 19–22, 2006.

played a role; third was "entertainment"; fourth was "passing the time"; fifth was information; and sixth was "professional advancement".[22] These motivations can also be presumed to be behind literary works posted online in the countries that I study. Self-expression and social interaction seem to be the most important factors in posting creative content online. In the survey that I conducted with users from some of the GCC states, writers say that they also blog because they want to practise their writing to be more professional.[23] Many of the participants in the survey mentioned that they wanted to give expression to their thoughts and feelings and share them with an audience. Three out of 32 participants specifically mentioned that online publishing is the easiest way to get feedback on thoughts.

Being able to distribute without many restrictions was also one of the reasons for going online. Participants made it clear that censorship was an important issue for them.[24] Online publishing is an alternative when an author lacks opportunities to have his or her works distributed in print—and also because it can evade state censorship. Motivations for distributing online are plentiful. Most important is the possibility of distributing cultural products and receiving feedback from other users. For Gauntlett, another important aspect of participatory culture is that users engage with the world and help create a positive environment.[25] The participants in my survey also mentioned the aspect of meeting like-minded people.[26] As a caveat, the previously mentioned research is not my area of expertise and hence its findings can, at best, serve as a point of reference for other research. The online survey demonstrates how learning about users' intentions help grasp regional distinctions in participatory culture.

---

[22] Louis Leung, "User-generated content on the Internet: An Examination of Gratifications, Civic Engagement and Psychological Empowerment", in *New Media & Society*, 2009, pp. 1327–1347, p. 1328 f.

[23] In 2010, I conducted an online survey with 35 participants of different ages, contacting them via email, in forums, and by twitter.

[24] Survey data, 2010.

[25] David Gauntlett, *Participation Culture, Creativity, and Social Change*, November 29, 2008, http://www.youtube.com/watch?v=MNqgXbI1_o8&feature=related, accessed November 11, 2011.

[26] Survey data 2010.

Interpersonal Experience, Time, and Space

Interaction with the audience is influenced by notions of time and space that will be outlined in the following. The temporality of online distribution is closely connected to communication with users and producers.[27] Users can be connected without being physically in the same location. Finally, an additional form of communication can be seen in the interactive process of reposting and changing already existing cultural products such as audio files, films, and texts.

It is evident that interpersonal experience is essential for online participatory culture. Especially in parts of the Gulf, where genders do not mix outside of work or family setting, this form of communication is an alternative to offline spaces. Relationships can be established, either between bloggers and other bloggers or between bloggers and readers. A unique characteristic of the medium is that instant contact between writer and reader is possible. One of the connecting instances for writers is the *Arab Union for E-Writers*, which unites authors from all over the Arabic-speaking world. On the Union's online site, authors are able to create their own profile sites with contact data, pictures, and samples of their works. Only a small group of bloggers and online writers are actual members of the Arab E-Writers' Union. Since online platforms or writers' unions promote authors, online literature also functions as a platform for like-minded people and help them to communicate with one another. For example, the Arab E-Writers Union supports communication among authors by hosting meetings and conferences.[28]

Whether in Arabic-speaking countries or the rest of the online sphere, an essential benefit of interactivity online is the option to collaborate in a variety of temporalities without being restricted to a particular physical location. Annette Markham (2003) highlights how crucial the temporality of online literary texts and other cultural works is. Online distribution can

---

[27] Communication through online writing was also analysed in the research field of Chinese digital literature by Xiaomeng Lang in the article *Der Dialog der Kultur und die Kultur des Dialogs: die chinesische Netzliterat* on http://dokumentix.ub.uni-siegen.de/opus/frontdoor.php?source_opus=398&la=de, last accessed January 3, 2012.

[28] More information on the union can be found on the website www.arab-ewriters.com/, last accessed January 11, 2011.

work in "real time"[29] as well as in "delayed time".[30] This means that posts can deal with past events as well as with current events, published as live streams or tweets. Responses to these posts depend on the audience. They can either interact in "real time" by commenting directly on shared material; or they could come to know about the material at a later time and subsequently respond whenever their schedule permits. A delayed reply is influenced by changes that happen in the time that has passed since the original publication. This can have an effect on the interaction between producer and recipient. In print literature, this speed of interaction is impossible to attain and interaction in general is rather uncommon. The author is less accessible and more static, which creates a gap in communication between audience and author. The physical location and the time of interaction between authors and readers are flexible. The following example shows that readers' responses to postings in forums and blogs are rarely in "real time". Still, responses to blog postings often come within a few hours or days, meaning interaction is much faster than was possible with earlier media.

Another essential advantage of online media is that interaction does not depend on being in the same physical location. Maddalena Pennacchia Punzi (2007) points out that de-territorialised groups created by mass media "imagine and feel together", no matter which location they are physically at. She continues by quoting Raymond Williams to underline the argument that locality can be produced by technology. Williams states that groups can produce and work together, independently of their actual location.[31]

Technology such as telephones, instant messaging, and chat rooms, as well as forums, can create a common space. It is a virtual space, but it is still a location where participants from different physical places can interact. It differs from earlier media in that the communication is not between just two persons, but among many. Additionally, users communicate although they do not know each other from other contexts. This is advan-

---

[29] By "real time" I mean the actual instant communication experienced in phone connections and chat rooms.

[30] Annette N. Markham, *Internet communication as a tool for qualitative research*, November 18, 2003, markham.internetinquiry.org/writing/silvermangalleyproofs.pdf, accessed November 11, 2011.

[31] Maddalena Pennacchia Punzi, *Literary intermediality: the transit of literature through the media circuit*, New York 2007, p. 248.

tageous for connecting not only people from different places, but also people whose movements are restricted by societal obligations. Some blogs use a chat box to facilitate instant communication.[32] Chat boxes allow instant communication on blogs without the need to submit personal information to one's interlocutors. They underline the bloggers' desire for interaction with the readership. Another form of communication may be seen in the act of reposting and remixing stories, which will be presented in the following section.

Links as a Form of Communication

Part of the interactive mode online is the use of links. Links have several functions. For producers, they help to contextualise and place themselves. Users or readers recognise links as a means of navigation. Links can visually express relationships to other bloggers and show fields of interest. By linking to specific pages and blogs, a writer situates himself and displays his personal interests and connections. Gert Lovink states that social networks are not a parallel reality but "reflect and accelerate tendencies that already exist".[33] The online representation of networks mirrors connections that have already existed offline or those that have developed through similar interests or admiration. Links, as the name implies, aim to make connections to different writers, but also to websites that might be valuable to readers or writers. Additionally, links are embedded within blogs to refer to texts published earlier on the same blog that are related to and provide background knowledge for the current post. On the blog http://al-zain.blogspot.com/, bloggers link to each other's blogs but also comment on each other's blog posts. Following links to these other bloggers, the user finds further comments from writers who are connected within a wider network of bloggers and online writers. A structure of networks among different writers is evident. As can be seen in Layal's blog (http://layal7.blogspot.com/), these links can also connect to Arabic-writing bloggers from countries outside the Gulf, such as Morocco and Egypt.

---

[32] An example can be found on the blog http://rarain.blogspot.com/.
[33] Geert Lovink, *Zero Comments: Blogging and Critical Internet Culture*, New York 2007, p. 236.

Authors of Online Literature

As for the role of the author in online writing, it is important to distinguish between the situation in the Gulf, Egypt, and Lebanon, and the world in general. Most research on online writing is conducted in the context of European and North American writing, which is one-sided. Although most research on online literature is not conducted in the Arabic-speaking world, it is essential to examine authorship. Access to Web 2.0 has changed perspectives on authorship as well as on the replication and alteration of cultural products. I found four aspects that distinguish digital authorship from authorship offline: (1) the writer has a stronger impact on the outcome of the work because of a newly gained independence, (2) anonymity is much more present in online writing, (3) from a narrative perspective, a blurring and fading of the lines between *us* and *them* is apparent, and (4) users are empowered through writing.

1. In the past, it was more difficult for an author to publish. Usually, s/he was not self-published and the editor usually functions as the intermediary between writing and publishing. The author receives new freedom concerning a choice of style and content. The author is challenged with new tasks when publishing online such as dealing with formatting layout, but this means that s/he is also the maker of his/her own product when it comes to typesetting, graphic art, and editing of cultural products.[34] It is a characteristic of Web 2.0 and user-generated content that people can become their own authors, readers, and publishers at the same time.[35] But this unfiltered content means that quality and style of literary texts vary a lot. This is generally applicable to Arab countries and also the publishing processes of other countries of the world.

    Particularly against the background of the Gulf, the relative anonymity of and less censorship applied to online literature offer greater freedom in writing than in print media. But while writers are

---

[34] Loss Pequeno Glazier, *Digital poetics*, Tuscaloosa 2002, p. 29.

[35] Carolyn Guertin, "Handholding, Remixing, and the Instant Replay: New Narratives in a Postnarrative World", in Ray Siemens and Susan Schreibman (eds.), *Companion to Digital Literary Studies*, Oxford 2008, http://www.digitalhumanities.org/companion/view?docId =blackwell/9781405148641/9781405148641.xml&chunk.id=ss1-5-6, last accessed January 27, 2012.

regularly arrested for what they publish in Egypt and in some GCC countries, for example Saudi Arabia, in Lebanon and Kuwait authors have more freedom of speech.

2. A major phenomenon of online writing is the vast number of writers who distribute anonymously. This is especially true for the forums in the Gulf because anonymity shields the writer against social or governmental retaliation and punishment for unapproved content. Hence, it is important to distinguish between writers who distribute with their real names and others who work with a nickname or pseudonym. Usually, a writer does not distribute completely anonymously, but rather picks a permanent nickname that makes him or her recognisable for readers. Historically, publishing under a pseudonym is not an invention of online media. Much has been published anonymously in print. What *is* new is that it is easier online to *distribute* anonymously, due to the absence of instances that would want to know something about the original author, such as editors or publishers. Not distributing with a real name is usually linked to a fear of societal or state censorship and backlash. In forums, almost everyone writes anonymously, whereas in literary blogs the tendency is to publish under one's real name.[36] When online censorship and surveillance is intense, anonymity becomes both a crucial and beneficial tool. But simply using another name does not make a user anonymous on the net. If circumvention tools[37] are not used, it is easy to track an IP address back to the user. However, societal censorship is easily avoided by using a pseudonym. Albabtain (2008) emphasises that anonymity is beneficial for an open dialogue online. He states that it increases the users' willingness to communicate "without reservation".[38] This means an open dialogue can develop with unknown others, which might not happen on the same subject in an offline space.

---

[36] As found in my analysis of a wider selection of online literature from the region.
[37] More on this in Chap. 4.
[38] Afraa Ahmed Albabtain, "Downloading Democracy. Bloggers in the Gulf", in *International Relations and Security Network*, 2008, p. 62. http://www.isn.ethz.ch/isn/Current-Affairs/Security-Watch-Archive/Detail/?fecvnodeid=128146&ord588=grp1&fecvid=21&ots591=0c54e3b3-1e9c-be1e-2c24-a6a8c7060233&v21=128146&lng=en&id=90279, last accessed January 3, 2012.

James Bohman (2004) argues that this anonymity influences the relationship between the audience and author.[39] He states that anonymity alters the context and is "making speaker and audience not only indefinite but also indeterminate in its many-to-many form".[40] This stresses a point made about stories that I mentioned earlier, that spreading the message is becoming more important than the identity of the writer. This is observable at least in forums where one-to-many and many-to-many forms of communication are preferred. In forums, users often publish under a pseudonym, as will be shown in the table presented later in this chapter.

A different way of identifying a writer is presented in blogs. Authorship in blogs, in all countries studied in this monograph, tends to be strongly identified with a real or pseudonymous person by means of a user name or display name for each blog and blog entry, or using an "about" or profile section that gives information about the writer.[41] In my sources I observe that bloggers usually publish their stories under their real name.

The following section will deal with problems that appear when producers of texts do not publish with real names—for example when they present text under what is obviously a nickname—and with the challenges of sharing intellectual property.

For the Gulf, one example of anonymity in the redistribution of a single theme, often slightly altered in wording and layout, is "How was she killed? The complete story of an Emirati woman who was found dead in a well". In every single forum, a different user distributes the story. The users are male or female, and not all of them claim the story as their original product. Most of them do not mention where it originated, or they use an introduction that appears identical in several repostings. This introduction states that the story is based on hearsay.[42] Usually, the reader cannot be sure about the identity of the original author of the stories, because the stories are reposted so

---

[39] James Bohman, "Expanding dialogue: The Internet, the public sphere and prospects for transnational democracy", in John Michael Roberts and Nick Crossley (eds.) *After Habermas: New Perspectives on the Public Sphere*, Oxford 2004, pp. 131–155, p. 133.

[40] Ibid., p. 138.

[41] Mark Warschauer and Douglas Grimes, "Audience, Authorship, and Artifact: The Emergent Semiotics of Web 2.0", in *Annual Review of Applied Linguistics* 27, no. 1, 2007, pp. 1–23, p. 8.

[42] Find Example in *Visual Set-Up and Narration*, Chap. 1.

many times. Later in this chapter, in the section about remixing stories, a table shows changes in one and the same story that was redistributed several times. In every publishing platform anonymity ranks differently in relevance. Writing on blogs is not like writing in forums because the process of distribution is not the same. Usually literary texts on blogs are distributed exclusively on one blog and are not cross-posted elsewhere. Thus, authorship in blogs tends to be strongly identified with a real or pseudonymous person through a user name,[43] and it is clear to the readers who wrote the texts, often know earlier texts by the same author. In contrast, if the literary texts are published in a forum, the author's identity will likely be unknown because the texts are copied and republished in other forums at different times and in different countries, with either many people or no one at all claiming credit for the story.

3. The narrative of online literature is also affected by interaction. Guertin points out that there are new forms of digital narrative that do not clearly separate between "us" and "them", that is between the writer and the audience.[44] The accustomed distance gives way to the possibility of interacting with the audience. The Egyptian author Ghāda ʿAbd al-ʿĀl (Ghada Abdel Aal) explained the influence of this interaction at *The Emirates Airline International Festival of Literature* (EAIFL) in Dubai 2011. She said that she was always interested in seeing what the audience suggested—subsequently, she would change her next post to surprise the audience.[45] This move of unexpectedness helps keep readers stay interested in the blog. In print literature, such interaction is not possible—certainly not at the speed that is so distinct for online participatory culture.

---

[43] Mark Warschauer and Douglas Grimes, "Audience, Authorship, and Artifact: The Emergent Semiotics of Web 2.0", in *Annual Review of Applied Linguistics* 27, no. 1, 2007, pp. 1–23, p. 8.

[44] Carolyn Guertin, "Handholding, Remixing, and the Instant Replay: New Narratives in a Postnarrative World", in Ray Siemens and Susan Schreibman (eds.), *Companion to Digital Literary Studies*, Oxford 2008, http://www.digitalhumanities.org/companion/view?docId=blackwell/9781405148641/9781405148641.xml&chunk.id=ss1-5-6, last accessed January 27, 2012.

[45] Panel: Digital Revolution 1: Margaret Atwood, Ghada Abdel Aal, China Mieville. Real Readers, Virtual Communities: A revolution in the way authors are connecting with readers, Emirates Airlines Festival of Literature (Dubai), March 11, 2011.

Larry Friedlander (2008) emphasises that "in the digital realm, authorship is dispersed, collaborative, and understandable".[46] He suggests that the problem of recognising new forms of stories is also related to the "conventions of modern authorship" which is not contemporary anymore.[47] More on this new role of the author is also discussed in the chapter on participation culture relating to anonymity in distributions of literary texts.

The Dynamics Public and Private

In the following I will provide an overview of the academic discourse relating to the dynamics of the public sphere. This is part of most discussions of online media and as Kristina Riegert already points out, it can be concluded that the internet is not a public sphere in the Habermasian sense.[48] Hannah Arendt, Jürgen Habermas, and many others have given many definitions of what a public sphere is. Generally, it is defined as a public space where individuals discuss societal matters. Bohman (2004) holds that the conservative criterion that a public sphere must be a face-to-face space for communication should be relaxed.[49] That means that communication not occurring in a physical room should be defined as public as well.

Researchers have presented various arguments on how online participation leads to a blurring of public and private spaces. Guertin (2008) claims that, in a technological age, our "very notions of public and private are being eroded".[50] On a general note and placing public and private spheres in a cultural context, Uwe Boker and Julie A. Hibbard (2002) point out

---

[46] Larry Friedlander, "Narrative strategies in a digital age. Authorship and authority", in Knut Lundby (ed.), *Digital Storytelling, Mediatized Stories. Self-representation in New Media*, New York 2008, pp. 177–196.

[47] Ibid., 183.

[48] Kristna Riegert, "Understanding Popular Arab Bloggers: From Public Spheres to Cultural Citizens", *International Journal of Communication* 9(2015), 458–477, p. 460.

[49] James Bohman, "Expanding dialogue: The Internet, the public sphere and prospects for transnational democracy", in John Michael Roberts and Nick Crossley (eds.), *After Habermas: New Perspectives on the Public Sphere*, Oxford 2004, pp. 131–155, p. 133.

[50] Carolyn Guertin, "Handholding, Remixing, and the Instant Replay: New Narratives in a Postnarrative World", in *Companion to Digital Literary Studies*, Ray Siemens and Susan Schreibman (eds.), Oxford 2008, http://www.digitalhumanities.org/companion/view?docId=blackwell/9781405148641/9781405148641.xml&chunk.id=ss1-5-6, last accessed January 27, 2012.

that every culture draws this line differently.[51] While researchers such as Jodi Dean explain "Why the Net is Not a Public Sphere" (2003), other researchers outline distinct aspects of the internet as a public space. Dean sees the internet rather as rooted in a notion of networks. Tyler Curtain (2006) also describes the interactive aspect of the medium, with an ongoing and unfolding interaction between readers and writers in blogs. Bohman (2004) argues that the internet is a public of publics and not a unified public sphere. This public of publics still needs to enable communication among an "indefinite (although not unitary) audience" that must first become a series of publics connected with an institutional context of other publics.[52]

For authors, it is important to decide what to make public and what to keep private. What can be posted online and what is material that should not be shared; "online media" is mostly understood as an open sphere that *everybody* can access.[53] Studies show that not every user sees the online sphere as a public space. Studies conducted usually did not examine online behaviour in the Gulf, but rather in Europe and North America. As an example from outside the Gulf, Zizi Papacharissi's study (2007) analysed 260 blogs and found that many of them were directed to family members and friends.[54] This is the users' personal perception, since blogs are actually public. Writers in the world at large sometimes assume that their online audience is limited to friends and family and no one else would be interested in reading their works. According to the data from my survey, writers distribute online because they want readers to have access to their works. They do not mainly publish for people they know personally, even though they know some readers, either from before from "real life" or through interaction online.[55] Some of the female bloggers are well aware of the openness of the web and protect their blogs with passwords, so that only their friends can read and comment. This clearly shows that the

---

[51] Uwe Boker and Julie A. Hibbard, *Sites of Discourse—Public and Private Spheres—Legal Culture: Papers from a Conference Held at the Technical University of Dresden, December 2001*, Amsterdam/New York 2002, p. 9.

[52] James Bohman, "Expanding dialogue: The Internet, the public sphere and prospects for transnational democracy", in John Michael Roberts and Nick Crossley (eds.), *After Habermas: New Perspectives on the Public Sphere*, Oxford 2004, pp. 131–155, p. 152.

[53] Everybody who has the needed skills and hardware, that is.

[54] Zizi Papacharissi, "Audiences as media producers: Content analysis of 260 blogs", in M. Tremayne (ed.), *Blogging, citizenship, and the future of media*. London 2007, pp. 21–38.

[55] Survey data 2010.

perception of private and public varies in different cultures as well as offline and online.[56] It also shows that users try to create their own boundaries in a space that can be described as rather free and unrestricted, in order to preserve the privacy of data and material rather than making all their information universally accessible.

"Nada", a female blogger from Saudi Arabia, used to have a blog that was accessible for everybody, but later changed the blog's privacy settings to protect her privacy. "Nada" does not restrict her posting to literary texts, but a lot of her textual production is literary. Her blog is hosted by *Wordpress*. The author is well connected to female writers all over the Gulf and is interlinked with blogs and on *Twitter*. Her posts regularly in literary form and in diary form about things that happen in her life. Her texts are mostly in Arabic, but sometimes in English as well.

Now the reader needs to log-on into a password-protected form before being able to reach her stories and poetry. It is not clear why this blogger switched to private settings, since she is in active contact with other bloggers and on *Twitter*. However, it is interesting that already established bloggers also sporadically shift their blogs into a private mode. Similar shifts can be observed with the Omani blogger Muawiyah, who switches between public and private settings. Sometimes his blog is not accessible at all, though it is not clear whether he or an institution is blocking access. Gail Ramsay witnessed similar behaviour in her own studies. In contrast to the above discussants, it can be argued that computer-mediated communication is the contrary of a public sphere because of the possibilities to limit access to a restricted audience and to maintain anonymity.[57] This anonymity can either promote freedom of expression or undermine it.[58] Connected to the discussion of public and private is also the blurring of fiction and fact that may appear in autofictional text distributed on blogs or in forums. Autofictionality is discussed in the chapter on language and narration.

As the example of "Nada" and the different perspectives on public space online show, it is difficult to make distinctions between notions of public and private on the net. Even if the internet is not a public sphere, it is still

[56] Uwe Boker and Julie A. Hibbard, *Sites of Discourse—Public and Private Spheres—Legal Culture: Papers from a Conference Held at the Technical University of Dresden, December 2001: Vergleichenden Literaturwissenschaft*, 2002, p. 9.
[57] Ibid., p. 132.
[58] Ibid., p. 138.

public and accessible to a broad range of users. Thus, bloggers seem to be aware of the difficulties that come with publishing online. That means the audience is one important part to consider when writing for the net.

The Role of the Audience

The following outline of the role of the audience is a summary of findings that are applicable to literary production and distribution of digital artworks all over the world. However, these findings are also important for reading online literature from my field of research. It needs to differentiate between participants of forums and those in the blogosphere.[59] An advantage of a blog is the writers' knowledge about the number of readers, since he can actually see how many people have read his story or at least clicked it. Knowing the numbers can encourage a blogger to write more because they are aware of their popularity. In the following paragraphs, the role of the audience in blogs serves as an example of interactions; I will discuss forums in the context of remixing and reposting of stories.

Blogging, if practised in the most successful way, can reach a very large audience.[60] However, not every blog or forum post that is produced attracts a considerable audience. Warschauer and Grimes (2007) make clear that just a small number of "A-list bloggers" dominate the blogosphere.[61] Even if this finding is based only on blogs from a different region, it is equally relevant. In each country, some A-list bloggers dominate the blogosphere, and their blogs get more comments on blog posts than others. According to statistics, they also have a higher number of visitors/readers.[62] Popular blogs are read not only by users from their own country, but also by people all over the Arabic-speaking world and from other countries. Ramsay and Riegert filtered the samples for their research according to popularity and ranking. Because authors who publish their works online intend to share their content and interact with the audience, distributing literary text online is often connected to an expectation of feedback from the audience, as many participants in my survey also mentioned.[63]

---

[59] The term "blogging" is the processes of distributing on a blog.

[60] For example the Egyptian Uprising 2011.

[61] Mark Warschauer and Douglas Grimes, "Audience, Authorship, and Artifact: The Emergent Semiotics of Web 2.0", in *Annual Review of Applied Linguistics* 27, no. 1, 2007, pp. 1–23, p. 6.

[62] Technorati is a company which regularly measures these numbers, Technorati.com, last accessed January 3, 2012.

[63] Survey data 2010.

Several researchers deal with the function and value of an audience in online distribution. Kirby (2009) underlines the value of the recipient of texts as "fetishized". He sees the reader as part of the texts. The audience becomes "part of the text" by participating in comments and feedback. Kirby's idea considers the audience to be a significant component in the completing of online literature—but this also withdraws credit from the original author. The writer is no longer seen as the one and only creator of an artwork. A process of interaction forms a new cultural good. Kirby sees "fetishising" the audience in contrast to a postmodern "fetishising" of the author. This emphasis on the importance of the recipient in his findings can be seen as democratising culture or as generating "excruciating banality and vacuity" in cultural products.[64] Analysts differ in their judgement of the audience's importance in correlation with their general views of online media. Optimistic voices might see the audience's importance and increasing value as an interactive process of democratisation in literature. More pessimistic researchers might judge the influence of the audience negatively because they fear that the quality of these cultural products will suffer if produced solely for the enjoyment of the readership. Guertin also emphasises the role of the audience by stating that without its "acts of conversation" there is no work of art.[65] She sees the act of "re/seeing it" as already a part of the text. Guertin regards digital media as much more interactive than its predecessors (e.g. TV and books). This interaction makes it difficult to separate between audience and producer. Thus, reading literature online can be seen as an active process.

While critics might focus on the recipient from a theoretical perspective, writers have a more practical relation with their audience. My online survey on online writing in the Gulf showed that some writers embrace contact with and feedback from the audience.[66] This proves the influence of the audience on online writers.

One act of conversation between audience and author was mentioned in the last chapter. Zain the blogger posted a poem that received a reply in the form of another poem. The blog text was as follows:

[64] Alan Kirby, *Digimodernism: How New Technologies Dismantle the Postmodern and Reconfigure Our Culture*, London 2009.

[65] Carolyn Guertin, "Handholding, Remixing, and the Instant Replay: New Narratives in a Postnarrative World", in *Companion to Digital Literary Studies*, Ray Siemens and Susan Schreibman (eds.), Oxford 2008, http://www.digitalhumanities.org/companion/view?docId=blackwell/9781405148641/9781405148641.xml&chunk.id=ss1-5-6, last accessed January 27, 2012.

[66] Survey data 2010.

كوني كجميله ليحبك

كوني رقيقه القلب هينة المعشر ليحبك
كوني ربة منزل وطباخه ماهره يشهد لك بالبنان ليحبك
كوني مدبرة لأموره اليومية والمعيشيه والماديه ليحبك
كوني ام حنون وزوجة رؤوم .... ليحبك
كوني سخيه معه واحفظي ماله وعرضه وبيته في غيابه ليحبك
ظلمك التاريخ يا حواء ... وباع لك سيرة الجواري بقليل من الحب
سؤال على هامش اللائحة التي قد تطول
اين النصائح المقدمة له!![67]

Be beautiful so that he will love you
Be gentle-hearted and easy to live with so that he will love you
Be an excellent housewife and cook […] so that he will love you
Be a manager of his daily living and financial affairs so that he will love you
Be a loving mother and a forgiving wife … so that he will love you
Be generous with him and protect his wealth and honour and house/family in his absence so that he will love you
History has not been just to you, O Eve … and it sold you the stories of female slaves in return for a little love
A question on the margins of the list that might be too long
Where are the advices given to him!!

This reply can be found in the comment section:

كوني رقيته
كوني نسمه
كوني بسيطه
زيوون ،،، دخلت جو مع أنغام كلماتج
أنامل تسطر حب
لو ما كتبتي في الحب
نغم
ياخذني بعيد
وانتي بعيده عني
أحبج*:
انتي كل الحب:)

---

[67] http://al-zain.blogspot.com/2011_02_01_archive.html, last accessed December 26, 2011.

> Be gentle
> Be (like) a breeze
> Be easy
> Zayyoun … you have added Joe to the beat of your words
> Fingers that chart love
> If you don't write about love
> A tune
> Takes me far away
> And you are far away from me
> I love you :*
> You are love itself :)

It clearly shows that readers are involved in the process of collaborative writing and the text receives an additional element through the commentators reply. In the chapter on participation culture, more on interaction in online writing is discussed.

Reposting and Remixing of Works of Art Online

This section focuses on forums because remixing and reposting are much more common with content posted in forums than with content in blogs. Cory Doctorow, an internet activist and writer of novels published in print as well as electronically, emphasises that copying is part of contemporary art: he even says that art that is not copied is not contemporary.[68] As a consequence, copyright is a widely discussed subject as on the one hand, cultural products are easy to copy and disseminated nowadays and producers might gain more popularity to the possibilities. On the other hand, they do not get financial rewards as reproduction often happens without a contribution to the original source.

One form of communication and interaction online manifests itself in the re-editing and reposting of original cultural products such as audio files, films, and texts. The best-known form of communication by changing an original cultural product is found in the remixes posted on YouTube, the most representative interactive space for user-generated content. This platform allows users to upload videos. A variety of communication forms can be observed; there is often interaction, either through the comment function, the "thumbs-up" button, or a video reply from other users.

---

[68] Reason TV, *Cory Doctorow on The War on Kids, Boing Boing, & His Next Novel*, July 15, 2010, http://www.youtube.com/watch?v=LLf3nldagXc, accessed November 11, 2011.

Here, the audience is also a creator because content can be created, exchanged, and also remixed. Michael Wesch, a media anthropologist, researched this aspect of *YouTube* in depth in his "An anthropological introduction to YouTube" in 2008, which is itself distributed on *YouTube*.[69] Wesch made it clear that, when spreading from one place to another, a cultural product keeps its original meaning, but also becomes transformed into something more personal. According to Wesch, the new media are a tool to connect people and make them interact.

Remixing and reposting of short stories is often carried out in forums in the Gulf, where stories are constantly published and rewritten. Immediate interaction takes place and stories can also "travel" and develop. Replicating and spreading stories, as users do with literary works in the Gulf, is therefore a means of this communication. Although participatory culture invites the audience to contribute or remix art works, the original author is still important for the initial creation and inspiration. Without the initial cultural product there can be no remixing of it. In contrast, it is not common that blog posts are remixed.

The following table presents an example of a story that was reposted several times in different forms in various repostings. This is a summary of the story: a third-person narrator tells the story of a young Emirati woman who is tortured and finally killed by her husband. As a stylistic choice, most of the story is told in questions. The narrator asks in an accusatory tone why and how the villain was able to commit the crime. The story introduces two characters: the evil husband, a policeman who violently kills his wife; and contrasting with him is his wife, the innocent victim. The narrator underlines the victim's pureness and innocence by noting her virginity and her reputation in society, as well as her family background. The description of the criminal act of violence is detailed. The story is posted in more than 50 forums and varies slightly in layout, title, pictures, and description. Its earliest publication can be traced back to May 28, 2009. It was most frequently distributed in June and July 2009. Depending on the time and platform on which it is posted, it is redistributed with different titles. To find more examples of the same story, I picked a random sentence ("How was he able to stab her with such shaaaaaarp and painful tools?")[70] and looked up the first 50 hits on Google, but there were many

---

[69] Michael Wesch, *An anthropological introduction to YouTube*, July 26, 2008, http://www.youtube.com/watch?v=TPAO-lZ4_hU, accessed November 11, 2011.

[70] The original sentence was كيف استطاع أن يطعنها بأدوات حاادة مؤلمة بهذا الشكل .

more redistributions than I was able to include in my analysis. The search engine asked whether the sentence in use was misspelled and provided an alternative[71] which did not lead to any additional redistributions. This emphasises the importance of the use of a distinct vernacular and internet language. Language in use is rather colloquial, and repeating a letter several times for emphasis is an example of a different use of written language among young people on the internet. Language in online literary text has already been discussed in greater detail in the chapter on language and narration.

The story claims to be true, which might make it more interesting to read for the audience, whose voyeurism is better satisfied if a story is labelled true rather than fiction. For the analysis of and further dealing with this story, it is not relevant whether it is fictional or true (Table 4.1).

Most striking in the different distributions is the use of pictures supposedly taken at the crime scene. Surprisingly, all but one redistribution of the story makes use of the same pictures, but not all of them use all of the pictures provided in the first posting of the story. Photographs were no longer included in distributions of the story later than the mid-June 2009. A very striking version of the story went online in June 8, 2009 in the forum *Uaetd.com*.[72] This story differs immensely from other repostings: the introduction is not the same and the pictures in use are completely different. Instead of the pictures showing the location of the brutal act, a drawing is presented that displays the message: Stop the violence. The introduction mentions other violent events against women. After this introduction the story is reposted.

The visual appearance of the story varies also because the layout and choice of fonts vary. The font can be very plain and sober with black script on a white background or, in contrast, very colourful texts can be found. Changing font colour for emphasis appears to be a common choice in changing layout.

As already mentioned above, it is striking that the story is reposted by many different users. I did not find any repetition of user names in my analysis of sources. The titles of the story are changed in many repostings. The title of the story sometimes includes the location of the crime scene or the nationality of the victim. The nationality of the victim is always

---

[71] كيف استطاع أن يطعمها بأدوات حادة ومؤلمة بهذا الشكل, that is, without the emphasis on *ḥādda* "sharp".
[72] http://www.uaetd.com/vb/showthread.php?t=57662.

Table 4.1 Example of a story that was reposted several times in different forms in various repostings

Date	User	Title	Pictures	Forums	CO[a]	Changes	City
May 28, 2009	Dam3tshog	How was she killed. A tragedy that I narrate	With links of pictures at photobucket	http://www.adbuae.com/vb/archive/index.php/t-4491.html	26	• Is introduced with "In the name of God" • Introductory phrase: "I do not know where to start and I do not know how to start" • Additional note: "Sat ,,, 23-May-2009 ,,, 3:14 pm ,,, in the bus ... from fuj to alAin ,,, BY: Dam3tshog ~"	
May 29, 2009	شـابـَة ظـبيانيـة	How was she killed. A tragedy that I narrate.	No pictures	http://www.alwasluae.com/vb/showthread.php?t=133307&langid=2	54	Introductory phrase: "I do not know where to start and I do not know how to start"	Dibba
May 29, 2009	بنتي اصل ادنيه	How was she killed. A tragedy that I narrate	no pictures	http://www.do7atkom.com/vb/showthread.php?t=11729	23	Introductory phrase: "I do not know where to start and I do not know how to start"	
May 31, 2009	ورد جوري	"How was she killed? The complete story of an Emirati woman who was found dead in a well"	No pictures	http://www.dhnuae.com/forums/archive/index.php/t-26.html	18		Fujairah

(continued)

Table 4.1 (continued)

Date	User	Title	Pictures	Forums	CO[a]	Changes	City
Jun 1, 2009	رصد مدينتي	"How was she killed? The complete story of an Emirati woman who was found dead in a well"	No pictures	http://www.arabmet.net/vb/showthread.php?t=26546&page=1	17		
Jun 1, 2009	زوبع	How was Maha killed (RIP)??? A crime in the city of Ditba in the UAE	Three pictures	http://www.al7nan.com/vb/t26106.html	3	Introductory phrase: "I do not know where to start and I do not know how to start"	Dibba
Jun 1, 2009	toota	"How was she killed? The complete story of an Emirati woman who was found dead in a well"	No pictures	http://www.shrquae.com/vb/showthread.php?t=5470	1		
Jun 3, 2009	كذبة 999	"How was she killed? The complete story of an Emirati woman who was found dead in a well"	No pictures	http://www.zaimuae.com/alain/showthread.php?p=2176960	25	Text in different colours	
Jun 6, 2009	شك 2	A crime in the city of Dibba in the UAE	Links to pictures do not work	http://fr1.startimes2.com/f.aspx?t=17249957	0		Dibba
Jun 7, 2009	زان	Picture of the well where Emirati woman was found dead	No pictures	http://bint-uae.mam9.com/t1480-topic	2		Fujairah

						Fujairah
Jun 8, 2009	العيون	The killed young woman in Fujairah	No pictures	http://www.women.uaeec.com/showthread.php?14586-%C7%E1%DD%CA%C7%C9-%C7%E1%E3%DE%CA%E6%E1%C9%C8%C7%E1%DD%CC%ED%D1%C9	23	
Jun 8, 2009	المصفور ة مقاول مشفير	"How was she killed? The complete story of an Emirati woman who was found dead in a well"	Completely different pictures: The first picture is a drawing that shows a protest of women and one man holding a banner which says "stop the violence". The second picture shows a photograph which displays a man beating a woman.	http://www.uaetd.com/vb/showthread.php?t=57662	23	Completely different introduction: a list of recent rapes of women and girls in different places is introduced. The narrator alludes to events in Egypt that then transferred to the UAE where violence against women can be found during the events of this story.
Jun 9, 2009	مبارك بن لندن	"How was she killed? The complete story of an Emirati woman who was found dead in a well"	All but one pictures	http://www.zayedbinhamdan.com/vb/showthread.php?p=178089	31	

(*continued*)

Table 4.1 (continued)

Date	User	Title	Pictures	Forums	CO[a]	Changes	City
Jun 10, 2009	ابو اليقين	"How was she killed? The complete story of an Emirati woman who was found dead in a well?"	No pictures	http://shabaaaab.hooxs.com/t376-topic	0	A picture is inserted as a header that greats the readers and additionally includes the formula "In the name of God".	
Jun 12, 2009	اسير الخذلان	Location where an Emirati woman was found dead in a well in *Fujairah* with real pictures	Three pictures	http://www.3yobi.com/vb/showthread.php?p=87398	8		
Jun 12, 2009	الشقيرة ة	Emirati young women who was killed in a well in *Fujairah* "pictures"	No pictures	http://saleh-saad.com/vb/showthread.php?p=61304	5	Includes an animated (gif) rose and coloured fonts	*Fujairah*
Jun 12, 2009	الجرحى	Picture of the well where Emirati woman was found dead	No pictures	[b]	9		
Jun 13, 2009	بنت الامود	Emirati young women who was killed in a well in *Fujairah* "pictures"	No pictures	http://www.alkhawatir.com/vb/archive/index.php/t-8258.html	9		*Fujairah*
Jun 15, 2009	جاسم محمد	Location where an Emirati woman was found dead in a well in *Fujairah*	Pictures	http://www.rafha2.com/vb/showthread.php?t=35515		Coloured fonts	*Fujairah*

Jun 20, 2009	وجه الخير	"How was she killed? The complete story of an Emirati woman who was found dead in a well"	No pictures	http://www.oman10.com/vb/showthread.php?t=740&page=9	6	
Jun 20, 2009	بنت الزعيم	"How was she killed? The complete story of an Emirati woman who was found dead in a well"	Links to pictures do not work	http://3inawi.yoo7.com/t265-topic	2	
Jun 21, 2009	زهور الريف	How was Maha killed (RIP) with pictures	Links to pictures do not work	http://www.afif.ws/sahat/archive/index.php/t-142563.html	10	Introductory phrase: "I do not know where to start and I do not know how to start"
Jul 19, 2009	جنيف نت	"How was she killed? The complete story of an Emirati woman who was found dead in a well"	No pictures	http://dibba-al-hisn.com/vb/showthread.php?p=9888	9	Dibba
Aug 12, 2009	متشبب فعال	"How was she killed? The complete story of an Emirati woman who was found dead in a well"	No pictures	http://www.yaf33.com/vb/showthread.php?p=117499	5	Introduced with personal greeting
Sept 29, 2009	ملاك الورد	"How was she killed? The complete story of an Emirati woman who was found dead in a well"	No pictures	http://www.lil-3.com/vb/archive/index.php/t-15916.html	10	

(*continued*)

Table 4.1 (continued)

Date	User	Title	Pictures	Forums	CO[a]	Changes	City
Oct 6, 2009	alaany_999	The truth of … a young woman killed in Fujairah	No pictures	http://vb.we3rb.com/archive/index.php/t-41847.html	9	Introductory phrase: "I do not know where to start and I do not know how to start"	
Mar 19, 2010	حقي ع بناتي ظبي	"How was she killed? The complete story of an Emirati woman who was found dead in a well"	No pictures	http://www.mo7adtha.com/vb/180311-post1.html	0		
Jul 14, 2010		"How was she killed? The complete story of an Emirati woman who was found dead in a well"	No pictures	http://www.roadeed.net/showthread.php?t=15757	3		
Jul 16, 2010		"How was she killed? The complete story of an Emirati woman who was found dead in a well"	No pictures	www.mmmoh.blogspot.com	3		

[a]CO = number comment

[b]http://www.3nabi.com/forums/showthread.php/171732 %D8%B7%C2%B5%D8%B8%CB%86%D8%B7%C2%B1-%D8%B8%E2%80%9E%D8%B8%E2%80%9E%D8%B7%C2%A8%D8%B7%C2%A6%D8%B8%B7%C2%B1-%D8%B7%C2%A7%D8%B8%E2%80%9E%D8%B8%E2%80%9E%D8%B9-%D8%B7%C2%A3%D8%B8%E2%80%9E%D8%B8%E2%80%9A%D8%B8%E2%80%B0-%D8%B8%D9%BE%D8%B8%D9%81-%D8%B7%C2%A7%D8%B8%E2%80%9E%D8%B8%D9%BE%D8%B7%DA%BE%D8%B7%C2%A7%D8%B7%C2%A9-%D8%B7%C2%A7%D8%B8%E2%80%9E%D8%B8%E2%80%9A%D8%B7%DA%BE%D8%B8%CB%86%D8%B8%E2%80%9E%D8%B8%E2%80%A1?p=3286276

Emirati, but the setting of the story shifts between Dibba and Fujairah, which are both cities in the UAE and are not far from each other.

An analysis of readers' participation shows that a large number of comments were posted within the first days of distribution. The first posting of the story received 26 comments, and the second one received 54 comments, which is high compared with the later numbers of comments. Comments are usually not on the story's style or setup, but rather emphasise the reader's sympathy for the victim or are critiques of the Emirati society.

The actual text does not change much. In some redistributions, the story starts with the sentence "I don't know where to start and I don't know how to start." In others, this sentence is left out. Rarely, the story starts with the formula "In the name of God", which is commonly used in the Gulf when writing. In the first appearance of the story, this sentence precedes the introduction. The first posting also includes a striking note in English above the forum post:

> Sat ,,, 23-May-2009 ,,, 3:14 pm ,,, in the bus ... from fuj to alAin ,,, BY: Dam3tshog.[73]

The story itself was distributed five days later. This remark suggests that the story either was first heard or was first created on the bus from al Fujayrah to al-ʿAyn. The remark may have been made to underline the story's authenticity.

Thus, stories are redistributed by a variety of users at different times. This coincides with Wesch's aforementioned findings on YouTube videos. Images are an important factor in the redistribution of stories, but later these pictures are abandoned and users focus more on the text itself. Often users change the distributed story a little, but in ways that do not affect the plot of the story.

This chapter discussed the advantages and challenges of Web 2.0 and participatory culture online. The medium has an impact on cultural products through its many ways of interaction and reuse and through its promotion of the changeability of text. Authors are challenged by seeing their works changed and remixed by others as well as by dealing with repostings that do not give credit to the original author. Additionally, producers must decide what should be public and what private online.

---

[73] http://www.adbuae.com/vb/archive/index.php/t-4491.html, January 2, 2012.

Related to public and private space is the distinct feature of online interactivity that influences contemporary online writing. Authors and audience both make use of the interactive aspect of online distribution. Both sides benefit from this interaction and both might incidentally form a cultural product as a collaborative process.

Interactiveness can lead to a process of changing texts. Thus, changeability can be mirrored in remixing and reposting stories in forums; a vast number of users do this.

Participatory culture is also subject to criticism. For example, if a blog's privacy settings are changed, texts can suddenly disappear for a broader audience, remaining visible only for a smaller selected audience. Online distribution also poses the problem of infringement of intellectual property rights.

Although the distribution of cultural products has increased, user-generated content is not entirely new, for example, it is part of Xeroxing culture. However, distributing online means authors no longer need to send their products to mainstream media to make their works accessible. But this can also mean that content is published regardless of its actual literary value for a larger audience.

The role of the audience and its perception is shifting; observers do not agree on its importance. Some say the stronger focus on the readership is encouraging a democratisation of literature; others say that this is weakening the literature's quality.

Cultural production and participatory culture online are still in their infancy. Web 2.0 has existed for less than ten years and participants need time to learn to control quality and deal with interactivity and privacy issues.

In this chapter, it was important to outline circumstances of distribution as they influence writing and publishing. Certainly, a variety of other circumstances of online writing can be studied in future research.

CHAPTER 5

Who Are the Actors? Portrayal of Heroes

In this chapter I will offer a frame of references related to the representation of gender identity, globalisation and individualisation processes within the sources. The protagonist's struggle over identity can be understood as a critique of social norms. Analysis of self-representation is fundamental to this chapter because characters often situate themselves in their cultural contexts.

WHO ARE THE ACTORS? PORTRAYAL OF HEROES

This chapter deals with the various ways heroes (as in the protagonist of a story) are described or describe themselves in online literature from some of the Gulf countries, mostly Kuwait and the Emirates, and a comparison to heroes in blog posts from Egypt. Having looked at the language, narration in socio-political contexts, as well as medial make-up of online literary texts—and having examined participatory culture and communication with the audience, I now return to the topic of social discourse, here in connection with the portrayal of protagonists.[1] Studying a

---

[1] The term "discourse" is used here with the definition that it has in critical discourse analysis, that is, a form of language use in writing and speech that is seen as a "social practice" and displays social identities. CDA sees discourse—language use in speech and writing—as a form of "social practice". Describing discourse as social practice implies a dialectical relationship between a particular discursive event and the situation(s), institution(s), and social structure(s) that frame it: the discursive event is shaped by them, but it also shapes them. That is, dis-

© The Author(s) 2019
N. Lenze, *Politics and Digital Literature in the Middle East*,
https://doi.org/10.1007/978-3-319-76816-8_5

variety of perspectives on online literature reveals components of discourses in society. Discourses in society are strongly related to the manifestation of identities because the formation of identities is possible only within societal norms and boundaries[2]; subsequently, a story can represent a character's identity in its relationship and interaction with the social surroundings. It is important to mention that internet activities do not restructure public discourse,[3] meaning that the two worlds are not separated from one another and changes usually take place off-screen rather than online. Studying heroes in literature involves understanding fictional characters in fictional settings. The study of heroes in fictional stories merely highlights discourses that seem to be of relevance for writers, which means that certain subjects, of value to the writers, are composed and distributed as literary texts. This chapter focuses on the analysis of representations of heroes in short literary texts in online forums and blogs. In the second part of this chapter, the examples given are focussed on Gulf countries, but I will compare them to publications from other countries based on Gail Ramsay's and Teresa Pepe's research. An important field of examination is the depiction of gender roles which may also be linked to processes of individualisation in the region that influence the representation of identity in literary texts. Further, I explore global impacts that change society as exemplified in a variety of short stories. This means that all the aforementioned topics are recurring themes that online writers find important to express. In the texts that I studied, more than half of them address at least one of the subjects that I analyse here. Other aspects of the portrayal of heroes such as class or nation will not be examined in detail because they play a minor role in my sources. These elements, whilst

---

course is socially constitutive as well as socially conditioned—it constitutes situations, objects of knowledge, and the social identities of and relationships between people and groups of people. It is constitutive both in the sense that it helps to sustain and reproduce the social status quo and in the sense that it contributes to transforming it. Since discourse is so socially consequential, it gives rise to important issues of power. Discursive practices may have major ideological effects—that is, they can help produce and reproduce unequal power relations between (for instance) social classes, women and men, and ethnic/cultural majorities and minorities through the ways they represent things and position people (Fairclough and Wodak, 1997: 258).

[2] Rom Harré discusses the conceptualisation of personal being and here embeds the self in a social context that suggests a more important role for the (narrative) understanding of self. R. Harré, *Personal Being*, Oxford 1983.

[3] Yochai Benkler, *The Wealth of Networks: How Social Production Transforms Markets and Freedom*, New Haven 2006, p. 271.

important, are subjects of much less than half of the texts that I looked at. I will shed light on the discursive construction of social actors and processes and aim to study social actors and phenomena while framing the discourse and position the heroes' and/or narrators' point of view.

Perspectives on Online Identity

Closely related to the portrayal of heroes is the presentation of identities, which is discussed in research on online media users. Many researchers describe the online sphere as a unique space for creating and portraying identities. Representation of identity is certainly present in offline or physical space but the anonymity of the internet allows for new possibilities. Two researchers who write on the subject are Susanna Paasonen and Jenny Davis. In Paasonen's *Figures of Fantasy* (2006), which examines discourses of femininity in cyberspace, part of her research focuses on self-representation. She finds that users often do not limit themselves to presenting one identity on the net; instead, "multiple identities may flourish".[4] This means that the same user may distribute literary texts through more than one online identity. Such practices might be especially easy in forums, where users act much more anonymously than in blogs and usually disguise their true identities with nicknames. Building on Paasonen's argument, Davis, who works on the same subject but focuses on MySpace,[5] underlines the flexibility of creating identity online. In the article "Architecture of the Personal Interactive Homepage: Constructing the Self Through MySpace" (2010), she states that "the internet (…) can be seen as a prevalent means for creating and negotiating our identities",[6] emphasising the possibilities to enhance and rearrange identity on the net, including representing oneself as the "ideal self". With the flexible tool, people can present "one piece" of their identities. This self-representation is limited to the boundaries set by the platform where they are published, in addition to the boundaries that are set by users. Boundaries are for example established in design choices.

---

[4] Susanna Paasonen, *Figures of Fantasy. Internet, Women and Cyberdiscourse*, New York 2005, p. 107.

[5] *MySpace* is a social network that allows connecting to others as well as distributing music.

[6] Jenny Davis, "Architecture of the personal interactive homepage: constructing the self through MySpace", in New Media & Society November 2010, first published on May 4, 2010, pp. 1103–1119, 1106.

While Paasonen talks about multiple identities, Davis restricts herself to the negotiation of a single identity. Neither focuses on the Middle East. Still, patterns of use in the US or Europe can serve as a benchmark and help identify those in the countries studied. According to my findings, users' behavioural patterns do not differ much when it comes to the interactive communication aspect of using online media. For the following examination, my material mainly consists of blogs and stories in forums. Representation of identity can also be found in a lot of other texts which do not need to necessarily be literary. As the focus of this book is Arabic online literature, I limit my field to literature distributed on the internet. Instead of focusing on the content producers' profiles or "about" pages, which would help form a picture of these authors, I will look into the representation of identity or portrayal of heroes within the stories. The following examples from my sample texts will serve as a basis for discussion of the aforementioned perspectives on identity representation. Not every sample fits all of the chosen aspects of the discourse, but some of them share a variety of themes that are worth analysing. We can find similar topics to be discussed in Egyptian and Lebanese writings; however, they must be read in their own cultural and political contexts.

Sample Texts

The sample texts for this chapter are from Kuwait and the Emirates, and I compare them to heroes in blog posts from other countries at the end of the reading of the sample texts. Showing a wide range of socially relevant topics, these stories deal with body image and beauty standards, cultural norms and stereotypes, abuses, longing and love, arranged marriage, racism, and classism. Three examples are from Kuwaiti blogs, two of which are published by the same blogger under the name "7osenman": "Fantasy world" (*ʿĀlam khayālī*) and "What shall we eat?" (*mādhā naʾkul?*). One blog post is from Salatmaiwa.com: "Your nose belongs to you, so what?" (*Anfik minnik—wa-law!*). Additionally, I selected two examples from forums: "How was she killed? The complete story of an Emirati woman who was found dead in a well" (*al-Qiṣṣa al-kāmila li'l-fatāt al-imārātiyya allatī ʿuthira ʿalayhā fī biʾr maqtūla^{tan}*) and "Ḥiṣṣa and the Taxi Driver" (*Ḥiṣṣa wa-rāʿī al-taksī*). I first came across these stories through their distribution in forums in 2009 and 2010; after some research I found that they had been circulated on other forums at earlier and later times as well.

Two stories distributed through the blog 7osen-man.blogspot.com are worth showing as examples of the representation of identity. In his BlogSpot profile titled "Below Zero", 7osen-man describes himself as a Kuwaiti male. He mentions that his favourite book is *Mawsim al-hijra ilā 'l-shamāl* (*Season of Migration to the North*, 1966) by al-Ṭayyib Ṣāliḥ (Tayeb Saleh), which gives the reader a hint about his literary preferences. His blog is still active, but he has continuously decreased publications since 2011, limiting them to as little as one or two blog posts a year in comparison to publishing between 40 and 60 texts annually in the years between 2007 and 2010.

(a) Fantasy World

The first story that I want to present is "Fantasy world", posted on June 18, 2011. In this story, the narrator describes an evening he spends in the cinema together with a friend. The two male friends watch a romantic comedy. The protagonist describes the situation at the cinema as "We are a diverse society in everything", explaining that the things that bind people together are the same as those that separate them.

التفاوت الكبير في الأوضاع الاجتماعية يظهر بصورة جلية بين الناس عبر الأشكال طريقة اللباس الحديث .. المعاملة "نحن مجتمع متفاوت بكل شيء، الأشياء التي تجمعنا هي ذاتها التي تفرق بيننا."[7]

> The big gap in social status is evident between people from their looks ... the modern style of clothes ... the treatment ... "We are a diverse society in everything, the things that bring us together are the same as those that set us apart ..."

The protagonist is waiting for his friend to come to buy Nachos and M&M's, which his friend does habitually every time he goes to the cinema. This makes the protagonist reflects on "the curse of habits" and concludes that "change is the best".

كنت أنتظر صديقي الذي ذهب لشراء بعض "الناتشوز" و"الأم أند أمز" كما هي عادته دائماً، قلت في نفسي: تباً للعادات التي تبقينا عبيداً لها دون أن نشعر، ياليتنا نستطيع أن نتغير، التغيير أفضل ما يمكن أن نصنعه في حياة شديدة الغرابة والوضوح معاً."[8]

> I waited for my friend who went to buy some Nachos and M&Ms, like he always did, and I said to myself: God damn these traditions that keep us as slaves without knowing; I desire we could change; change is the best thing we can do in this very strange and at the same time clear life.

---
[7] Blog post from 18.6.2011, http://7osen-man.blogspot.com/2011/06/blog-post_18.html, last accessed December 28, 2011. The syntax in this text is not completely clear.
[8] Ibid.

The story continues with the main character going inside and seeing a young woman who is wearing clothes that accentuate her figure, which he finds attractive. The protagonist asks his friend if he has ever fallen in love before; the friend laughs this off and tells him to just sit down. The film triggers emotions in the protagonist and he describes the wish to cry after the movie ends. To extend the evening, he asks his friend if they can take the long ride home instead of the regular way. The protagonist's thoughts during the car ride are described.

بدت لي الطريق الاسفلتيه معبدة على نحو غريب .. وشعرت بلحظة ما أن بأمكان المركبة أن ترتفع وتلج بنا أبواب ذلك العالم المنتظر .. العالم الكبير ، المثالي، الصادق، الذي بأمكانه أن يمنحني دفء الحياة الغائب ابدأ ..
كنت أتمنى أن تُختصر كل الحياة في هذه اللحظة. أن ينتهي العمر وأنا سارح في خيالات تطير من الارض وتحط في السماء.
قطع صديقي حبل أفكاري المشدود .. وقال ، :"البطلة كانت جميلة جداً لها شفتين تقتلان"ضحكت بصفاء طويلاً .. وقلت: "هناك فقط بأمكانك أن تشعر بالحياة ".[9]

The asphalt road looked strange to me ... I felt for a moment that the car could fly and sweep us to the doors of the awaited world ... the big, ideal and honest world that can give every absent warmth of life.

I wished that all life would come down to this moment, that life would end while I am chasing fantasies that take off from the earth and land in the sky.

My friend interrupted my trail of intense thought and said: "The heroine was very beautiful with killer lips…" I laughed so hard and then said: "Only there you can feel alive."

While the protagonist is contemplating life and giving his imagination free rein, the friend talks about the movie. The story ends when the protagonist arrives at home:

حين دلفت إلى غرفتي كانت خطوات الفجر الاولى تتقدم بتأني ساحر .. صليت الفجر .. وتكورت داخل فراشي طلباً للنوم قبل أن يبدأ يوم طويل أخر .
فجأة قفز مدير عملي إلى مخيلتي رأيته يستفسر عن الواجبات التي ينتظر مني أن انهيها تذكرت ايضا الأوراق الكثيرة التي تنتظر على مكتبي .. وحالة النعاس والأرهاق في منتصف اليوم ... حلت هذه الأشياء فجأة كعاصفة مباغتة واقتلعت كل ماهو جميل في نفسي كان الحب والحكمة والمتعة والحياة أخر ما أفكر فيه في تلك اللحظة.[10]

---

[9] Blog post from June 18, 2011, http://7osen-man.blogspot.com/2011/06/blog-post_18.html, last accessed December 28, 2011.

[10] Blog post from May 25, 2011, http://7osen-man.blogspot.com/2011/05/blog-post_25.html, last accessed November 22, 2011. When I wanted to access the blog post again on December 28, 2011, it had been deleted.

When I entered my room, the first crack of dawn was creeping up with a captivating slow pace ... I prayed the dawn prayers ... and crawled up into my bed to sleep before another long day started.

Suddenly, my manager jumped to my mind. I saw him inquiring about the duties that he waited for me to finish and I also remembered the many papers that awaited me on my desk ... and feeling sleepy and exhausted in the middle of the day ... these things suddenly gripped me like a sudden storm and uprooted everything beautiful inside me.

Love, wisdom, pleasure and life were the last things on my mind at that moment.

The story is addressing several topics, one of which is the emancipation from traditions. Further in the story, it describes the old and the new, a liberal perspective and a conservative one. The narrator tries to tackle deeper issues but ends abruptly when everyday life is catching up with him.

(b) What Shall We Eat?

The second story by 7osen-man that I find relevant to present within the topic of the portrayal of heroes is the story called "What shall we eat?" that was posted on May 25, 2011. The story starts off with the narrator telling the reader about an emotional pain he feels. The pain appears at night.

> لم تكن هذه الليلة الوحيدة التي يمر ني بها هذا الشعور ، بل الليالي السابقة كلها، منذ أن أبتعدت عن عالمي الذي احبه بسبب سلطة المجتمع الذي أنتمي إليه وأنا اتشظى إلى نتف صغيرة في كل ليلة ، أعانق الألم بصمت، وأتمنى أن تجود نفسي بماء الروح عليّ أرتاح لكنها صامتة وجافة مثل أيامي.[11]

This was not the only night I felt this way, I [had] felt it every night before that, since I left the world that I loved because of the authority of the society I belonged to, and I am torn into tiny pieces every night, embracing the pain in silence and wishing that my soul would be so kind to me as to give me some peace, but it remains quiet and dry just like all my days!

The narrator tells his story of wanting to get married to a female colleague with whom he has fallen in love. He asks his father to marry him to her, but his father refuses because the woman is not from the right family and his family's reputation might be harmed. After hearing his father's words, the protagonist feels tears coming to his eyes. He says that he does not know why it is necessary to still stick to the old rules.

[11] Ibid.

لماذا يجب عليّ أن أقترن بإنسانة لا أعرفها، لماذا يجب أن أتزوج من العائلة، أي قانون هذا، وأي عرف مهترئ من يتحكم بمصائرنا.[12]

Why should I marry someone I don't know? Why should I marry someone from the family? What law is this and what outdated tradition is this that controls our destinies!

The narrator describes his personality as non-confrontational because he fears dealing with the consequences.

لم أثور ولم أقاوم كلمة والدي بل أنصعت له بكل هدوء رغم رفضي الداخلي لجميع مظاهر مجتمعي.[13]

I did not rebel and I did not resist my father; rather I quietly obeyed him in spite of my internal rejection of everything in my society.

He describes the traits of his beloved, to whom he feels attracted.

وحين أقتربت منها كثيرا وبدأت أتحدث معها ذهلت من كمية المنطق التي تمتلكها، وادهشتني نظرتها التحليلية للحياة، كان منطقها قريبا من المنطق الذي يقبع في داخلي، كانت تقول ما تؤمن به دون إنتظار لرأي أحد، تحترم حق الجميع في ممارسة قناعاته دون التدخل في قناعات الاخرين، متمسكها برأيها وبذات الوقت مستعده أن تقتنع برأيك أن اقنعتها، كانت فتاة جدية جدا صاحبة شخصية قوية ومسيطرة، تستطيع أن تصد كل متملق و تافه وما اكثرهم في عالمنا بكل بساطة وأدب.[14]

When I got to know her better and began to talk to her, I was amazed by the amount of logic that she had, and her analytical view of life amazed me … her logic was closer to the logic inside me. She said what she believed without waiting for other people's opinions and held on to her opinion. At the same time, she was ready to believe your point of view if you convinced her. She was a very serious girl with a strong dominating personality who could easily and politely stand up to any hypocrite or idiot—and how many idiots there are in this world.

After describing her character he moves on to descriptions of her physical appearance. The narrator alludes to her family's openness when she states that her father has always taught her the values of freedom and respect. He mourns the separation while complaining about his father's and his community's customs and convictions.

---

[12] Ibid.
[13] Ibid.
[14] Blog post from May 25, 2011, http://7osen-man.blogspot.com/2011/05/blog-post_25.html, last accessed November 22, 2011. When I wanted to access the blog post again on December 28, 2011, it had been deleted. The words التحليلة and إنتظرا seem to be spelled differently from the norm.

أحببتها جداً بكل بساطة قلبي وغرابة أحساسي، أحببتها بإنسانية خالصة بعيداً عن تجاذبات القناعات والاعراف، إلا أن الأخيرتين هما من يحدد مصائرنا على نحو بالغ الأثر ، وشخصاً في مثل وضعي لا يمكنه مواجهتما، أعرافنا وقناعات مجتمعي ووالدي الرجل القوي ، وضعفي الذي يصور لي أحيانا كل ما أفعله على إنه مجرد حماقات ملعونة ، جعلاني ارضا بحكم الفراق بيننا، وأستسلم للقدر الذي يراه والدي مخلصا لي من كل "نزوات العقل".15

I loved her very much with my simple heart and strange feelings. I loved her with pure humanity that is free from the attractions of convictions or norms. However, the latter immensely determine our destinies and a person in my position cannot stand up to them … Our norms and the beliefs of my society and my strong father and my weakness that sometimes makes me believe that everything I do is nothing but damn idiocy. They beat me to the ground, given the huge differences between us, and make me surrender to the fate that my father decided for me, free from all the "whims of the mind".

After telling his female colleague at work about his father's response and that he will work elsewhere, they agree to stay friends but not to be lovers. Except for two SMS that he sends some months later, their contact ends. The protagonist decides that he wants to get over it and asks his family to find him a suitable wife whom he then marries. He finds her obedient and attractive. Many years later, he goes to a restaurant with his family and happens to meet his former beloved, who is there with her husband and children. They look at each other and introduce each other to their families as old friends. The story ends with an awkward moment as the protagonist asked his wife: "what shall we eat?"

فرأتنا وأبتسمت ببراءة ، صافحتني وعرفتني على زوجها الذي ابتسم بأدب وحياتي ، تبادلنا كلمات معتادة قليلة ثم توادعنا ونحن نشكر الصدفة الجميلة. عندما مضوا سألتني زوجتي بشيء من الانزعاج من هذه ، قلت بعدم أكتراث زميلة قديمة، قالت بتهكم وهي تقصد زوجها فعلا الطيور على أشكالها تقع. إبتسمت بعدم مبالاة وقلت لها وانا اشير إلى قائمة الطعام " ماذا نأكل"..16

She saw me and smiled innocently and shook my hands and introduced me to her husband who smiled politely and greeted me. We exchanged the usual small talk and then said goodbye, grateful for this great coincidence. When they [had] left, my wife asked me with some annoyance who she was,

---

[15] Blog post from May 25, 2011, http://7osen-man.blogspot.com/2011/05/blog-post_25.html, last accessed November 22, 2011. When I wanted to access the blog post again on December 28, 2011, it had been deleted.

[16] Blog post from April 6, 10 http://www.salatmaiwa.com/2010/04/blog-post_05.html, last accessed on November 22, 2011. When I wanted to access the blog post on December 28, 2011 the settings had been changed to privacy mode.

and I said carelessly: an old colleague. She cynically blurted out, while in reality meaning her husband: birds of a feather flock together. I smiled carelessly and said as I pointed to the menu: "What shall we eat?"

Again the narrator picks up on challenges of traditions and living according to the obligations of society and family. This time the story presents the protagonist's heartbreak to the audience. He is portrayed as a dreamer, someone who wishes and desires but does not act. The story also shows the narrator in a social context. Consequences of taking actions against society's ideals are never mentioned, but the fear of them is great enough for the protagonist to conform.

Both stories of the blogger are about longing and desiring what is far away. In both stories the protagonist shows his vulnerabilities and opens up to the audience. Cultural norms and traditions are questioned but eventually given into.

(c) Your Nose Belongs to You, So What?

The Kuwaiti blogger Sullat Maywah[17] has been blogging on salatmaiwa. com since 2009. On April 6, 2010, she distributed the story "Your nose belongs to you, so what?" The narrator tells the story of a young woman, 23 years of age. It starts with a female protagonist, stopped at a red traffic light, realising that a man in another car is looking at her. This makes her self-conscious and leads her to touch her nose because she thinks it is exceptionally unattractive, while her eyes are portrayed as beautiful. The narrator tells us that the protagonist dislikes pictures of herself and that she covers her nose when photographed and that she dislikes the picture on her ID card. She is so unhappy that when she received a car as a birthday gift from her father she started crying because she preferred to hide in the back seat with a driver in the front so that no one could see the profile of her nose.

فأكبر عقاب لها هو مطالعة بطاقتها الشخصية! تتذكر عيد ميلادها الثامن عشر ، حين اهداها والدها سيارة بكت ليلتها كثيراً لأنها لم تكن تنوي القيادة، فلا تريد أن تكون على مرأى من ناظري أحد، بل كانت تخطط الجلوس في أحد الكراسي الخلفيه لسيارة يقودها سائق![18]

---

[17] The name of the blogger might be translated with "fruit basket". This nickname might lead to a variety of associations. Maybe one of the most striking one is freshness. However, there are surely other ways of interpreting this blogger's name.

[18] Blog post from April 6, 10 http://www.salatmaiwa.com/2010/04/blog-post_05.html, last accessed on November 22, 2011. When I wanted to access the blog post on December 28, 2011 the settings had been changed to privacy mode.

Her biggest punishment is looking at her personal identity card! She remembers her eighteenth birthday when her father gave her a car. She cried so hard all night, not because she did not plan to drive, but because she did not want to be seen by others. She planned to sit in the back seat of a car driven by a driver!

When another student at college asks her whether her nose is crooked, she decides to wear a *niqāb* in order to hide her nose and highlight her eyes.

لكنها منذ تلك اللحظة قررت أن تلبس النقاب!
كانت نقلة كبيرة في حياتها، فلا شعر متناثر حول وجهها، بل قطعة قماش سوداء تغطي نصف وجهها الذي تكرهه، لكن ذاك القماش الأسود كان خلاصها، فيه إختبأت عن العالم، فما أن تضعه حتى تنسى أنفها وتطل من عينيها الجميلتين حولها، لتوهم الناس بجمالها،مدها ذاك النقاب بالثقة مدها بما كانت تحتاج إليه لتنهي دراستها دون خجل.

But since then, she decided to wear the *niqāb*!
This marked a great transformation in her life, for there was no hair covering her face, but rather a piece of black cloth covering the one half of her face that she hated. That black cloth was her salvation, behind which she hid from the world; and soon, as she put it on, she forgot about her nose.
And she would look around with her beautiful eyes to delude people with her beauty; that *niqāb* gave her confidence and what she needed to complete her studies without being shy or evading her colleagues.

One day she decides to take the *niqāb* off once and for all and to finally face her nose. She goes to a beauty clinic to get her nose "fixed". While she waits for her turn, she leafs through magazines and reflects on a TV presenter who could not work with an "ugly" nose. In her thoughts she already plans to get a new picture taken for her ID card.
Later she takes the bandage off her nose and discovers it is still the same nose. This realisation makes her shout for the doctor and nurses and tell them that the nose is still the same. She starts crying bitterly.

بخوف فتحت عينيها لتراه، صرخت بهم !!!!ماهذا!!!!
و!!انظركل من الدكتور والممرضة إلى بعض!
لم تغيرو انفي!! مازال كما هو!![19]

With fear she opened her eyes to look at it ... she yelled at them!!!!
What is this!!!!
The doctor and the nurse glanced at each other!
You did not change my nose!! It still looks the same!!

---

[19] Ibid.

When shown pictures, she admits that the nose feels different. Still, the protagonist sees her nose the same way it was before and is disappointed. In the end she realises that her nose will always be her nose and decides to cover it with the *niqāb* again.

هو انفها .. هو هو .. مهما غيروا فيه هي تراه كما كان، ذات الأنف القبيح .. عادت تقف أمام المرآة لترتدي النقاب وتعاود الإختباء خلفه .. وفكرة واحده تدور في رأسها (انفك منك ولو كان أجدع).[20]

(…) it is her nose … the same old nose … no matter how much they changed it, she still sees it the same … the same old ugly nose … she stood in front of the mirror to wear the *niqāb* and hid behind it once again …
With one thought running through her head: (Your nose is yours, even if it is made smaller.)

The short story describes a common phenomenon of people feeling uncomfortable with their bodies.

It is clear that giving into beauty standards does not change the protagonist's self-perception, rather she goes through body dysmorphia and later tries to deal with it. Catering to social ideals of beauty does not change her self-perception. It seems that only when she wears hijab is she comfortable with her facial features, which suggests her self-perception being influenced by beauty standards.

Only at the end of the story, self-acceptance is seen as a solution to the problem. It is interesting to see how the story develops and different emotional stages are presented. The heroine seems isolated in her struggle throughout the short story.

(d) How Was She Killed?

The next story differs very much from the ones above. This crime story has appeared in many forums and been commented by a lot of readers. Its title is "How was she killed? The complete story of an Emirati woman who was found dead in a well" (referred to below as "How was she killed?"). The story already served as an example in the chapter on setup and narration because of its multimedia features.

A third-person narrator tells the story of a young Emirati woman who is tortured and finally killed by her husband. The short story starts out by describing the female victim as a virgin and a moral person and then

---

[20] Ibid.

continues, stating that the victim's husband physically abused her. The setting is described as in the middle of the mountains. This narration is to a large extent in the form of rhetorical questions.

كيف له أن يضربها ويضربها وهي تقاوم ... تصرخ ... ترتجي الرحمة ؟!
كيف استطاع أن يطعنها بأدوات حاااادة مؤلمة بهذا الشكل ؟
كيف لعاقل أن يخطط لجريمة قتل بهذا القبح ؟![21]

> How could he beat and beat her as she resisted ... screamed ... begged for mercy?!
> How could he stab her with such painfully sharp tools?
> How could any sane person plan such a heinous crime?

When her husband wants to kill her, the woman tries to escape, but she stumbles and falls. Her husband then hits her on the head with a stone and pours corrosive acid on her. The husband is described as a policeman who is supposed to protect the nation and the family. He leaves her, injured and in pain, in the middle of the night in a hole that is 25 metres deep. The victim wishes to die instead of suffering from the torture. The husband returns to his house and pretends that his wife ran away. He goes out and pretends to search for her, too, and is later interrogated by the police. A search for the victim is depicted and the crime scene is described in detail in words and pictures.[22]

The narrator accuses the authorities of not protecting women sufficiently. A description of the crime scene is present in text form and underlined with a picture.

هذه الحفرة .. حوافها تحمل بعض الدماء اليابسة ..
بعضها تبدو كمسحة أصابع مليئة بالدماء .. وبعضها تدل على أنها تطايرت بعد ضربة قوية .. لترسم على الحجر دليلا لمدى الشناعة التي من الممكن أن يصل لها الإنسان ..
وقريبا من ذلك البئر .. بقعة أو اثنتين .. لمادة اختلطت بالرمل وجفت .. تبدو صفراء اللون ..
استنتجنا أنها الحمض.[23]

---

[21] http://www.adbuae.com/vb/archive/index.php/t-4491.html, last accessed December 28, 2011.

[22] The role of the pictures in this story is examined in the chapter on participatory culture.

[23] http://www.adbuae.com/vb/archive/index.php/t-4491.html, last accessed December 28, 2011.

This ditch … its edges have some dried blood
Some spots look like the swipe of bloodied fingers … and some indicate that they splashed after a severe blow … to etch on the stone a testimony to how horrible human beings can be …
Near the well … lies a stain or two … of a material that mixed with the sand and dried … it looks yellow…
We concluded that this was the acid.

The narrator states that it is God who decides on life or death. The story ends with calls to God. This widely distributed story shows a severe case of domestic violence that turns into murder. It is presented in the manner of a crime story or thriller. The heroine is hunted down and her emotional state is described in detail. The complete inability of the victim to escape and the detailed description of the case keep the reader interested and create a climax of the story.

(e) Ḥiṣṣa and the Taxi Driver

An often-redistributed short story from forums is "Ḥiṣṣa and the Taxi Driver". The earliest version of the story that I found was published in the forum alghat.com on January 3, 2006. It goes like this:

One day three young women need to take a taxi because their car has broken down and the driver is unable to fix it. The same day a guy who owns a taxi but is not actually a taxi driver has the same problem: his car has broken down. So he takes the taxi, which he owns but is usually used by one of his employed drivers. The girls happen to get into his taxi; he drives them, pretending he is an Indian driver, even trying to talk like an Indian.

One of the girls forgets her phone in the taxi and the driver and the girl have to meet again. She forgets the phone a second time in the taxi, both feel uncomfortable with the situation because by this time the girls already know that the driver is a local and not a real taxi driver. So the phone will be deposited at a local Starbucks.

حميد : هيه
حصة: إذا مافي تعب عليك.. وده الأستار بوكس .. وعطه اللي على الكونتر .. وقوله وحده بتي تأخذه .. وأنا الحين بتصل فيهم.
حميد: إنشاء الله
حصة: شكرآ اخويه وأنا أسفه على الإزعاج.[24]

[24] http://www.alghat.com/archive/index.php/t-614.html, last accessed December 28, 2011

Hamid: Yes
Hissa: If it is not tiring you ... you can leave it at the Starbucks ... and leave it for me at the counter [using the English word] ... and tell him a girl will pick it up ... and I will call them now.
Hamid: Inshallah
Hissa: Thank you, my brother, and I am sorry for the inconvenience

Sometime later they see each other again in a mall. They don't talk to each other, but they look at each other and accidentally touch shoulders on the way out of a shop. Later that day they start communicating via mobile phone. The story has a happy ending where the two come together.

وتصلو آهل حميد بأهل حصة وصار النصيب وتزوجا في نفس الصالة اللي وصلهم فيها حميد يوم كان راعي التاكسي.[25]

And Hameed's family called Hissa's family and the relatives visited each other and they got married in the same hall in which they met on the day when Hameed was the taxi driver.

Several social issues are addressed in the story. Classicism and racism are two aspects, which are accentuated in dialogues between the protagonists. All through the story the racial aspects are expressed in how communication is presented, as well as there is a focus on class when describing the role of the driver as well as taking a taxi in the first place instead of taking a private car. Additionally, the obstacles in dating or finding love in a conservative society are also part of the story. This theme of societal control was already on display in the earlier mentioned stories. Nevertheless, this story has a happy ending, not only because the two protagonists have found each other but also by educating the audience about not judging a book by its cover. The narrator shows this in changing her attitude towards the love interest and by uncovering a background story of the protagonists. This is a happily ever-after ending.

Depicting Heroes
After introducing the above examples, it is time to examine the general trends in the portrayal of heroes. In online short stories and blog posts, heroes' features are described when showing behaviour and thoughts. Features attributed to the heroes are intentionally constructed to reflect distinct changes in society. However, the sources make certain leanings of

[25] Ibid.

heroes' characteristics apparent. The focus in this analysis lies on portrayals of the new generation and where they feel they belong in terms of gender, societal norms and taboos, individualisation, and other factors such as globalisation and local culture. The older generation in the stories is usually described as a contrasting foil to actions by younger heroes. When heroes are portrayed in stories, personality and physical appearance, settings, description of social behaviour, emotions, and many other factors come into play. A majority of stories published on blogs seem to portray struggling *male* protagonists; these heroes are not able to overcome obstacles set up by the system. In forums, on the other hand, more often *heroines* take an active role. Many writers pick up on topics such as racist stereotyping, cultural traditions, and generational conflicts.

Portrayal of Individualisation

The new generation in the Gulf was brought up differently from their parents, who in turn were brought up very differently from their grandparents, due to the changes in the economy over the last 60 years. These changes have become topics of online literature. In this part, I would like to reflect on how the developments through individualisation are mirrored in the sample texts.

Again, I emphasise that stories do not serve as authentic representations of realities and they were not intended to educate a foreign audience. In this way they have to be seen as a work of literature without having the intention of serving as manifestations of social transformations. However, even reading them as digital short stories shows us concerns and desires of the young writers.

Connected to the portrayal of individualisation is an increase of ICT (Information and Communication Technology) usage. It may be vital to outline the impact of ICT on the process of individualisation.[26] In the story "Ḥiṣṣa and the Taxi Driver", the frequent use of modern communication technology is a reference to current reality essential to describe all of the rather young protagonists. A major part of communication between the characters is conducted on mobile phones, which helps to keep communica-

---

[26] Either ICT is part of the communication between actors of the stories, or it is mentioned in a side note that the original story was typed on a mobile phone or notebook.

tion private, as in Saudi Arabia gender segregation is customary. Individualisation in this story is mirrored in ICT usage. The use of ICT is to influence the individualisation process in two ways: on the one hand, it enables users to have private interactions with one another via online media or mobile phones without control or pressure from the surrounding society, including friends or family. On the other hand, online media in particular enables users to express themselves, present their ideas, and (re)present their identities. Outside of short stories this case is studied, reaffirming that the use of ICT can lead to greater individual autonomy.[27] Bradley argues that two processes are happening at the same time: individualisation and users' increased private interaction. Certainly, the process of increasing individualisation is not only related to ICT but also to globalisation and increasing financial independence of women and men from their families. Individualisation can be seen as part of an overarching development in societies all over the world. The transformation from a life lived within family structures to one more individually experienced is the subject of research for scholars of various cultural studies.[28] It can be seen as part of the recent generations' development in general. As individualisation is taking an increasingly important position in social and academic discourses, it is interesting to ask about the degree to which individualisation is a subject of literary texts in the Gulf. As an increasing degree of globalisation is found everywhere, it is also part of the socio-political development in Egypt and Lebanon.

To this end, "individualisation" first needs to be defined. According to Zygmunt Bauman (2001),

---

[27] Gunilla Bradley, "The Convergence Theory on ICT, Society and Human Beings", in *tripleC—Cognition, Communication, Co-operation*, Vol 8, No. 2, 2010, pp. 183–192. Valerie Frissen and Hermineke van Bockxmeer (2010) also emphasise the shift that appears in society when people increasingly use ICT. Valerie Frissen and Hermineke van Bockxmeer, "The Paradox of Individual Commitment. The implications of the Internet for social involvement", in *Communication Strategies*, no. 42, 2nd quarter 2001. Neither Bradley nor Frissen and van Bockxmeer conducted research in the Gulf, but Bradley included research on Asian countries and argues that this is a global development.

[28] Examples for this trend can be seen in publications as *Sticking Together or Falling Apart: Solidarity in an Era of Individualization and Globalization* (2010) by Paul de Beer and Ferry Koster; *The Individualization of Chinese Society* (2010) by Yunxiang Yan; *Individualization: Institutionalized Individualism and Its Social and Political Consequences* (2002) by Ulrich Beck and Elisabeth Beck-Gernsheim; *Paradoxes of Individualization* (2011) by Dick Houtman, Willem de Koster and Stef Aupers, just to mention a selection of works that all deal with same ideas.

individualization consists in transforming human identity from a given into a task—and charging the actors with the responsibility of performing that task and for the consequences (also the side-effects) of their performance.[29]

Individualisation is strongly related to the emancipation of an individual. Individualisation is usually seen in opposition to collectivism. Therefore, in order to review literature for expressions of emancipation, we need to ascertain the degree to which protagonists act within collective societal limits and the process of emancipation is depicted within the texts. Hazim Saghie edited a collection of articles on individualisation, "The Predicament of the Individual in the Middle East" (2000), which claims that no real individualisation process has happened so far.[30] These articles had been written before uprisings took place in Arab countries, and some of the ideas might be challenged after recent events. The European Science Foundation hosted a research project on the subject of "Individual and Society in the Mediterranean Muslim World" from 1996 to 2001, where it was dealt with many aspects of the subject.[31]

Stephan Guth (2007) highlights some changes that can be observed in the representation of identity in late twentieth-century Arabic and Turkish literature. He states that in these printed texts, which some ascribe to a period he calls "postmodernism", "real individuality [...] consists in an acceptance of your *un*individuality, a *fragmented self* made up of *multiple identities*"[32]; he continues:

> Accepting yourself as a composite being, however, frees you from the burden of having to search for a fixed and definite identity and of committing yourself to the tight and almost strangling corset of an ideologically prefabricated self. With the freedom you gain by accepting yourself as a composite being you also gain fun, because only now will you be able to live life truly and wholly, with all its fascinating aspects, no more having to suppress any of the elements of yourself, of whatever origin they may be.[33]

---

[29] Zygmunt Bauman, *Liquid modernity*, Cambridge 2000, p. 31 f.

[30] Hazim Saghie, *The Predicament of the Individual in the Middle East*, London 2000.

[31] More on this can be found on the website of the project http://www.esf.org/activities/research-networking-programmes/humanities-sch/completed-rnp-programmes-in-humanities/individual-and-society-in-the-mediterranean-muslim-world.html, last accessed January 19, 2011.

[32] Stephan Guth, "Individuality lost, fun gained. Some recurrent motifs in late twentieth century Arabic and Turkish novels", in *Journal of Arabic and Islamic Studies*, Volume 7, Number 1, 2007, pp. 25–49, p. 32.

[33] Ibid., p. 33.

These observations are made about texts from Arabic and Turkish literature from the period immediately preceding (1990s) the one this book deals with. A lot of my text sources do not show the same characteristics as the novels that Guth analyses.

The story "Your nose belongs to you, so what?" is a good example of one way the process of individualisation manifests, because the protagonist is stuck in her subjective perception of what is going on around and with her. Not even when the outside world effects a change of her physical appearance, namely altering her nose does her "inside" is reached. Additionally, the protagonist seems to be left alone with her thoughts. Minor characters of the story, like her father, the other student, and the staff of the clinic, do not interact with her in depth. She does not seem to be embedded in social surroundings such as her family or a circle of friends. The protagonist is part of a family unit, but she appears to be completely isolated. On the other hand, she does not separate herself from society, either. In fact, she tries to blend in and to fit the beauty standard of her surroundings to avoid attracting negative attention. Her wish to assimilate even renders her to cover her face with a *niqāb* in order to hide her "ugliness". This story also reveals post-postmodern notions of heroes' portrayal. The character, unlike the postmodern understanding of a hero, strives to be like everybody else, instead of wanting to be different from the mainstream. The main character has internalised societal norms and values, and she desires to fit in. The opposite of individualisation is represented in the wish for conformity. Only at the end of the story the self is accepted as it ends with "Your nose belongs to you, so what?" Of course, this individualised self is accepted after it becomes apparent that even a physical change of the nose cannot change her view of herself. The heroine's struggle to accept her nose marks the process of individualisation as painful; she does not appear to be completely free of internalised beauty standards. However, this story may be interpreted as presenting a change in literary development and might serve as a metaphor for a blueprint of a change in society to make it more self-accepting.

The story "Fantasy world" could be seen as an example of making individualisation part of the discourse in online literary text. The narrator reflects on the society he lives in as "We are a diverse society in everything", which highlights room for a variety of individualised ways of living. The narrator is usually stuck in his imagination but clearly sees differences in society.

Many of the stories posted in forums and blogs describe individualised characters. Often there seems to be no connection between these characters and their families. The family might be mentioned in a side note or in their function of restricting certain actions of the protagonists, but most often the characters lead their lives quite independently and individually. Still, the opposite is shown in the story "What shall we eat?" (b), in which the main character is still trapped in a hierarchically organised family system with no choice of his own to find happiness by marrying the woman he loves. This story is about a quest for individuality that the protagonist is not strong enough to pursue. He wishes to follow his own desires, such as marrying the woman he wants, but is trapped by family claims on his marital life. The protagonist faces an internal struggle.

The examples discussed earlier describe an alienation of protagonists from the established system of norms and values. Choices of either breaking with or accommodating the system are shown through actions like changing one's appearance, protesting circumstances, or giving in to norms like in the story "How was she killed". These examples make it evident that there are various forms of representation of individualisation in online literary texts. Heroes are portrayed through their struggles with the family collective. Other discourses visible in the sources may shed light on the depiction of individualisation. With showing characters being helpless or surrender to their fate vulnerabilities are exposed that present criticism of traditional norms. In the following part, the portrayal of gender roles will be examined. In the Egyptian novel to be examined, the protagonist faces pressure from society but turns it into humour.

Gender Roles: Some Examples

Individualisation might also be seen in the portrayal of subversive gender roles in the making; here gender roles are altered and new ideals or definitions can be imagined. Since gender representation differs in its forms, I will discuss this topic in two sections. First, I will introduce the representation of heroines and second the portrayal of heroes. Womanhood is portrayed in a variety of forms, for example, in the context of gender segregation, of differences in social interaction.[34]

In this section, some examples from the sources introduced above will illustrate the depiction of femininity in literary texts.[35]

---

[34] Nawar Al-Hassan Golley and Miriam Cooke's *Arab Women's Lives Retold: Exploring Identity Through Writing* (2007) studied the literary representation of women. Within the examination of autobiographical writing by female authors, boundaries in self-representation become apparent.

[35] Sabry Hafez developed a terminology for evaluating gender roles in modern Arabic literature. Hafez analyses a variety of novels written by female authors and divides his examination into the categories feminine, feminist, and female which he sees in corresponding with

In the story "What shall we eat?" a male narrator identifies two young women. On the one hand, there is the beloved whom the protagonist intends to marry but is not allowed to because of his father's opposition. The woman whom the protagonist loves is characterised as being analytical, strong, and dominant in her nature. Still, her appearance is depicted as feminine with beautiful black hair, conforming to rather conventional norms of female beauty:

كانت نحيفة جداً وطويلة، شعرها أسود فاحم يسترسل على كتفيها بإهمال متقن، غالباً ما ترتدي الجينز والتي شيرت بطريقة عملية وأنيقة، عينيها ضيقة وتكاد تختفي عندما تضحك، أنفها صغير وشفاهها مكتنزة ومغرية، وجهها دائري جميل وبشرتها تميل إلى السمار.[36]

She was very slim and tall, her black hair falling on her shoulders with perfected negligence; most often she wore jeans and T-shirt in a sporty and elegant way. She had narrow eyes that almost disappeared when she laughed, with a small nose and full sexy lips and a beautiful round face and browny complexion.

On the other hand, the description of the protagonist's actual wife is much shorter, because she is not the one he desires. She is depicted as a decent wife who is obedient and physically attractive.

تراجعت درجات العذاب قليلاً بعد الزواج فالفتاة التي اقترنت بها كانت جميلة فعلاً ومطيعة، كنت أكن لها كل الاحترام والتقدير لكنها فتاة أخرى، رقم من جملة الأرقام الملتصقة بالناس. فقط أولئك الغير موصومين بالأرقام بإمكانهم أن يوصلونا إلى غاياتنا المرجوة.[37]

The severity of the suffering eased a little after the marriage, as the girl I married was indeed beautiful and obedient. I had a great deal of respect and appreciation for her, but she was another girl, just another number. Only those who are not marked with numbers can lead us to our desired goals.

It is clear that the more independent and strong female character is more attractive to the protagonist. This is not a difference in the person's personality but a difference in rating the person due to limited affection

---

the development of national identity. He finds it necessary to develop a classification system of Arabic literature written by women because their work should not be studied with expectations applied to literature written by men. His way of analysing literary text written by women is valuable in itself but will not be applied in my examination as online literature is varying from his sources. Sabry Hafez, "Women's Narrative in Modern Arabic Literature: A Typology", in Roger Allen et al. (eds.), *Love and Sexuality in Modern Arabic Literature*, London 1995, pp. 154–74.

[36] Blogs-post from May 25, 2011, http://7osen-man.blogspot.com/2011/05/blog-post_25.html, last accessed November 22, 2011. When I wanted to access the blog post again in December 28, 2011 it was deleted.

[37] Ibid.

and admiration. There is a discrepancy between the hero's desires and actions, on the one hand, and the portrayal of society, on the other. As the narration suggests, a strong, independent, and attractive woman is more desirable than a woman who obeys. However, the narrator seems to criticise social norms, hence the sadness, or even "suffering" (*'adhāb*), of the protagonist living under circumstances that prohibit his love. The protagonist does not take further steps to reach autonomy. By criticising norms, the story may lead the audience to feel that injustice has happened and a change of norms is necessary. Criticism of norms may also be seen as a parallel to *nahḍa* literature that emphasises the importance of change within society. The emphasis is often reached by presenting emotional conflicts. One example for this can be found in the "first" Egyptian novel *Zaynab* (1913). The author M. Ḥ. Haykal illustrates a love story that shows conflicts related to class. The heroine in the story is not allowed to be engaged with a farmer but is instead married off to her rich neighbour.

One of al-Zain's blog posts that was discussed in earlier chapters deals with gender roles prescribed to women. Especially the discussion in the comment section picks up on this topic. The third part of one of her blog posts is arranged in the form of a poem, followed by a reply in the same form from a reader, which I will reproduce here in order to give an example of criticism of gender stereotypes. The sample shows the poetic text of the blogger.

كوني جميله ليحبك
كوني رقيقه القلب هينة المعشر ليحبك
كوني ربة منزل وطباخه ماهره يشهد لك بالبنان ليحبك
كوني مدبرة لأموره اليومية والمعيشيه والماديه ليحبك
كوني ام حنون وزوجة رؤوم.... ليحبك
كوني سخيه معه واحفظي ماله و عرضه وبيته في غيابه ليحبك
وباع لك سيرة الجواري بقليل من الحب.. ظلمك التاريخ يا حواء
سؤال على هامش اللائحة التي قد تطول
اين النصائح المقدمة له!![38]

    Be beautiful so that he will love you
    Be gentle-hearted and easy to live with so that he will love you
    Be an excellent housewife and cook [...] so that he will love you
    Be a manager of his daily living and financial affairs so that he will love you

---

[38] http://al-zain.blogspot.com/2011_02_01_archive.html, last accessed December 26, 2011.

Be a loving mother and a forgiving wife … so that he will love you
Be generous with him and protect his wealth and honour and house/family in his absence so that he will love you
History has not been just to you, O Eve … and it sold you the stories of female slaves in return for a little love
A question on the margins of the list that might be too long
Where are the advices given to him!!

Here again the comment addresses the issue of gender roles, listing "proper" mannerisms and personality traits that are suggested to women in order to be their best selves. In the last line of the poem, the commentator asks if the same kind of advice is given to men.

The story "Your nose belongs to you, so what?" presents a weak female character who used to suffer from low self-esteem. Beauty standards are a major focus of the story, in which the protagonist reacts to beauty standards by rejecting her own appearance. She wears a *niqāb* not for cultural or religious reasons, but as a cover for her perceived lack of beauty. Beauty standards are perpetuated by her peers as well as TV presenters and magazines. This story not only focuses on the loneliness of the protagonist but also criticises the obsession with (mostly euro-centric) beauty standards that are imposed on women. However, at the end of the story, the heroine's perspective changes after she learns that she suffers body dysmorphia disorder, she accepts herself. The process of acceptance means a process of maturity is outlined in order to suggest a decent role model to the readers.

The heroine of "How was she killed?" is depicted in the very first paragraph of the story as a young woman of good morals and a virgin. She is an innocent victim who is weak and in pain. Her suffering is caused by male domination and violence. Her feeble physical conditions make it impossible for her to fight back. Oppression in its most brutal form is shown in this story, which is also observed in *nahḍa* literature. Authors such as al-Manfalūṭī or Jubrān Khalīl Jubrān depict the brutal destruction of heroes by the authorities.[39]

---

[39] Stephan Guth, "fa-ġrawraqat ʿuyūnuhum bi-d-dumūʿ. Some notes on the flood of tears in early modern Arabic prose literature", in: Lutz Edzard and Christian Szyska (eds.), *Encounters of Words and Texts. Intercultural Studies in Honor of Stefan Wild on the Occasion of His 60th Birthday*, March 2, 1997, Presented by His Pupils in Bonn, Hildesheim, Zürich, New York 1997, pp. 111–123.

Even though the heroine is victimised, the story itself is told in a manner that condemns violence and abuse. Although no new ideal of women is formed, the story functions as a moral appeal. The readership is encouraged to condemn the brutal actions. The vast number of the story's redistributions and comments, which are discussed in the chapter on participatory culture (see above, p. 91), suggests that this story inspires discussions of such incidents of domestic abuse.

A completely different representation of female characters is found in the story "Ḥiṣṣa and the Taxi Driver". All of the female characters here are rather independent, funny, chatty, witty, and proactive. Short stories posted in forums often feature eloquence and wit of the protagonists. This can be compared to depictions of female protagonists in *Banāt al-Riyāḍ*—a novel written by a young Saudi woman who imitates an exchange in a Yahoo group as a stylistic tool. Here heroines are portrayed as cosmopolitan, witty, and funny as well as being independently acting women who take the initiative.

These young women are described as living between their own curiosity and outgoingness, on the one hand, and wanting to protect their reputation on the other. This dualism is apparent in the heroine's change of tones when communicating with the driver as soon as she realises that he is a local, and also in other parts of the story where three young women do not want to be seen leaving by a taxi. On the one hand, they make their own choice to reach their desired destination by any means, including taking a taxi. On the other hand, taking a taxi is not generally considered appropriate or in compliance with societal standards. The author seems to intend to uncover a form of mild rebellion within the social behaviour of female protagonists. This is described in a positive way of narrating actions taken by heroines. It appears that a general tendency towards female empowerment is endorsed and presented as something that should be strived for in order to reach happiness. Inner conflicts are illustrated and breaking with conventions is depicted as something worth doing as they find love. A similar description of heroines can also be seen as an idealisation of strong individual woman outlined above in the example of "What shall we eat?" We can find representations of strong females within the description of the desired colleague. A brief examination of the examples shows that there is not only a single typical form of representation of femininity in online literary texts from the Gulf. As observed, a wide variety of female portrayals are represented. Heroines can be weak or strong, attractive or not, witty, chatty or silenced as victims.

Now that the portrayal of female characters has been briefly outlined, I will examine the representation of male protagonists in short stories and blog posts. Like femininity, masculinity too can be represented in many ways. My sample texts display a variety of descriptions of male emotions.

In his article "Mohamed 'El-Limby' Saad and the Popularization of a Masculine Code" (2011), Koen van Eynde describes the changing ways of masculinity representation in Egyptian cinema. Paul Amar approaches the subject from a meta-perspective when he discusses the perception of masculinity in a variety of Arab countries in his article "Middle East Masculinity Studies: Discourse of 'Men in Crises', Industries of Gender in Revolution" (2011). In a collection of articles on *Imagined Masculinities* edited by Mai Ghassoub and Emma Sinclair-Webb in 2006, the authors highlight topics such as fear, body hair, and homosexuality in the military. The problem with contextualising representations of masculinity in the Gulf is that not much research has been done in the field and even less when it comes to literature. Research on masculinity is very limited even in other Arab countries, and it is unfortunately not applicable to the Gulf. Culture and tradition in Egypt and Gulf countries are not the same, and even within the Gulf countries it is not possible to talk about one homogeneous culture. Examples of a more popular way of examining masculinity in the Gulf can be found in newspaper essays. Journalist Yousra Samir highlights the cultural distinctiveness of "Kashkha" in her brief article where she outlines the importance of men's grooming in Gulf society, which carries different connotations from in Europe or North America.[40] Another journalist Ali A. Al-Tarrah outlines perspectives on masculinity in Kuwait in his article "Socialization and Masculinity Values in Kuwaiti Society".[41]

As already suggested in the section on generational differences, "What shall we eat?" presents two male characters who are unalike. The son is weak and does not stand up for himself; he is non-confrontational because he fears consequences. On the other hand, the father is strong and dominant.

---

[40] Yousra Samir, "A Qatari Man and His Kashkha", http://www.qatarvisitor.com/index.phcID=412&pID=1639, last accessed January 3, 2012.

[41] Ali A. Al-Tarrah, "Socialization and Masculinity Values in Kuwaiti Society" http://pub-council.kuniv.edu.kw/jss/english/showarticle.asp?id=760, last accessed January 3, 2012.

والدي القبلي المتشدد، كبير الأسرة، ذو الكلمة النافذة والسلطة المطلقة على الجميع.[42]

My father, the tribal and strict one, is the head of the family and his commands are orders and he has absolute power over everyone.

Given the fact that the father in the story is assigned the role of the opponent, it seems that this portrayal aims to emphasise a change of representation of male identity. It can also be argued that the characters' contrast is a representation of the *in-betweenness*, because the son is trying to fight back, though he is not able to. Another challenge for the hero is the struggle with himself, knowing his role as to obey instead of rebelling against the patriarchal system.

شعرت بعد هذه الاحداث بالمهانة لكنني لم أحرك ساكنا، صحيح إنه لم يتغير شيء في عالمي، فأنا أقوم بخدمة ضيوف والدي كل يوم في "الديوانية" على أكمل وجه.[43]

After all these events, I felt humiliated but I did not lift a finger. It is true that nothing in my world changed, since I served my father's guests every day at the "Diwanyia" perfectly well.

These authors' implicit rejection of old role models seems to be based on general humanistic ideals and the condemnation of physical violence and other injustices, for example, the denial of permission to marry the desired partner in compliance with social norms and traditional values. The stories appear to promote the value of finding individual fulfilment without exploring why norms and values are as they are in society; nor is there a direct attack on these norms. Rather, it appears that the readership is expected to have internalised a common understanding of justice.

It appears that these writers want to trigger emotions among readers so as to make them understand specific societal conditions, leading them to feel with the stories' victims or heroes and calling for change. This is a form of narration that makes readers draw their own conclusions instead of accepting the writer's prefabricated conclusions. Still, this strategy is intended to make readers arrive at the conclusions writers expect. As mentioned above,

---

[42] Blogs-post from May 25, 2011, http://7osen-man.blogspot.com/2011/05/blog-post_25.html, last accessed November 22, 2011. When I wanted to access the blog post again in December 28, 2011 it was deleted.

[43] Ibid.

this stylistic feature of appealing to emotions to call for change has already been employed in earlier literature that appeared in the *nahḍa*.

Both stories on 7osen-man's blog present male characters who are emotional, and both characters feel tears coming at some point. Emotions are presented as rather natural. The heroes are not ridiculed for their expression of feelings, instead it appears that their sensibility is appreciated. This kind of sensibility is also presented in literature from the *nahḍa* as well as in the Saudi novel *Banāt al-Riyāḍ*.

Another example of the representation of masculinity can be found in the story "How was she killed?" Here, the male character is portrayed as a cruel aggressor who is nothing but violent. His cruelty and brutality are described in detail in torture scenes. The disapproving depiction of brutality implies the author's rejection of this behaviour and advocacy of humane treatment. Two features are ascribed to the male protagonist that would seem to make him a protector: his job as a police officer and his other role as a husband. Both roles are implied in the story and are usually supposed to be filled by caregivers. In this story, however, the protagonist does the opposite of what is expected of him, torturing his wife until she dies from his violent acts. Male oppression of women is presented to the fullest extent in this short story. A different kind of masculinity is presented in the story "Ḥiṣṣa and the Taxi Driver". Here, the male character is emasculated when the young women assume that he is an Indian driver. He is not seen as a man, as can be observed in the way the young female protagonists talk to him. So here it seems that because of his ethnic identity, his individuality is not understood in terms of his gender. Additionally, it is mentioned that the young women do not wear their veils properly in the car. Later in the story, the male protagonist becomes more active and when it is discovered that he is a local, he also receives his masculinity back. At this point I will not further discuss the role of social class and ethnic belonging, but in this particular story class code overrules gender code.

Although the above examples are too few as to cover the variety of literature distributed online, they nevertheless can be regarded as typical of the attitudes towards masculinity, encountered in the texts analysed in this study. A variety of male characters are depicted in the stories. Some seem strong and dominant; others are weak. It is also important to highlight that most of the selected stories are written by female authors or authors that present themselves as female. This might also have had an influence on the depiction of male characters.

The stories examined all have an educational element to them. The reader learns about a variety of male and female roles and their struggles of conforming to society's demands.

Narration of Gender and the Normativity of Traditions

Ideologies transported in literary texts can either establish and maintain unequal power relations or question them. Taboos and norms are often part of the discourse in online literature. They are related to gender or generational issues but also to traditional values. This power imbalance is expressed through an asymmetric relationship between social actors. Many of the texts that I read are sites of social struggle and represent different ideological struggles related to dominance and hegemony.

In the story "Ḥiṣṣa and the Taxi Driver", inappropriate contact between men and women is best exemplified in the scene in which the "taxi driver" and the young woman meet in the mall by chance. The description of the encounter is part of the end of the story shortly before it is clear that the two protagonists will get married. In the context of traditions and customs the meeting can be seen as an inappropriate situation. That means with depicting the contact the encounter between the two challenges the norm. Here, two discourses are linked. An inter-discursive manifestation forms with two interwoven topics: how migrant labour is perceived and how gender roles are established.

The story "What shall we eat?" points to another set of social norms, in which the need to maintain the family's reputation leads to the protagonist's regret of being able to marry the woman he loves. Social norms here are the need to get married to somebody with appropriate class status and family lineage. The protagonist agrees with these norms and traditions and does not challenge them. However, it becomes apparent that he regrets his decision of not acting on his desires. When breaking down criticism of societal norms in online literary text from the Gulf, a majority of the texts deal with issues of love, such as the struggles to communicate or see each other.[44] Many stories describe how two lovers want to get married but cannot because of obstacles society puts in their way. The problem of being handicapped in pursuing love because of traditions and norms is also subject of *Banāt al-Riyāḍ*.

---

[44] This is especially observable in a number of short stories published in forums.

The online literature from the region does not paint a homogeneous picture of men or women. Gender roles are part of the stories, but all kinds of normative gender identities are presented. The context here is generally heterosexual. In mainstream blogs and forums, homosexuality does not appear in the stories. This does not mean that it is not present at all—there are niches for dealing with this subject—but mainstream online literary distribution does not pick up the subject of homosexuality. By mainstream online literature I mean stories on forums and blogs that seem to represent mainstream norms and are read by a larger audience. I have not looked into niche blogs that might deal with non-mainstream subjects. Gender is one aspect of how protagonists' identities are marked, but it is not the only one. Another perspective on heroes' criticism of social norms will be discussed in the following.

Criticism of Social Norms

Criticism of social norms in online literary text should be viewed in its political and cultural context. It is also necessary to examine whether criticism of social norms is actually part of a literary text or if it is rather presented in essays and the commentary form.

In my selection of stories, criticism appears in relation to issues such as restrictive societal conventions, expatriate workers, and the relationship between women and men. Depending on the platform of distribution and the individual writer, criticism on forums is often not a direct attack on societal values and in this way also reproduces and reinforces societal discourses. On the other hand, blogs present explicit criticism of societal problems. Criticising social norms is strongly connected to forming and representing identity in online literary texts from the Gulf because protagonists always situate themselves within and against these norms. The texts debate the protagonists' perceptions of themselves and others.

All of the examples introduced above seem to criticise or at least address society and norms, so the readers can form opinions and position themselves in relation to these issues. Among the examples, the stories presented by Nashiri illustrate rather conservative views, while in "What shall we eat?" the critique of a patriarchal system is direct and straightforward. There, this patriarchal system is portrayed to be a direct obstruction of the individual's happiness. The story "What shall we eat?" describes regret but also acceptance of circumstances. This is the opposite of the Egyptian writing of Ghada Abdel Aal in *Ayza Atgawez*, where the protagonist ridicules these norms and her suitors.

In the story "Ḥiṣṣa and the Taxi driver", initiatives that the young women take for themselves show their independence. However, steps that are taken are always in accordance with the aim of protecting the women's reputation. Boundaries are occasionally traversed but within the limits of a normative understanding of how an honourable woman should behave.

One recurring theme in online literary texts from the Gulf is the vast change in the region brought about by globalisation. A dichotomy between social norms and new global influences is part of the representation of identity in many ways, for example, in the choice of settings, language, and portrayal of the heroes.

The tension between globalisation and local or national heritage is part of a wider framework of topics studied by many researchers.[45] One way of connecting heritage and contemporary development in literature and the arts is poetry. In the Arabic-speaking world, poetry is a popular form of art in the public consciousness. Usually the style of this kind of poetry is traditional and local. Nismah Ismail Nawwab (2008) attempts to show "how poems evolve with the rendering of societal and political factors".[46] She states that, for example, in Saudi Arabian poetry, themes of societal discourses are prominent. Recent poems, she states, "capture life in present-day Arabia" (p. 92).

"My journey into poetry, in particular, is an example of how much the society—be it the local Saudi or the ever-wider and closer global community—is reflected in the themes, evolutions, styles and voice of the poems,"[47] Nawwab says. This means that traditional forms of literary production deal with contemporary issues and themes. This integration of traditional poetry in the media and its consideration of contemporary issues is a fusion of contemporary developments in literature and the arts on the one hand and reviving or maintaining the heritage on the other. Another form of fusing the culture of the past with the present is the transmission of stories in the form of storytelling.

---

[45] Cf., for example, Clement Moore Henry and Robert Springborg (2010); Bassel F. Salloukh and Rex Brynen (2004); David Held and Kristian Ulrichsen (2011).

[46] Nimah Ismail Nawwab, "The Social and Political Elements that Drive the Poetic Journey", in Alanoud Alsharekh and Robert Springborg (eds.), *Popular Culture and Political Identity in the Arab Gulf States*, London 2008, pp. 85–96.

[47] Ibid., p. 86.

Local culture and heritage help to shape representation of identity, which is in turn susceptible to the impact of globalisation. Partly this has already been dealt with in other chapters where global influences on language are documented. Globalisation influences not only the use of language but also other aspects such as in literature, the arts and human interactions. According to Maddalena Pennacchia Punzi (2007), global impact can be found in the authors' work in the way they envision new perspectives on the current situation. Print and online media and works of imagination such as plots and design can be embedded in a global frame while producing a local feeling within the text, thereby presenting a local perspective on global issues.[48] Aside from language, global impact on stories can be found in the descriptions of settings, brands, or the presence of foreign labour, for example.

In the Gulf, globalisation is much more visible in everyday life compared to many other places of the world. The presence of expatriate workers alone, who usually form the majority of the population in Gulf states, means that people from a wide variety of nationalities live in just one country. In some cities, the percentage of expatriates is very high.

Nada Mourtada-Sabbah et al.'s article "Media as Social Matrix in the United Arab Emirates" (2008) deals with young people's approaches to media use in the UAE. They state that the "new generation" has more in common with each other around the world than with their parents' or grandparents' generation.[49] This is true when it comes to popular culture, but also in the use of interactive communication devices. Popular culture is a superficial bond between the global youth and represents just one layer of identity. Regional cultural distinctions are still present and relevant for everyday life. These values do not disappear, but stay visible in regional and global cultures. Even when popular culture and ICT are connecting the youth worldwide, it is apparent that the use of ICT is culturally influenced and distinctive in its context. Mourtada-Sabbah et al. clarify that the young generation understands ICT differently than their parents' generation, because digital media was not available during the older generation's

---

[48] Maddalena Pennacchia Punzi, *Literary intermediality: the transit of literature through the media circuit* Bruxelles/Bern/Berlin/Frankfurt am Main/New York/Oxford/Wien 2007, p. 248.

[49] Nada Mourtada-Sabbah, Mohammed al-Mutawa, John W. Fox and Tim Walters, "Media as Social Matrix in the United Arab Emirates", in Alanoud Alsharekh, Robert Springborg and Sarah Stewart (eds.), *Popular Culture and Political Identity in the Arab Gulf States*, London 2008, pp. 121–142, p. 126.

formative years, and thus, and they did not grow up as "digital natives". ICT creates a social matrix for young people. This is mirrored in the use of online forums, chat rooms, social networks, and other interactive online media, as well as the widespread use of mobile phones.[50] The sense of collective memory also differs across generations.

The influence of globalisation is a regular theme of the stories. Globalisation is not criticised as an extraterritorial attack, but rather described and reflected upon as accepted element of life. Fast food chains like "Hot Burger" and "Starbucks", as settings for the story, are landmarks of globalisation.[51]

The frequent appearance of expat labourers in the stories also highlights globalisation. In "Ḥiṣṣa and the Taxi Driver", the taxi driver is supposed to be from India. As mentioned earlier, class code trumps gender code in the story. The form of language, communication, and attitude between the young women and the male protagonist changes as soon as it becomes clear that he is local.

The story "Fantasy world" is partly set in a cinema at a mall and the main character's friend indulges in American snacks. They watch a romantic comedy and the narrator lets the audience know that he is fond of change in society. These details are not necessary for understanding the complete plot, but they emphasise the globalised dimensions of everyday practice.

The connection between the heroes' portrayal and globalisation is illustrated in detail, materialised in venues and products. The short stories analysed here mirror these developments.

Valentine M. Moghadam states that social change and development "come about principally through technological advancements, class conflict, and political action" and are "located within and subject to the influences of a national class structure, a regional context, and a global system of states and markets".[52] The terms mentioned here are superficial indicators of a general opening to the global economy and a natural understand-

---

[50] Ibid.

[51] In the short story "And Rebecca Asks Me About the Wali" the technical term "French Manicure" is used and not transliterated into Arabic. Another example can be found in the short story "British Airways". The name of the company as well as the term "economy class" are used in English. http://www.alabudaiah.com/vb/showthread.php?p=17807, last accessed January 26, 2012.

[52] Valentine M. Moghadam, *Modernizing Women: Gender and Social Change in the Middle East*, Boulder 2003, p. 2.

ing as a part of ordinary social life. Embedding global influence in short literary texts helps to define identity in its context of a globalised society. Here, identity is not represented by gender roles or social norms but within an understanding of changes in the local infrastructure. This enhances the understanding of the self in contemporary times, no longer restricted to a self-image conveyed by literary culture from earlier times, as it was set in Bedouin life and the poetry of the desert. In the works of Pepe and Ramsay political dimensions of online writing are further discussing texts from Egypt and Lebanon.

Texts are cautiously interpreted because online literature as an emerging cultural expression needs more examination from a wider variety of perspectives. Therefore, examples were rather tentatively interpreted in order to avoid premature judgement. In further research of this field, in-depth interpretation can be approached. However, these text examples and their analysis show that a variety of factors influence identity representation in online literary texts from the Gulf. It can be observed that heroes portrayed in forums differ from those depicted in blog posts: change is desired in many stories on blogs, and in the stories in forums change is more actively approached. In these stories, individualisation can be interpreted as a way of finding one's own self-acceptance. The stories posted on the e-publisher's website are more conservative than those on blogs and forums.

In blogs and forums, it appears that there is a desire to get rid of old ideas and create new ones. The struggle for new ideals meets resistance from established norms. Proactiveness, as a personality trait, serves as an ideal type of acting in society but is seldom actualised. In some of the stories, protagonists begin to take the initiative for change, but are unable to carry through.

The representation of gender is part of the literary text. There is no homogeneous representation of womanhood. Female identities differ in various ways. Tendencies towards a preference of stronger, active female protagonists can be observed in some of the stories, but other forms of female identity—weak characters—are also present. The general tendency is towards an ideal of a "new woman".

The representation of male heroes is also an important part of short stories from the region. Male characters are sometimes presented as vulnerable and indecisive, showing their emotions. On the other hand, strong characters are also presented. These could be a violent husband or powerful father figure who controls his families.

In stories like "What shall we eat?" or "How was she killed?" male characters take up the role of the villain. These male characters embody stereotypical masculine features such as physical and emotional strength. Villains oppress heroes in these stories and harm them mentally or physically. The hero is depicted in contrast. In "What shall we eat?" a sensitive young man is in love and shows his emotions, expressed through sadness and tears. In "How was she killed?" the heroine/victim is described as innocent and pure with a good reputation in society. Readers here may sympathise with the emotional and pure heroine who suffers oppression and abuse. In "Your nose belongs to you, so what?" the heroine is exposed to an aesthetic understanding that takes the evil role, making her feel forced to adopt beauty standards. The heroine struggles with the imposed expectation and her emotions and fears are portrayed in opposition to societal forces. These stories are easily comprehensible for the reader, because the roles of the protagonists are clearly presented and it is not difficult to choose a figure to sympathise with.

The sources show a heterogeneous society described in a variety of texts, in which the portrayal of heroes is bound to multiple factors. Societal discourses are picked up and embedded in all of the blog posts and stories posted in forums.

Social norms and globalisation are both part of identity representation in online literary text. Global influences are represented in language settings and cultural expression. Social norms influence identity representation as much as globalisation does, since both shape the way of living.

CHAPTER 6

Challenges of Online Distribution

Authors turn to online publishing for many reasons. One of them is the possibility to distribute their works with a relatively low barrier for publication—this means that texts do not need to be approved by either editors, publishers, or governmental institutions. This chapter will identify challenges to online literature, such as the impact of digital media on political conditions, as well as the influence of authoritarian regimes on literary texts. These texts are strongly influenced by internet censorship as well as global and local influence on Information and Communication Technology (ICT) use. Some authors turn to writing online because they write on sensitive topics, while others find greater freedom of expression on the internet. This chapter begins by detailing the peculiarities and politics of censorship in various countries before concluding. The second part of the chapter deals with the challenges that occur through publishing in digital media. These challenges include issues of redistribution of literary works as well as crediting the original source.

CHALLENGES OF ONLINE DISTRIBUTION

This section examines the context of literary production (i.e. constraints and challenges) distributed in digital media. As my examination is a first attempt to capture the cultural phenomenon from a variety of perspectives, it is necessary to include restrictions in publications. This chapter is connected to an earlier examination of participatory culture as well as perspectives of identity representation, especially the latter's consideration of anonymity, intellectual property, and repostings of stories.

Two major challenges facing online literature production are autocratic forces that affect authors and online literary texts, and the authors' encounters with copying (reproduction) of intellectual property and the reposting of stories. In order to understand the intensity of ICT usage in the Gulf, Lebanon, and Egypt, patterns of use will be briefly introduced. Additionally, the mutual influence of online media and politics will be outlined by evaluating reasons for censorship. One of the perceived advantages of online media is its function as a source of uncensored information, which enables people to organise against states.[1] But the internet is not a space that is entirely free from censorship—governments in most countries have means to tap into and control ICT use and close down forums and blogs. Still, compared to print media, it is much easier to distribute digital media of any kind. In *The Wealth of Networks: How Social Production Transforms Markets and Freedom* (2006),[2] Yochai Benkler characterises this newfound freedom and subsequently online activism as increased autonomy supplemented with greater information and critical perspectives.[3] The use of ICT as the medium through which literature is written and read influences literary text production. Marshall McLuhan studied the relationship between medium and message (in 1964 and 1967), and emphasised that perception of a message is always impacted by the medium that it is sent through.[4] The following sections deal with the adaptation of ICT, global and local influences on its use that are especially pertinent to the sub-chapter on opinion making, and opportunities from having a "global voice". Further, the issue of creative commons licence and other distinct ways of dealing with intellectual property will be examined. The chapter begins with a brief description of censorship imposed by authorities and the political aspects that come into play in ICT use. Because all Gulf countries are ruled by autocratic regimes, it is much easier to enforce restrictive laws on media and publishing. In subsequent sections, the impact of online media on politics

---

[1] Helen V. Milner, "The Digital Divide: The Role of Political Institutions in Technology Diffusion", in *Comparative Political Studies* 39, no. 2, 2006, pp. 176–199, p. 184.

[2] Yochai Benkler, *The Wealth of Networks: How Social Production Transforms Markets and Freedom*, New Haven 2006.

[3] Ibid., p. 92.

[4] Marshall McLuhan, *Understanding Media: The Extensions of Man*, New York 1964. And *The Medium is the Message*, New York 1967.

will be discussed. Of all GCC countries, Freedom House only ranks Kuwait as "Partly Free", while all other countries are rated as "Non Free".[5] In Egypt, internet activists had already been arrested before the Uprisings of 2011. Egypt is rated as "Non Free" by Freedom House rankings while Lebanon is rated "Partly Free".[6] Lebanon is so far more free when it comes to rights of expression and freedom of speech. However, this status has deteriorated since 2014.[7]

The Impact of Online Media on Political Conditions

Highlighting the mutual impact of online media and political conditions sheds light on the nature of literary works from the region. Literature often reflects societal discourses and challenges as well as inspires debates on many aspects of life. As mentioned in earlier chapters, online literature can be seen as more democratic than those in print because it is more amenable to active usage and interaction between writers and readers. The following discusses the internet as a tool for hosting more opportunities for the freedom of speech and inspiring debates. I will start by looking at the broad debate around the net's influence on democratisation processes and political change, as well as on literary production in print and online since circumstances surrounding publication can and do affect the text itself.

In the early stages of research on online media in the Arab world, it was widely believed that the mere introduction of the internet might lead to political change, particularly in terms of the ability of the internet to spur democratisation and/or development in undemocratic countries.

Online media were used by citizens to spread information, communicate, and organise collective action during the uprisings in countries such as Tunisia and Egypt.[8] While online media facilitated social mobilisation for a limited period of time (before the internet was shut down), it was not

---

[5] https://freedomhouse.org/report/freedom-net/2015/united-arab-emirates, https://freedomhouse.org/report/freedom-press/2015/oman, https://freedomhouse.org/report/freedom-press/2015/kuwait, https://freedomhouse.org/report/freedom-world/2016/bahrain, https://freedomhouse.org/report/freedom-world/2016/saudi-arabia, last accessed December 29, 2017.

[6] Freedom House Report 2015, https://freedomhouse.org/report/freedom-press/2016/egypt, last accessed December 29, 2017.

[7] Freedom House Report 2015, https://freedomhouse.org/report/freedom-press/2015/lebanon, last accessed December 29, 2017.

[8] This is also true for other countries that had uprisings in 2011.

the only force fuelling these events. Veva Leye (2007) holds that ICT by itself will not lead to a change of institutional settings "as there are no changes in political decision-making processes"[9]—although this observation was made prior to the 2011 uprisings, it nonetheless holds true. What changed decision-making processes in Egypt and Tunisia was people taking collective action, rather than blogging individually. Thus, the events of 2011 bore out Leye's findings. After the internet and cell phone connections were shut down in Egypt for two days (January 27–28, 2011), the uprising continued to work even without access to ICT. Access to ICT has also been key to the organisation of social movements not just locally but also globally. This was evident in the 2011 uprisings where uproar over the self-immolation of Mohamed Bouazizi and subsequent toppling of Tunisian president, Zine El Abidine Ben Ali, led to a domino effect in Egypt. Yet this domino effect should not be overstated. In his book *Zero Comments* (2007), media researcher Gert Lovink makes the point that movements online are started by local events rather than by general ideas.[10] In other words, in Tunisia as well as in Egypt, while there was widespread desire to mount a revolt against the existing ruling power, locally based events were equally if not more important in triggering the revolt. In particular, online initiatives were key in documenting the events and helping gather vast numbers of people for an actual protest away from the screen (i.e. offline). Hence, the offline domain can be a necessary condition for political change.

The impact of online activities on offline livelihood witnessed in Tunisia and Egypt generally does not, however, apply to the Gulf region. This means that online political activism does exert a corresponding effect on offline political dynamics—at least not until someone permits such a transfer. Afraa Ahmed Albabtain has researched internet forums in Saudi Arabia in the article "Downloading Democracy" (2008), where he states: "Although forums play an important role in promoting political awareness, they have not yet developed to an extent that pushes the forum member to positive political and social action, which means his participation is limited to the virtual world." These findings undergird Leye's argument that change has to be effected *outside* the virtual world, that is, in political decision-making. One exception in the Gulf countries was the uprisings in Bahrain in 2011, which

---

[9] Veva Leye, "UNESCO, ICT corporations and the passion of ICT for development: modernization resurrected", in *Media Culture Society*, 29, no. 6, 2007, pp. 972–993, p. 983f.

[10] Gert Lovink, *Zero Comments: Blogging and Critical Internet Culture*, London 2007.

were however violently put down by the Bahraini regime with support from the armies of the neighbouring countries Saudi Arabia and the UAE.[11] Omar Al-Shehabi offers a more detailed overview on political movements in Bahrain.[12] One might argue that one could find exceptions in Kuwait as well, such as the Orange movement in 2006.[13] What is of great interest for this study is that in Bahrain, poetry was one form of protest on Pearl Square, the venue where people gathered.[14] Such oratory performance or spectacle highlights the political value of literary art forms in everyday life in the Gulf.[15] In Egypt, political activities on the web were taking clearer shape during the Kifaya movement from 2004 onwards. Bloggers such as Mahmoud Salem "Sand Monkey" have been arrested.[16] During the Uprisings, on Tahrir Square, poetry was recited, which gained momentum from the public, as the video of a poem related to the "virginity tests" of the police during the uprisings went viral online.

THE INFLUENCE OF AUTHORITARIAN REGIMES ON LITERARY TEXTS

Literary texts are influenced by the medium in which they are published through as well as external forces that shape its content and form of dissemination. This is true not only for digital literature but also for literature published in print. Differences between print and online literature are highlighted in the chapter on narration, as well as in the chapter on participatory culture, and will not be further discussed here.

---

[11] Ethan Bronner and Michael Slackman, "Saudi Troops Enter Bahrain to Help Put Down Unrest", in *New York Times*, March 14, 2011, http://www.nytimes.com/2011/03/15/world/middleeast/15bahrain.html?pagewanted=all, last accessed January 16, 2012.

[12] Omar Al-Shehabi. "Political Movements in Bahrain Across the Long Twentieth Century (1900–2015)." *Oxford Handbook of Contemporary Middle-Eastern and North African History*. Amal Ghazal and Jens Hanssen (eds). April 2017. http://www.oxfordhandbooks.com/view/10.1093/oxfordhb/9780199672530.001.0001/oxfordhb-9780199672530-e-27?mediaType=Article.

[13] Jon Nordenson, *We Want Five!: Kuwait, the internet, and the public sphere*, Saarbrücken 2010.

[14] Sarah Hoffmann, "Give Us Back Our Bahrain", on pen.org, June 9, 2011, http://www.pen.org/blog/?p=71, last accessed January 16, 2012.

[15] See also Nele Lenze, "Protest Poetry On- and offline: trans-regional interactions in the Arabian Gulf: An example from Bahrain" In N. Lenze, C. Schriwer & Z. Abdul-Jalil (Eds.), *Media in the Middle East Activism, Politics, and Culture*. Palgrave, New York. pp. 203–222.

[16] Award winning blogger, best Middle East blog in 2006, BOB best English Blog in 2011 http://www.sandmonkey.org/.

Media in most of the authoritarian Gulf countries such as television, radio, newspapers, magazines, books, and the internet requires approval from the local authorities before they are consumed by the masses. In Lebanon, the Constitution guarantees freedom of press, but media content has to be in accordance with "national ethics".[17] The approval of a cultural product therefore depends on its content; this is especially true if a country has just suffered from a period of political turmoil and opposition.[18]

Credible constraints on the freedom of expression can also inculcate a Foucauldian "automatism" or self-censorship among producers of literature in order to protect the authors and audience—this ensures that information and ideas already conform to state-sanctioned narratives and boundaries before even reaching the public sphere. Common red lines pertain to religion, political leaders, and sexuality—the three big taboos discussed already by Marina Stagh for printed literature in Nasser's and Sadat's Egypt.[19] William A. Rugh (2004) illustrates the above through

[17] Freedom House Report 2015, https://freedomhouse.org/report/freedom-press/2015/lebanon, last accessed December 29, 2017.

[18] For example, in Egypt, censorship and surveillance were further constrained following the uprisings. In 2015, it ranked as the world's second worse gaoler of journalists. Freedom House Report 2015, https://freedomhouse.org/report/freedom-press/2016/egypt, last accessed December 29, 2017.

[19] For the Gulf countries, the following framework of censorship has to be taken into account:

KSA: Saudi Arabia filters sites related to opposition political groups, human rights issues and religious content deemed offensive to Muslims. Pornographic and gay sites are pervasively filtered, as are circumvention tools and online privacy tools. Bloggers have been arrested, and blogs and sites run by online activists have been blocked. http://opennet.net/research/profiles/saudi-arabia, last accessed January 25, 2012.

OMAN: The Sultanate of Oman engages in extensive filtering of pornographic websites, gay and lesbian content, and anonymizer sites used to circumvent blocking. The censors have added to the blacklist content that is critical of Islam and websites on illegal drugs. Although there is no evidence of technical filtering of political content, laws and regulations restrict free expression online and encourage self-censorship. http://opennet.net/research/profiles/oman, last accessed January 25, 2012.

QATAR: The censors in Qatar admit to filtering pornography, political criticism of Gulf countries and material deemed hostile to Islam. The authorities also pervasively filter gay and lesbian content, sexual health resources and privacy and circumvention tools. Political filtering is highly selective, but journalists self-censor on sensitive issues such as government policies, Islam and the ruling family. http://opennet.net/research/profiles/qatar, last accessed January 25, 2012.

KUWAIT: Though the media in Kuwait are among the most outspoken in the Gulf states, journalists self-censor on issues related to the royal family. The primary target of Internet

Saudi Arabia's print censorship: "Newspapers publish on sensitive subjects such as crime or terrorism only after news has been released by the government through the official Saudi news agency SPA, or from government official." Rugh adds that foreign printed media is censored, depending on its "offending" content.[20] Strategies of state censorship vary across countries. Self-censorship is impossible to measure. In a survey I conducted with 27 respondents, 12 participants thought censorship was important to them, 11 did not find censorship important, 1 participant asked what kind of censorship was meant, and 1 stated that it was not very important; 1 participant made it clear that there is only social censorship, and another emphasised the importance of self-censorship.[21] Ola Erstad and James V. Wertsch (2008) highlight aspects of self-censorship in online writing in Iran and emphasise that the individual sets his or her limits of censorship.[22] In the Gulf region, social censorship is also an influential and active buttress of state censorship. Since people can ask for websites to be blocked, they have the power to increase censorship. Robin "Roblimo" Miller, former editor in chief of various Linux-related websites, points out that it is not difficult to bypass the Saudi internet filter. It took him less than 30 minutes to do so in the late 2000s. He interviewed Eyas S. al-Hejery who was head of the ISU (Internet Service Unit) in the Kingdom of Saudi Arabia at that time. During this interview, al-Hejery admitted that he knows how easy it is to bypass the blocked sites, but the filter is a necessary protection for children "and other innocents from Internet evils".[23] He

---

filtering is pornography and, to a lesser extent, gay and lesbian content. Secular content and websites that are critical of Islam are also censored. Some websites that are related to religions other than Islam are blocked even if they are not critical of Islam. http://opennet.net/research/profiles/kuwait, last accessed January 25, 2012.

BAHRAIN: Bahrain is a regional ICT leader and is one of the most Internet-connected countries in the Middle East. The country's Internet filtering regime focuses on political websites that are critical of the Bahraini government and ruling family, but also targets pornography, content related to gays and lesbians and content that is critical of Islam. http://opennet.net/research/profiles/bahrain, last accessed January 25, 2012.

[20] William A. Rugh, *Arab Mass Media: Newspapers, Radio, and Television in Arab Politics*, Westport 2004, p. 71.

[21] Survey data 2010.

[22] Ola Erstad and James V. Wertsch, "Tales of mediation: Narrative and digital media as cultural tools", in Knut Lundby (ed.), *Digital Storytelling, Mediatized Stories. Self-representation in New Media*, New York 2008, pp. 21–40, p. 35.

[23] Cf. Robin 'Roblimo' Miller: "Meet Saudi Arabia's most famous computer expert", 2004, http://www.linux.com/articles/33695, accessed September 7, 2009.

points out that the system has wide public support, as is demonstrated by the fact that the Internet Service Unit currently receives over 200 "legitimate" requests to *block* sites every day, but only a "trickle" of requests to *unblock* sites that members of the society feel are being hidden illegitimately.[24] This is common in many of the Gulf countries and some requests by the general population to ban content is present in the offline world as well. For example, the content of Rajāʾ ʿAbdallāh al-Ṣāni's novel *Banāt al-Riyāḍ* (The Girls of Riyadh) offended religious people.[25] Subsequently, al-Ṣāni received threatening mails and death threats. In addition, two Saudi men asked the Ministry of Information to revoke permits to distribute the novel in Saudi Arabia and demanded that the author be punished.[26] It was argued that the novel misrepresented the lifestyle of young Saudis and gave them a bad reputation all over the world. In this case, it was neither the religious police nor the Ministry of Information that worked to suppress the novel, but conservative members of society who asserted their moral standards on society. Marc Lynch states that there is a general tendency for religious actors to impose censorship on the media, as is witnessed in the Arab public sphere[27]—since religious doctrines mostly seek increasing censorship rather than otherwise, they can be said to have only adversary powers with respect to the freedom of expression.

The question of censorship of literary texts is publicly debated, for example at book fairs and in public panel discussions. The following example from print literature is a general example of people's awareness of censorship in Arab countries and outlines two contradictory positions in this debate. When I attended a panel discussion with two winners of the "International Prize for Arabic Fiction"[28] (the so-called Arabic Booker Prize) at Abu Dhabi International Book Fair in March 2011, the topic of writing under censorship came up. The audience asked whether censor-

---

[24] Ibid.
[25] Raid Qusti, "Court Rejects Case Against Rajaa Al-Sanea", in *Arab News*, October 9, 2006, http://arabnews.com/?page=1&section=0&article=87886&d=9&m=10&y=2006&pix=kingdom.jpg&category=Kingdom, accessed January 4, 2012.
[26] Ibid.
[27] Mark Lynch, "The Structural Transformation of the Arab Public Sphere", in: *Voices of the New Arab Public: Iraq, Al-Jazeera, and Middle East Politics Today*, New York 2006, p. 86.
[28] Event: Meet the Winners of the International Prize for Arabic Fiction 2011, Venue: KITAB Sofa, Abu Dhabi International Book Fair, ADNEC, March 14, 2011, Participants: Mohammed Achaari and Raja Alem.

ship had influenced the text and writing of the two winning authors. The authors' responses presented two opposing ideas. The Saudi author Raja Alem (RajāʾᵡĀlam) held that there was no censorship and it was up to the author to self-censor literary works. The Moroccan author Mohammed Achaari (Muḥammad al-ʾAshʿarī), on the other hand, stated that censorship does influence literary production. These two standpoints highlight differences in the perception of authoritarian influence. Both writers were moderate in their opinions in comparison with Joumana Haddad (Jumāna Ḥaddād), a Lebanese writer and the editor of the literary magazine "Jasad" (Body). Haddad strongly criticised censorship not only in her manifesto "I killed Scheherazade" (2010) but also during a public discussion at the Emirates Airline International Festival for Literature in Dubai in 2011. In her harsh condemnation of censorship she writes: "Some Arabs speak of the virtuous mission of literature while denying writers freedom of expression. Is there a more whorish act than depriving an author of his/her words? Let's call things by their names: censorship is an act of RAPE."[29]

Later in the same manifesto she emphasises that censoring books contributes to their popularity and praises the possibilities of circumventing print censorship through online media: "For what can censorship really hope to achieve, when banning a book guarantees it notoriety and widespread success? Why impose censorship in an age when, at the press of a button, we can get all the information we need and more?"[30]

Writers can employ various strategies to deal with censorship. Paul Starkey (2006) points out that, to circumvent censorship, writers of print literature can set their stories in another historical period and use the historical disguise to allude to present conditions.[31] In doing so, they draw on a long tradition of metaphorical writing in classical Arabic literature, some of them even imitating the style of medieval Arab writers (cf., e.g., Jamāl al-Ghīṭānī in his famous novel *al-Zaynī Barakāt* of 1974).

Surely, authorities are aware of the advantages of distributing literary and political texts online. They deal with it not only through censorship, but also by supporting projects that act in accordance with the rules. Government and government-affiliated organisations are involved in online activities. They can influence opinions through their distribution of

---

[29] Joumana Haddad, *I Killed Scheherazade: Confessions of an Angry Arab Woman*, London 2011, p. 69.
[30] Ibid., p. 86.
[31] Paul Starkey, *Modern Arabic literature*, Edinburgh 2006, p. 144.

state subsidies.[32] This is most easily achieved with media prizes awarded to active online creators/producers who work in accordance with the guidelines of common agendas. In the UAE, this can take the form of honouring projects, for example the *Sheikh Majid Youth Media Award*, which was first announced in 2008.[33] In Kuwait the e-publishing house Nashiri was granted the *Internet Contest Award 2005* by Sheikh Salem Al-Ali Al-Sabah of Kuwait.[34] Nashiri allows online literature to be distributed if it follows guidelines, which include the use of Modern Standard Arabic as well as the avoidance of offensive content.

Internet Censorship in Gulf Countries, Lebanon, and Egypt

This part will sum up what internet censorship is about in the Gulf countries, Lebanon and Egypt. Compared with some offline public spaces, the internet is still a space for open discussions in terms of political and social sensitive subjects. Online media did not initiate uprisings in the Gulf, but it was used as a tool to spread independent information and enable communication. For example, during the uprisings in Bahrain and[35] Saudi Arabia, it fuelled demonstrations[36]; and also in Kuwait, where demonstrators even stormed the parliament.[37]

The *Reporters Without Borders* 2007 annual report makes it clear that the situation is difficult for journalists in Saudi Arabia. Newspapers are shut down and journalists who write about subjects that the government disapproves are dismissed.[38] The *Open Net Initiative* also provides infor-

[32] Eric Louw, *The Media and Cultural Production*, London; Thousand Oaks/New Dehli 2005, p. 46.

[33] More information about the award can be found on http://www.sheikhmajidawards.com/about-sheikh-majid-media-award.aspx, last accessed January 4, 2012.

[34] More on this on Hayat Alyaqut's personal website http://www.hayatt.net/, last accessed January 2, 2012.

[35] Global Voice online offers an overview on activities in Bahrain in the post "Bahrain Protests 2011", December 19, 2011, http://globalvoicesonline.org/specialcoverage/bahrain-protests-2011/, last accessed December 29, 2011.

[36] "Saudi Arabia bans protest rallies", March 5, 2011, http://www.aljazeera.com/news/middleeast/2011/03/201135143046557642.html, last accessed December 29, 2011.

[37] "Protesters storm Kuwaiti parliament", November 16, 2011, http://www.bbc.co.uk/news/world-middle-east-15768027, last accessed December 29, 2011.

[38] Reporters without Boarders published their last Annual Report on Saudi Arabia in 2007. http://arabia.reporters-sans-frontieres.org/article.php3?id_article=20775, last accessed May 28, 2009.

mation on censorship in individual countries.[39] On the website on Bahrain, it is clarified that "Bahrain allowed relatively unfettered access to the Internet, especially compared with its neighbours", but that there is no transparency when it comes to filtering of content.[40] On Kuwait, it is said that surveillance and censorship are observable and that journalists self-censor.[41] The reports about Oman say that "extensive filtering" is conducted and self-censorship is encouraged. It is emphasised that "the authorities impose legal and physical controls to ensure that the Internet community does not access or publish objectionable or unlawful material".[42] In the description on conditions in Qatar, the report points out that in addition to the censorship that is also conducted in its neighbouring countries, filtering of circumvention tools is processed and the internet is "heavily censored".[43] Circumvention tools can be VPNs[44] or proxies[45] that allow users to connect to the internet outside of the censored ISPs. Going online through these tools might also enable users to escape surveillance. It additionally helps to circumvent geofiltering, which Google applies on its video platform *YouTube*.[46]

---

[39] http://opennet.net/, last accessed December 29, 2011.
[40] "Bahrain", http://opennet.net/research/profiles/bahrain, last accessed December 29, 2011.
[41] "Kuwait", http://opennet.net/research/profiles/kuwait, last accessed December 29, 2011.
[42] "Oman", http://opennet.net/research/profiles/oman, last accessed December 29, 2011.
[43] "Qatar", http://opennet.net/research/profiles/qatar, last accessed December 29, 2011.
[44] VPNs help to guarantee access to the net through an often encrypted network that prevents disclosure of private information. More on how a VPN works can be found in the video *Virtual Private Networks (VPNs)*, posted April 6, 2010, at http://www.youtube.com/watch?v=jJdW0_yB9vo&feature=related, last accessed December 29, 2011.
[45] Acting online through a proxy server enables users to access data that would be inaccessible due to restrictions through geofiltering or other forms of restrictions by ISPs. More on how proxy servers work can be found in a brief summary on the website of Indiana University in *What is a proxy server?*, May 3, 2011, http://kb.iu.edu/data/ahoo.html, last accessed December 29, 2011.
[46] A geofilter limits access to data online according to the physical location of the user. More on geofiltering can be read in: Geofiltering: Jillian C. York, *How to Alienate Business Customers Without Really Trying*, March 3rd 2009 on OpenNet Initiative, http://opennet.net/blog/2009/03/geofiltering-how-alienate-business-customers-without-really-trying, last accessed December 29, 2011.

The report on Saudi Arabia shows similar conditions with those in Qatar. For online actors in Saudi Arabia, it can be said that "Bloggers have been arrested, and blogs and sites run by online activists have been blocked".[47] Surveillance measures are also applied in internet cafes. It is highlighted that "the state has extended its filtering scheme to the Dubai free zones, which previously enjoyed unfettered Internet access".[48] Efforts are made to monitor activities in internet cafes, and also for electronic surveillance that should monitor objectionable online activities. This would be publicly acknowledged by the authorities.

Despite all these restrictions, online media in the Arab world provide space for expression and independent distribution of news about current events that is much less restricted than offline facilities. It is not a safe space to publish but a *possible* place to distribute and kind of information. While there are no gatekeepers online in the same sense that we can find them offline, producers of critical or sensitive content will still be punished for their activities online. However, censorship can be circumvented through virtual private networks (VPNs). Circumvention of censorship is much more difficult for printed goods or cable television. In the following, I will introduce forms of internet censorship and procedures of conducting surveillance online. It is vital to present forms of censorship because it affects literary production and might also explain the vast popularity of publishing literature on the net. Online censorship differs in each GCC country, but it shares a number of similarities the way it challenges users. In as early as March 1997, the regimes of the GCC countries gathered to discuss a common approach to the internet.[49] This was even before the internet was widely accessible in all of the Gulf countries and shows that the medium and its influence were, and are, taken seriously.

In the kingdom of Saudi Arabia, general online censorship in the form of internet filters and the blocking of specific pages limits access to and the production of online literature. Many Arab states set up internet filters, primarily to censor content.[50] The internet is censored in GCC countries

---

[47] "Saudi Arabia", http://opennet.net/research/profiles/saudi-arabia, last accessed December 29, 2011.

[48] "United Arab Emirates", http://opennet.net/research/profiles/uae, last accessed December 29, 2011.

[49] Henner Kirchner, "Internet in the Arab World: A Step Towards 'Information Society?'", in Kai Hafez (ed.), *Mass media, politics, and society in the Middle East*, Cresskill 2001, p. 150.

[50] Cf. OpenNet Initiative, entry: Saudi Arabia, http://opennet.net/research/profiles/saudi-arabia, accessed September 7, 2009.

before it reaches users. Internet service providers (ISPs) are usually owned by the state or by members of the ruling families. The cases of online censorship in Saudi Arabia and the UAE can be taken as typical also of the other Gulf countries. In the UAE, for example, Etisalat and DU (telecommunication companies) distribute internet access.[51] Albrecht Hofheinz (2007) points out that Saudi Arabia does not keep internet censorship a secret. Making censorship public and known may incentivise the state in the way that users already censor their behaviour themselves. The Ministry of the Interior runs an Internet Service Unit (ISU) situated in the environment of King Abdul-Aziz City for Science and Technology in Riyadh and is in charge of the process.[52] Keeping ISPs and ISUs a public function enables the state to control the medium in a way that would not be possible if it allowed private companies to offer internet access. But the system functions also to reflect users' feedback. In addition to the state's general filtering, users can ask an official institution to either censor websites or unblock them if it is claimed they do not do harm, for example, medical sites that use censored terms. Hence, everybody is encouraged to participate in making the internet a "morally suitable" zone. For the UAE, the following site is shown when content is censored. Reasons for censorship are presented in Arabic and English. The cartoon character taken from an Emirati-produced popular TV show called "Freej" trivialises censorship (Fig. 6.1).

However, it is possible to access censored content by using circumvention tools.

The reason that the authority gives for internet censorship is to "protect cultural identity".[53] Websites that could interfere with moral views on religion and politics or provide pornography are censored. Stagh (1993) studied limits of freedom of speech in Egypt in the time of Nasser and Sadat.[54] This study was conducted in a different time period; yet, it highlights subjects that may

---

[51] Etisalat is 60 percent government-owned and 40 percent public-traded. DU is 40 percent government-owned, 20 percent belongs to Mubadala, which is completely owned by the Abu Dhabi Government, and 20 percent is owned by TECOM, which is a subsidiary of Dubai Holding. The rest, 20 percent, is publicly owned.

[52] Hofheinz, Albrecht, "Arab Internet Use: Popular Trends and Public Impact", in Naomi Sakr (ed.), *Arab Media and Political Renewal: Community, Legitimacy and Public Life*, London 2008, pp. 56–79, p. 57.

[53] Henner Kirchner, "Internet in the Arab World: A Step Towards 'Information Society?'", in Kai Hafez (ed.), *Mass media, politics, and society in the Middle East*, Cresskill 2001, p. 151.

[54] Marina Stagh, *The Limits of Freedom of Speech: Prose Literature and Prose Writers in Egypt under Nasser and Sadat*, Stockholm 1993, pp. 127–132.

Fig. 6.1 Website displayed when a site is not accessible (Source: http://opennet.net/sites/opennet.net/files/WestCensoringEast5.jpg, last accessed January 25, 2012)

be difficult to publish even today. She refers to the three taboos of "sex, religion, and politics" but rephrases them into "obscenity, blasphemy, and political opposition".[55] In her analysis, she emphasises the growing impact of censorship on publishing in Saudi Arabia and other Gulf states since the 1970s.[56] Today, book fairs are popping up in all of the GCC countries, some with harsh censorship and some with censorship temporarily lifted for the time of the event. In most Arabic-speaking countries literature is being censored. This means that literary websites and blogs can also be closed down or made inaccessible by filters, thus leaving readers and writers denied of access to the web pages. The blog of "Saudi Eve" is an example. This blogger wrote in English and Arabic and at times her texts could have an erotic tinge. As she wrote on her blog, she discovered that her blog had been banned in Saudi

---

[55] Ibid.
[56] Ibid., p. 132.

Arabia when she returned to the country for a visit.[57] Saudi Eve stopped writing on her blog in 2009. In Egypt the approach to dealing with content deemed inappropriate has changed during and after the Uprisings. While the large book fair in Cairo was popular before the uprisings and the publishing industry was rather active, now the situation has changed. Writers are getting arrested and punished for their publications. One example is Ahmed Naji's arrest for writing "obscenities" in his novel Istikhdam *al*-Hayah (The Use of Life). This novel was already approved by the censoring institutions and only. Still, a trial was set up for the author, claiming he is writing against "against public morality". Cases like this show how unreliable and unpredictable the publishing situation is for literary writers.

Global and Local Influence on ICT Usage and the Potential of Opinion Making

This part deals with the possibilities and challenges of making use of a truly global media and the importance of user contributions in spreading messages and sharing literary works.

Online media offers the potential of accessing worldwide views on a huge variety of subjects, including politics and culture. This access is not restricted to mainstream media, because the tools provided by Web 2.0[58] allow many people to easily distribute their works. Web 2.0, a set of tools that facilitates user-generated content, has gained its popularity because of the audience and producers who contribute.[59] Users have to share their ideas, creations, and inspirations to make their blogs or social media account an attractive platform of discussion. The terminology in the research on this field is extensive and often changing; Axel Bruns (2008) emphasises the need to find new terms for user-led content and introduces the term *produsage*.[60] Online media offers the option for users to interact with members of almost every country in the world, but an important obstacle is the language barrier. This is one of the reasons why blogo-

---

[57] Blog post "Back and Blocked" from June 2nd 2006, http://eveksa.blogspot.com/2006/06/back-and-blocked.html, last accessed December 29, 2011.

[58] This term is explained in the chapter on participatory culture.

[59] Benkler points out that anyone can publish online "alongside the traditional mass-media environment." Yochai Benkler, *The Wealth of Networks: How Social Production Transforms Markets and Freedom*, New Haven 2006, p. 214.

[60] Axel Bruns, *Blogs, Wikipedia. Second Life. and Beyond: from production to produsage*, New York 2008.

spheres are often regionalised. Another reason for regionalisation is that the subjects of choice may differ from blogosphere to blogosphere. A blogosphere can be limited by subject of discussion, genre, language, region, or other factors. Later in this chapter, an example of how regionalisation works will be seen in the redistribution of a short story among different forums in the Gulf.

Deborah Wheeler stated (2004) that women rarely mentioned the concept of a "global voice" when using the internet. Her article was written before the uprisings in Arab countries like Egypt and Tunisia, and perspectives may have changed since then.[61] In 2017, her fieldwork-based results showed that this has changed and women are indeed using their voices online.[62] In the online survey I conducted, some of the participants explicitly mentioned that they considered it important to spread their thoughts and make their ideas read by and accessible to an audience. Their answer to the question why they write was most often that they felt the need to express themselves and they loved writing or that it helped them to breathe. More than half of the participants answered in this vein.[63] When asked why they distribute their texts online, they often answered that they wanted to share their thoughts and that online publishing was the easiest way of distributing them. Two participants explicitly clarified that the internet was the only way for them to publish without being constrained in their expressions.[64] They did not specifically mention a global audience, but this might be because they all write in Arabic, a language not read by users from all over the world. However, there is a worldwide Arabic diaspora that might also serve to spread messages.

Distributing thoughts online may also lead to a position of influence in public discourse. If an online writer is popular and thus visited by many users, their messages can spread. If authors have a larger audience, they may act as trendsetters or role models. That means the author can be an "opinion maker", someone who sets the tone. In the movements of the Arab Uprisings, it was possible

---

[61] Deborah Wheeler, "Blessings and Curses: Women and the Internet Revolution in the Arab World", in Naomi Sakr (ed.), in *Women and media in the Middle East: power through self-expression*, London 2004, pp. 138–161, p. 160.

[62] Deborah Wheleer. "You've Come A Long Way Baby: Women's New Media Practices, Empowerment, and Everyday Life in Kuwait and the Middle East" In N. Lenze, C. Schriwer & Z. Abdul-Jalil (Eds.), *Media in the Middle East Activism, Politics, and Culture*. Palgrave, New York, pp. 45–67.

[63] Survey data, 2010.

[64] Survey data, 2010.

to spot popular political blogs that encouraged and inspired wider discussions. For example, bloggers like Mahmoud Salem (http://www.sandmonkey.org/) and Wael Abbas (http://misrdigital.blogspirit.com) documented the Egyptian uprisings. Both received international attention for their comments and documentation of political on social events. Abbas's documentation of sexual harassment led to a nationwide debate.

Opinion making can operate on a direct level through explicitly marked blog posts that deal with current events and politics, but also through the more subliminal messages conveyed by stories or literary essays. A story can take up current debates and social issues and make them part of the plot. In the Gulf, love stories often serve as a basis for promoting discussions around contemporary topics. In these love stories, details describe social events, surroundings, norms and values, as well as political or societal conditions.[65]

The subject of my research is not how political blogs influence politics, but online stories that pick up ongoing social issues and it also includes general features of internet use as a tool of communication through literary texts. However, it is apparent that even literature has an impact on social change and public debate. It can also undermine authorities, as evidenced in the actions that were taken against writers in the region. This can only prove that authorities are undermining the writers. Authors are arrested because authorities condemn the content they publish. The undermining of writers by the state signals a de facto threat posed by these writers to the state.

One example is the Saudi Arabian case in which the poet Rushdi al-Dawsari was detained for eight hours. He had written a poem that included allegedly verses on sorcery. Before he was released, he had to sign a pledge vowing that he would not publish heretical or sorcerous poems online again.[66] The poem could potentially threaten authorities because it reached an audience that may have led to a public debate.

---

[65] Rosalind Gill, *Gender and the Media*, Cambridge 2007, p. 17.
[66] Cf. Sonia Farid: "No more online publishing, religious police demand Saudi poet busted for 'sorcery' poems", 2008, http://www.alarabiya.net/articles/2008/11/09/59794.html, last accessed September 7, 2009.

The Challenges of Anonymity, Intellectual Property, and Redistribution of Stories

This part connects the phenomenon of distributing anonymously in forums and the redistribution of stories, on the one hand, to the aforementioned restrictions placed on writers, on the other. As already explained, censorship in print and online greatly impacts literary production. Posting stories in forums might be a way to circumvent these restrictions for two reasons. Firstly, stories in forums are distributed with nicknames, so the real identity of a user is not exposed.[67] Secondly, the volume of postings in forums makes it difficult to maintain close surveillance on them. This means that the deleting or editing of stories is not excessive.[68] Additionally, if a story is entertaining for a vast audience, it will be redistributed in other forums and spread quickly. In the following, I will briefly introduce the debate on copying intellectual property online and then present an example of a story that has been redistributed many times.

An important issue debated all over the world is the copying of intellectual property. Mark Poster took up this subject in his book *What's the Matter with the Internet?* (2001). He emphasises that in the age of digitalisation of print, film, and audio media, "the media in which intellectual property appears alters the message of its legal integument".[69] Digital intellectual property is poorly protected. In an interview with an Omani blogger, I raised this issue and she told me about her concerns. During my interview I learned that producers of online literary texts simply turn to personal blogs. Copying literary goods is less frequent with texts published on blogs. In my survey, several participants explicitly mentioned the problem of copying stories.[70]

It is problematic for the original authors, because their stories are being copied and posted elsewhere with credit given to different authors. When I conducted an online survey with online writers from the Gulf in 2010, most of them pointed out that they are conscious of incidents where their works have been (re-)published without proper crediting. Some web pages, however, such as *alamuae.com*, do not allow users to copy texts from other websites by consistently blocking this function.

---

[67] This does not mean the state agency cannot trace the IP of the user and thus identify the user.

[68] However, by the time of publication of this book there are algorithms that can automatically filter out censored content.

[69] Mark Poster, *What's the Matter with the Internet?*, Minneapolis 2001, p. 3.

[70] Survey data, 2010.

These writers are aware of other people claiming these texts as their own, and so they sometimes turn to writing blogs, instead of publishing in forums, because blog posts are more personal and less frequently copied.

Two divergent positions can be taken on this subject. Copying intellectual property can be seen as stealing. Or, as Cory Doctorow, an internet activist and writer, puts it, it can be seen as proof that your work is contemporary,[71] that is, it has a value and is therefore worth being copied. He argues that if one's work is not copied, it is probably not contemporary. Indeed, a differentiation has to be made between copying intellectual property with giving credit to the original source and not mentioning the original author and claiming the cultural goods as one's own. On forums from the Gulf, where stories are widely redistributed, the problem of miscrediting is mostly ignored. This might be interpreted as showing the importance of spreading the message. The message here is prioritised before the individual's right on self-produced intellectual property. When McLuhan deals with authorship and copyright, he states that "Teamwork succeeds private effort."[72] But blogs often post notices that redistribution is allowed as long as the original source is mentioned in the reposting.

The following chart (Table 6.1) illustrates the reposting of one story as an example. It shows the date of publishing and the title of the story. The country that I assign to the forums depends either on the name of the forum or on user statistics from http://www.markosweb.com and http://www.websitelooker.com[73] which give visual expression to the forum's visitors from different countries.[74] This example shows the movements and popularity of a story. The short story that I chose to follow is not offensive and rather comical. The following brief outline.

A man enters a shop for used books. He browses through the books and buys one. When he opens it, he realises that a girl has written a letter

---

[71] Cory Doctorow on The War on Kids, Boing Boing, & His Next Novel, Reason TV July 15, 2010, http://www.youtube.com/watch?v=LLf3nldagXc, accessed November 11, 2011.

[72] Marshall McLuhan and Quentin Fiore, *The Medium is the Message. An Inventory of Effects*, Corte Madre 1996, p. 122.

[73] http://www.markosweb.com and http://www.websitelooker.com are commercial websites that measure details of users of websites and offer data analysis.

[74] There are many reasons why this result merely serve as a benchmark as user statistics are easily manipulated by a huge variety of factors. However, this is a simple way of at least trying to place forums regionally. More on that can be read here: Loren Baker, "Alexa: Worthless & Easy to Manipulate?" September 30, 2006, http://www.searchenginejournal.com/alexa-worthless-easy-to-manipulate/3847/, last accessed December 29, 2011, and here: http://www.searchenginehistory.com/, last accessed December 29, 2011.

Table 6.1 Reposting of a story since 2006

Title	Forum	User	Country	Date	COM	Distinctive additions
القصة تقول بطل	http://www.hdrmut.net/vb/t215789.html	قلب الرصاصة 77	KSA	Aug 08, 2006	13	
!!!! قصه حب... بطل سلان في كتاب	http://majdah.maktoob.com/vb/majdah30789/	رومانسية	KSA	Sep 03, 2006	5	
نقول بطل القصة	http://forum.arjwan.com/t33.html	صدى الاحزان	KSA	Feb 22, 2007	11	
نقول بطل القصة	http://forum.sedty.com/t41348.html	«®°·..°° جوريا الها..°®»	KSA	Jul 11, 2007	8	
علي نسخة الراوي	http://www.kshfi.net/forum/show.php?main=1&id=996	عبدالهادي القريشي مشرف	KSA	Apr 22, 2007	3	
نقول بطل القصة	http://forum.brg8.com/t10522.html	MAS KSA	KSA	Oct 11, 2007	15+	A statement about the authenticity of the story is added.
يقول بطل القصة مع انا !!!	http://www.arabchat.net/forum/t11321.html	العاشق المجروح	KSA	Oct 27, 2007	6	User states that this is his first time posting in the forum.
قانون العرض و الطلب	http://www.amwalnet.com/vb/showthread.php?t=1204	Laser2Purchase	KSA	Dec 01, 2007	1	User tells the audience that he read the story and found it funny.
يقول بطل القصة	http://www.souqaldoha.com/vb/t811.html	Leader	QATAR	Mar 03, 2008	9+	
يقول بطل القصة	http://www.bdr130.net/vb/t253794.html	نبع الحب	KSA?	Mar 29, 2008	5	

نقل بطل القصة	http://www.love-m.com/vb/t107133.html	منفذ أحلام البنات	KSA	Mar 30, 2008	6
ودردود الشمس	http://www.almsloob.com/vb/t9462.html	ودردود الشمس	KSA	Apr 29, 2008	5	User introduces the story through naming it sweet and funny but also with the advice to trust anybody.
نقل بطل القصة	http://forum.bantiraq.com/bnatiraq20687/	أميرة الورد	IRAQ	Aug 20, 2008	1	Small changes within the text.
هذه قصة الشخص بأنقول بطل القصة	http://www.m0dy.net/vb/t100896.html	طيف الورد	KSA?	Oct 07, 2008	5+
قصة حب على كتاب!!	http://www.ammartalk.com/?p=373	Ammar	QATAR	Oct 22, 2008	24
نقل بطل القصة	http://vb.ta7a.com/t146858/	تفوق الرصف	KSA	Dec 17, 2008	10
قصة حب غريب الخلو وشوق؟	http://forum.al-wlid.com/t46634.html	ودمير المنتدى	KSA	Jan 30, 2009	7
نقل بطل القصة	http://www.alhotcenter.com/vb/showthread.php?s=&tthreadid=2682	الوردة البيضاء	KSA	Jan 31, 2009	5
نقل بطل القصة	http://faisalfw123.jeeran.com/fw/archive/2009/10/959422.html	فيصل ال سلاتي	USA	Oct 23, 2009	12	Introduction by the user is changed and more personal.
نقل بطل القصة	http://www.omaniaa.net/avb/showthread.php?p=1367263	روعة جعفر	OMAN	Dec 12, 2009	6
نقل بطل القصة	http://www.madaralroh.com/vb/showthread.php?p=132089	Cadetblue	UAE	Dec 23, 2009	7

(*continued*)

Table 6.1 (continued)

Title	Forum	User	Country	Date	COM[a]	Distinctive additions
يقول بطل القصة	http://forums.graaam.com/271363.html	سيدة كل الغاركي	KSA	Jan 05, 2010	1	
يقول بطل القصة	http://www.7be.com/vb/t118651.html	عشقي سحاب	KSA	Jan 19, 2010	8	
يقول بطل القصة	http://www.so5on.com/showthread.php?p=59909	Cadetblue	KSA	Mar 01, 2010	5	
أنا بطل القصة	http://abuadah.forumarabia.com/t963-topic	ملك الرومنسية	KSA	May 02, 2011	3	

The chart does not show all redistributions of the story but rather serves as an example

Note: Data distributed in this table is selected. For practical reasons the first result for the first ten Google search pages (September 2011) were analysed. In addition, a search for subsequent years of distribution was conducted in order to get a broader idea of the story's redistribution over a longer period

inside the book. She writes about being bored and wanting to do something exciting by communicating via the used book. The girl who wrote the letter asks the young man to write back and to sell the book back to the used bookstore in order to allow her to buy it again to read the reply. The man answers the girl's letter and the book becomes a medium that goes back and forth, and a relationship is built up through the letters. The narrator explains to his readers that the person who benefits the most of this system is the owner of the bookshop. One day the young man comes into the bookshop with the intention to pick up his book, but it is not there anymore. He asks the bookseller where it is and he replies that it was sold. The protagonist leaves, disappointed, thinks about the situation, and comes to the conclusion that the bookseller was talking about another book that was not the medium he used to communicate with the young woman. He returns to the shop to clarify the mistake and witnesses the bookseller writing in the book he shared with the young women. He realises that his beloved was not real, but rather that the bookseller himself had written the letters to him in order to make money.

The table shows the reposting of the story since 2006. It presents the benefits of the medium for keeping a short story "alive" and exposed to many readers. The story's continuous reappearance shows that it has been entertaining the audience over five years. It also presents the distinctiveness of forums by showing a story whose original author is unknown. Coming back to the issue of copying stories without referring to the original author, it appears that repostings in forums are not perceived as problematic, at least judging by the comments underneath the repostings. My online survey showed that some of the participants were concerned about copying intellectual property in online platforms.[75] This behaviour is rather common in micro-blogging in platforms such as Tumblr, Twitter, or Instagram, where redistribution is encouraged. However, it is customary to refer to the original source on micro-blogging platforms, since retweets[76] and repostings usually credit the first user who published it.

The sample story in the table is clearly not political, nor does it offend anyone; yet, it is posted in forums, obviously because it is entertaining and attracts a rather wide audience, as can be seen in the number of redistributions of the story. The story itself is irrelevant for an examination of its

---

[75] Survey data, 2010.
[76] A distribution on *Twitter* is called a "Tweet", a re-distribution on Twitter is called a "Retweet".

"travelling" or redistribution. However, its popularity is due to the content and deserves to be briefly interpreted in the following. The story is written in colloquial language and includes several discourses that are already discussed in Chap. 3. These are discussing norms, gender roles, and globalisation. In the story of the used books, gender segregation is an essential part of the text. The two characters have to communicate in secret because society forbids contact between men and women. Two lovers overcome these social norms to pursue their own happiness. Ex-pat labour is frequently part of short stories, as the bookseller in this story is from Sudan. The salesman is incentivised to his actions by the thought of increasing turnover. The feelings of the main character are abused for the sake of generating income for the salesman. This could be interpreted as a funny way of criticising capitalist society for giving monetary values a higher importance then the value of love. The story seems to attract a larger audience because the secret love story may be exciting to read.

The table shows that the story was initially published in 2006 in Saudi Arabia and then slowly gained popularity. The same nickname is rarely used for redistribution; rather, the nicknames of users who repost the story change frequently. The reposted stories are not connected to the original author anymore. Larry Friedlander raises question concerning stories that are related to redistribution and remixing of short stories in online forums. He sees that the multiplicity of "the reader/user/player" identity takes over some of the functions of the original author.[77]

The story does not "travel" outside the Gulf countries, a fact that might be due to the story's distinct plot and also because it is written in colloquial Arabic from Saudi Arabia. Despite extensive distribution in a variety of forums, it has never received a large number of comments in one thread, but rather a modest number of comments in a wider selection of forums. Some of the users who redistributed the story clearly stated that it was not their own story but that they had heard it elsewhere or that someone had sent it to them and they thought it was worth sharing with others. This point may suggest that internet users have a different conception of intellectual property from how it is traditionally defined, which leads to different behaviour.

---

[77] Larry Friedlander, "Narrative strategies in a digital age. Authorship and authority", in Knut Lundby (ed.), *Digital Storytelling, Mediatized Stories. Self-representation in New Media*, New York 2008, pp. 177–196, p. 180.

By discussing the challenges of distribution in online literary platforms, two major factors are influential in online publishing in the Gulf. First, authoritarian pressure and power heavily restrict publication. In addition, social as well as self-censorship limit writers in their creative expressions. In response, different ways of dealing with these problems can be observed. One of them is to turn to distributing elsewhere, either online or in other countries. Online media is a convenient and less restricted space for publishing literary works. The second challenge appears in relation to intellectual property in online media. Two ways of dealing with this problem can be observed. One is turning to blogs, where copying content is less common and texts are often ascribed to one author. The other way is to accept the copying of cultural products as a given in digital times.

Conversely, both challenges, censorship and copying, show the benefits of the medium in that it offers more freedom and is read by a vast audience even without a publisher. Earlier chapters showed a wider selection of positive aspects of online distribution; this chapter has presented the difficulties in online writing and highlighted the challenges for the authors.

As we can see, there are great differences in how individual countries conduct censorship. While Lebanon and Kuwait have "partly free" environments of freedom of speech, Egypt and the rest of the GCC countries are more restrictive.

CHAPTER 7

Concluding Thoughts

I have chosen the perspectives on composition and setup, linguistic features, heroes' portrayal, ICT use, and restrictions because they are the most striking characteristics in the original sources. The results extracted from my research open up a view into new literary expressions, which can be applied to literary studies of the Arabic-speaking world.

The research field is new both in terms of its regional focus in Arabic-speaking countries and the novelty of research on online literature, because also in other countries online literature did not emerge until the last two decades. The following sums up my findings in order to shed light on the project as a whole and the variety of connections between the perspectives that have been at the focus of single chapters.

The form and appearance of online literary texts are the first two elements of my analysis. Examples in my presentation of text layout and usage of multimedial elements illustrate the integration of pictures and audio files. Results show, on the one hand, that multimedia features underline the message of texts and, on the other hand, that they exemplify details within stories. Another feature of layout is the use of applied elements, such as quotations and additional applications that structure blog entries. As the analysis shows, these stylistic tools serve the purpose of self-representation. Moreover, the other visual features, such as visitor counters, also function as self-representation by showing the popularity of blogs. As I have shown, multimedia elements are not employed in every literary blog from the region; many blogs exhibit a rather modest layout and a clearer focus on the literary text.

Blogs do not represent one genre of texts but rather embody a variety of subjects and writing styles. However, similarities can be observed in the setup of blogs, because they are all organised chronologically and make use of links and a comment section. Blogs and forums often need to be examined separately, because they differ in the style of writing as well as visualisation. An analysis of samples has shown that short stories are popular in forums. The frequent distribution of short literary texts might be due to the medium, which invites short texts. Reading on-screen is usually not popular for longer texts. In addition to the visual features used in online literature, in forums a distinct form of composing and reposting short stories is observable. The analysis of a selection of stories shows that many stories are introduced with a personal note by the user that explains the circumstances or background of stories, followed by the story itself, and then a discussion of the story in a separate section. The investigation of composition, redistribution, and rearrangement shows that this form of literary texts has some resemblances to storytelling. The resemblance manifests in the personal introduction by the user, interaction with the audience, and a retelling of the same story in other locations, meaning other forums.

One focus in my examination of original sources is the style of writing and narration. My analysis suggests that online literature may be seen as a continuation and part of contemporary literature, depending on its composition and style. An analysis of a number of blog posts makes it evident that internet literature has much in common with printed texts, mostly with regard to narration and language. Stories posted in forums are not as close to earlier printed literature as blog posts are, because they are less careful with grammar and seem to have as their major function the spreading of messages rather than pursuing aesthetic objectives. The narration does not differ strikingly from that of printed texts; the distinctiveness of online literature is rather found in terms of the participatory culture. Noteworthy is auto-fiction, which stands between fact and fiction and blurs the lines between personal narrations and literature; both blogs and forums reflect tendencies of auto-fiction. Ongoing research on this subject is conducted by Teresa Pepe.[1] As mentioned before, short stories in forums come with a personal introduction that is not clearly marked as authentic or fictional. Blogs describe personal opinions side-by-side with fictional texts, which often makes it difficult to decide what is fiction or fact. In this sense, sources from blogs and forums show the characters of the auto-fiction.

To contextualise this relatively new literary category and highlight the differences and similarities compared to earlier literature, I conducted a comparison with literary texts from the 1990s and postmodern perspectives. My comparison has shown that online literature tends to have a simpler narration and a more linear storyline, while its auto-fictional feature resembles that of earlier printed literature from the 1990s researched by Christian Junge.

The first chapter examined the use of language, which is essential when dealing with new forms of literature posted on the net. My analysis has shown that blogs tend to be written in Modern Standard Arabic, while forum postings are most commonly written in colloquial language. An examination of forum postings shows the significance of dialogues as a tool for incorporating humorous arguments. Analysing the features of online literature helps us understand blogs and forums and may also reveal new perspectives on recent published texts (in print). One of the most important aspects that contribute to digital literature's contemporaneity is its interactivity. But this poses certain challenges to authors: it influences text production from the region in many ways, as is exemplified in the process of remixing and redistributing short stories in forums. This process is part of cultural production in Web 2.0 and of participatory culture. The challenge to authors, however, is that texts are often reposted without giving credit to the original authors.

The interaction and communication between readers and writers are closely related to the notion of public and private spaces in online media. Since interactivity in open platforms such as blogs and forums is a form of communication in public space, notions of public and private come into play when examining interactive processes online. Additionally, this interaction impacts online writing. Authors and audience are both part of the pro-

---

[1] Pepe presented her result in presentations entitled "Autofiction on Screen: Self-representation of an Egyptian 'Spinster'", at *Technologies of the Self: New Departures in Self-Inscription*, Cork September 2011 and at *International Forum on 'Women and the New Media in the Mediterranean Region'*, Fez, June 2011.

cess of creating a cultural product as a whole because commentaries from both sides affect both current and future texts. The interaction also allows texts to be changed in a variety of remixes and repostings during their distributions in forums. On the other hand, distributing cultural products or intellectual property without naming the original source is a problematic trait of the medium. User participation in creating and remixing videos, audio files, and texts can be seen as one feature of the great freedom of possibilities on the web. Still, not everyone who creates and distributes works wants others to redistribute them. In my sources, redistribution in forums inspired discussions, as the number of commentators proves.

Writers can restrict the openness of personal presentation online; this does not contradict the idea of more freedom of publishing online, but is an aspect of this freedom. However, for readers this might be restrictive, since bloggers may limit access to their personal blogs to just a selected audience by turning the sites into the private mode. Another advantage of distributing literary texts online is the independence from institutional publishers. This independence offers benefits and challenges at the same time and also leads to the publication of unedited texts because of the lack of editors in blogs and forums. On the other hand, this independence might be beneficial to the audience, since texts can be distributed no matter what their content might be. It benefits the audience because it gains access to otherwise inaccessible material, enabling people to read and watch content that could otherwise be restricted. Nevertheless, it may lead to a lack of the quality control exercised by editors at publishing houses. This means that amateurish texts are part of online literary production. Scholar Alan Kirby comments on this polarising impact brought about by online publishing, arguing that while the strong impact of freedom in online media facilitates democratic processes in cultural production, these new possibilities are weakening literary quality.[2] In either case, online literary distribution allows publication apart from questions of profitability. Blog posts and stories in forums show that the literary quality varies, since some writers place a higher value on the literary quality of texts while others focus on the message they want to send to a broad audience. It is not only a question of will but also of capability. By democratising publishing, people with lower literacy levels may also partake in the distribution of information online, which accounts for varied literary quality of online literary texts.

---

[2] Alan Kirby, *Digimodernism: How New Technologies Dismantle the Postmodern and Reconfigure Our Culture*, London, 2009.

Examining the appearance, composition, and interactivity of the texts helps to prepare an analysis of content and recurring themes that provide deeper insight on important issues. Chapter 5 "Who Are the Actors? Portrayal of Heroes" examined fields of gender representation and globalisation as well as dealing with social norms and socio-political discourse. The analysis of sources has shown that the most frequently appearing subjects of popular online literary texts relate to gender and a variety of notions around globalisation. Both topics are often illustrated in the portrayal of heroes, which tends to be different in blogs from in forums. The portrayal of heroes in blogs illustrates an eager for societal change, but most often heroes cannot reach their ideals because they are handicapped by values and norms deeply rooted in their normative cultures. In forums, on the other hand, heroes and heroines not only desire a change in society but also actively work to reach their personal goals. Here, social rules are sometimes broken to strive for an ideal of self-acceptance. I have not yet found an explanation of this phenomenon, because not enough information on the writers and readers is accessible in my online literary sources.

An analysis of heroines in the short stories and blog posts from my materials has found no homogeneous image of heroines. There is a tendency to portray female protagonists as strong and proactive, but other forms of female identity—"weak" characters—are also present.

The representation of heroes is not homogeneous in online short stories from the region, either. However, two different types of male actors can be described. On the one hand, there is the vulnerable and indecisive character who is overcome with emotions, and on the other hand, a strong masculine figure. Stronger men are often portrayed as violent and controlling of their families. In some stories, the role of the villain is taken by a male character who embodies stereotypical masculine features such as physical and emotional strength. In these stories, villains oppress the stories' heroes and harm them mentally or physically.

As observed in the analysed texts, struggles with society are reflected in the description of the heroes; the narrative often directs readers to sympathise with the more emotional heroes who struggle against oppression, abuse, and societal controls. Heroes try to overcome these conflicts going by through a process of individualisation and coming to terms with themselves, gradually coming to self-acceptance. Another aspect of the portrayal of heroes can be seen when looking at the hero in a social context. Globalisation and societal norms are both part of identity and hero representation within many of the stories. Settings and cultural impact are often contextualised in the blog posts and short stories distributed in forums.

The last chapter highlights two particular challenges facing writers when distributing literary texts online: authoritarian forces that restrict publications and the copying of intellectual property. Firstly, societal censorship or self-censorship may limit writers in their creative processes. Everything published needs permission from the Ministry of Information, so the choice of content is restricted. Self-censorship and social censorship are personal and not a measurable restriction in online literature. Online writers seem to have developed a variety of approaches to deal with these issues. Online publishing is convenient because it is the least restricted space for distribution. Anonymity serves as a beneficial tool to avoid social censorship.

Secondly, the risk of abuse of intellectual property is present on the net. Authors handle the problem of being copied in a variety of ways. The two most common forms of dealing with this issue seem to be, first, that authors who frequently copied in forums may turn to blogging, where the likelihood of being copied is said to be less than in forums. The second is the possibility of accepting being copied, as is common in this medium, but also in contemporary culture in general. Copying and remixing are part of cultural production not only in digital media. One of the most successful artists of the last century, Andy Warhol, based some of his success on remixing and reproduction. Stories published in forums are often redistributed without changes. Nevertheless, it is also possible to see repostings with changes in narration, introduction, and media use.

My findings show that both challenges, censorship and copying, underline the benefits of online distribution because they emphasise the opportunities and freedom of expression and the writers' responsibility to reach a vast audience in real time. Redistribution has good and bad aspects to it. On the one hand, a story finds its way to many people, which may be the goal of writers who focus on spreading a message. On the other hand, authors will most often not be credited for their cultural contributions. Original authors become irrelevant, as the redistribution of stories still inspires discussions within the readership.

Perspectives

Online literature is a rather new phenomenon that has been growing since the mid-2000s continuously until 2014 which dates the end of my text analysis and also marks a steady decline of online literature publications in my sources. From blogs and forums it is developing in many directions. By 2018, writing literature online has steadily declined. Creatives have moved on to other outlets of online media, changed their interests, or published works in print. It is vital to examine developments and tendencies of future online literary production. Since wider cultural tendencies can be inferred from online literary texts, it is valuable to study a wider variety of samples and more discourses that recur on a long-term basis. Studying short-term trends will also provide a broader picture of developments. It remains to be seen if online literature continues to be written on a smaller scale, if it professionalises more, or if it vanishes completely. Online cultural production and participatory culture are still in their beginnings. There is much scope for research in the field of online literature in Arabic-speaking countries, for example, the huge variety of poetry that is distributed and discussed. Additionally, an analysis of literary production of texts distributed on Tumblr, Twitter, or Instagram might be enlightening. Also worthy of study is religiously or politically motivated online cultural production online.

Online literature is a global phenomenon. It allows new freedom in the distribution of unique digital works. Comparing online literature from different regions of the world will reveal a variety of motivations and aesthetic approaches. This could be modified versions of digital literature that contrast or show similarities as for example SMS and Twitter novels.

For future studies in the field, it would also be of great value to look at the activities and cultural developments of the reading public. That means how far the readership will participate in the writing process and what will be its new role.

This exploration of distinctive features of online literary texts attempts to interpret the cultural phenomenon as a continuation of recent developments in Arabic literature. My research has examined the cultural processes of online writing, mainly in forums and blogs. These processes needed to be highlighted from various perspectives to form an overall picture of how these practices work.

Bibliography

Books

Aarseth, Espen J. *Cybertext: Perspectives on Ergodic Literature.* Baltimore: The Johns Hopkins University Press, 1997.

al-Fahim, Mohammed. *From Rags to Riches. A Story of Abu Dhabi.* London: The London Centre of Arab Studies, 1995.

Al-Hassan Golley, Nawar, and Miriam Cooke. *Arab Women's Lives Retold: Exploring Identity Through Writing.* Syracuse, NY: Syracuse University Press, 2007.

al-Mughni, Haya. *Women in Kuwait.* London: Saqi Books, 2000.

Altorki, Soraya. *Women in Saudi Arabia: Ideology and Behavior among the Elite.* New York: Columbia University Press, 1988.

Anderson, Benedict R. *Imagined Communities: Reflections on the Origin and Spread of Nationalism.* London: Verso, 1991.

Bauman, Zygmunt. *Liquid Modernity.* Cambridge: Polity, 2000.

Benkler, Yochai. *The Wealth of Networks: How Social Production Transforms Markets and Freedom.* New Haven: Yale University Press, 2006.

Bruns, Axel. *Blogs, Wikipedia. Second Life and Beyond: From Production to Produsage.* New York: Peter Lang, 2008.

Crystal, David. *Language and the Internet.* Cambridge: Cambridge University Press, 2001.

Crystal, Jill. *Oil and Politics in the Gulf: Rulers and Merchants in Kuwait and Qatar.* Cambridge: Cambridge University Press, 1995.

Davidson, Christopher. *Power and Politics in the Persian Gulf Monarchies.* London: Hurst, 2011.

El-Ariss, Tarek. *Trials of Arab Modernity: Literary Affects and the New Political.* New York: Fordham University Press, 2013.
Gendolla, Peter, and Jörgen Schäfer. *The Aesthetics of Net Literature: Writing, Reading and Playing in Programmable Media.* Bielefeld: Transcript, 2007.
Ghaloom, Ibrahim Abdullah. *The Short Story in the Arab Gulf. Kuwait and Bahrain—Article and Analytical Study.* Basra: Arabian Gulf Center for Studies, 1980.
Gill, Rosalind. *Gender and the Media.* Cambridge: Polity Press, 2007.
Glazier, Loss Pequeno. *Digital Poetics.* Tuscaloosa: The University of Alabama Press, 2002.
Guth, Stephan, and Gail Ramsay, eds. *From New Values to New Aesthetics*, vol. II: *Postmodernism and Thereafter.* Wiesbaden: Harrassowitz, 2011.
Haddad, Joumana. *I Killed Scheherazade: Confessions of an Angry Arab Woman.* London: Saqi, 2011.
Harré, R. *Personal Being.* Oxford: Blackwell, 1983.
Hayles, N. Katherine. *Electronic Literature: New Horizons for the Literary.* Notre Dame: University of Notre Dame, 2008.
Held, David, and Kristian Ulrichsen, eds. *The Transformation of the Gulf: Politics, Economics and the Global Order.* London: Routledge, 2011.
Henry, Clement Moore, and Robert Springborg. *Globalization and the Politics of Development in the Middle East.* Cambridge: Cambridge University Press, 2010.
Keen, Andrew. *The Cult of the Amateur: How Blogs, MySpace, YouTube, and the Rest of Today's User-Generated Media Are Destroying Our Economy, Our Culture, and Our Values.* New York: Random House, 2008.
Kirby, Alan. *Digimodernism: How New Technologies Dismantle the Postmodern and Reconfigure Our Culture.* London: Continuum, 2009.
Kolk, Mieke (ed.), and Freddy Decreus (co-ed.). *Arabic Theatre Cultural Heritage, Western Models and Postcolonial Hybridity*, 2005. www.artsafrica.org/archive/documents/docu-01/002_comic.pdf, last accessed January 3, 2012.
Lenze, Nele. "Protest Poetry On- and Offline: Trans-Regional Interactions in the Arabian Gulf: An Example from Bahrain." In *Media in the Middle East Activism, Politics, and Culture*, ed. N. Lenze, C. Schriwer, and Z. Abdul-Jalil. New York: Palgrave, 2017.
Louw, Eric. *The Media and Cultural Production.* London, Thousand Oaks, New Delhi: Sage, 2005.
Lovink, Geert. *Zero Comments: Blogging and Critical Internet Culture.* New York: Routledge, 2007.
Lundby, Knut, ed. *Digital Storytelling, Mediatized Stories. Self-Representation in New Media.* New York: Peter Lang, 2008.
Mahne, Nicole. *Mediale Bedingungen des Erzählens im digitalen Raum.* Frankfurt am Main: Peter Lang, 2006.

McLuhan, Marshall. *Understanding Media: The Extensions of Man*. New York: McGraw-Hill, 1964.
———. *The Medium Is the Message*. New York: Bantam Books, 1967.
McLuhan, Marshall, and Quentin Fiore. *The Medium Is the Message. An Inventory of Effects*. Corte Madre: Penguin Books, 1996.
Moghadam, Valentine M. *Modernizing Women: Gender and Social Change in the Middle East*. Boulder, CO: Lynne Rienner Publishers, 2003.
Neuwirth, Angelika, Andreas Pflitsch, and Barbara Winckler, eds. *Arabic Literature: Postmodern Perspectives*. London: Saqi, 2010. Translated from the original German version: *Arabische Literatur, postmodern*, München, 2004.
Nordenson, Jon. *We Want Five!: Kuwait, the Internet, and the Public Sphere*. Saarbrücken: LAP Lambert Academic Publishing, 2010.
———. *Online Activism in the Middle East: Political Power and Authoritarian Governments from Egypt to Kuwait*. London: I.B. Tauris, 2017.
Paasonen, Susanna. *Figures of Fantasy. Internet, Women and Cyberdiscourse*. New York: Peter Lang, 2005.
Palfrey, John, and Urs Gasser. *Born Digital: Understanding the First Generation of Digital Natives*. New York: Basic Books, 2008.
Panovic, Ivan. "Arabic in a Time of Revolution: Sociolinguistic Notes from Egypt." In *Media in the Middle East: Activism, Politics, and Culture*, ed. Nele Lenze, Charlotte Schriwer, and Zubaidah Abdul Jalil. Basingstoke: Palgrave Macmillan, 2017.
Perthes, Volker. *Geheime Gärten: Die neue arabische Welt*. Berlin: Siedler-Verlag, 2009.
Poster, Mark. *What's the Matter with the Internet?* Minneapolis: University of Minnesota Press, 2001.
Punzi, Maddalena Pennacchia. *Literary Intermediality: The Transit of Literature through the Media Circuit*. Bruxelles/Bern/Berlin/Frankfurt am Main/New York/Oxford/Wien: Lang, 2007.
Ramsay, Gail. *Blogs & Literature & Activism: Popular Egyptian Blogs and Literature in Touch*. Wiesbaden: Harrassowitz Verlag, 2017.
Rizzo, Helen M. *Islam, Democracy and the Status of Women: The Case of Kuwait*. London: Routledge, 2008.
Rugh, William A. *Arab Mass Media: Newspapers, Radio, and Television in Arab Politics*. Westport, CT: Praeger, 2004.
Saghie, Hazim. *The Predicament of the Individual in the Middle East*. London: Saqi, 2000.
Salloukh, Bassel F., and Rex Brynen. *Persistent Permeability? Regionalism, Localism, and Globalization in the Middle East*. London: Ashgate, 2004.
Simanowski, Roberto. *Interfictions*. Frankfurt am Main: Suhrkamp, 2002.
Snir, Reuven. *Modern Arabic Literature: A Theoretical Framework*. Edinburgh: Edinburgh University Press, 2017.

Starkey, Paul. *Modern Arabic Literature*. Edinburgh: Edinburgh University Press, 2006.

Torstrick, Rebecca L., and Elizabeth Faier, eds. *Culture and Customs of the Arab Gulf States*. Westport, CT: Greenwood Press, 2009.

Turkle, Sherry. *Life on the Screen: Identity in the Age of the Internet*. New York: Simon and Schuster, 1997.

Wheeler, Deborah L. *The Internet in the Middle East: Global Expectations and Local Imaginations in Kuwait*. Albany, NY: State University of New York Press, 2005.

Wodak, Ruth, and Michael Meyer. *Methods of Critical Discourse Studies*, 3rd ed. London: Sage, 2016.

Zirinski, Roni. *Ad Hoc Arabism: Advertising, Culture, and Technology in Saudi Arabia*. New York: Peter Lang, 2005.

Articles

Albabtain, Afraa Ahmed. "Downloading Democracy. Bloggers in the Gulf." In *International Relations and Security Network*, 2008. http://www.isn.ethz.ch/isn/Current-Affairs/Security-Watch-Archive/Detail/?fecvnodeid=128146&ord588=grp1&fecvid=21&ots591=0c54e3b3-1e9c-be1e-2c24-a6a8c7060233&v21=128146&lng=en&id=90279, last accessed January 3, 2012.

Allen, Roger. "Fiction and Publics: The Emergence of the 'Arabic Best-Seller'." In *Viewpoints Special Edition. The State of the Arts in the Middle East*, Washington, 2009. www.mei.edu/Portals/0/Publications/state-arts-middle-east.pdf, last accessed January 2, 2012.

Al-Shehabi, Omar. "Political Movements in Bahrain Across the Long Twentieth Century (1900–2015)." In *Oxford Handbook of Contemporary Middle-Eastern and North African History*, ed. Amal Ghazal and Jens Hanssen. April 2017. http://www.oxfordhandbooks.com/view/10.1093/oxfordhb/9780199672530.001.0001/oxfordhb-9780199672530-e-27?mediaType=Article.

Al-Tarrah, Ali A. "Socialization and Masculinity Values in Kuwaiti Society." http://pubcouncil.kuniv.edu.kw/jss/english/showarticle.asp?id=760, last accessed January 3, 2012.

Baker, Loren. "Alexa: Worthless & Easy to Manipulate?" September 30, 2006. http://www.searchenginejournal.com/alexa-worthless-easy-to-manipulate/3847/, last accessed December 29, 2011.

Bohman, James. "Expanding Dialogue: The Internet, the Public Sphere and Prospects for Transnational Democracy." In *After Habermas: New Perspectives on the Public Sphere*, ed. John Michael Roberts and Nick Crossley, 131–155. Oxford: Blackwell Publishing, 2004.

Boker, Uwe, and Julie A. Hibbard. *Sites of Discourse—Public and Private Spheres—Legal Culture*. Papers from a Conference Held at the Technical University of Dresden, December 2001. Vergleichenden Literaturwissenschaft, 2002.

Bradley, Gunilla. "The Convergence Theory on ICT, Society and Human Beings." *tripleC—Cognition, Communication, Co-operation* 8, no. 2 (2010): 183–192.

Bronner, Ethan, and Michael Slackman, "Saudi Troops Enter Bahrain to Help Put Down Unrest." *New York Times*, March 14, 2011. http://www.nytimes.com/2011/03/15/world/middleeast/15bahrain.html?pagewanted=all, last accessed January 16, 2012.

Burkhart, Grey E., and Seymour E. Goodman. "The Internet Gains Acceptance in the Persian Gulf." *Commun. ACM* 41, no. 3 (1998): 19–25.

Connelly, Bridget, and Henry Massie. "Epic Splitting: An Arab Folk Gloss on the Meaning of the Hero Pattern." *Oral Tradition* 4, nos. 1–2 (1989): 101–124.

Curtain, Tyler. "Promiscuous Fiction." In *The Cybercultures Reader*, ed. Barbara M. Kennedy, David Bell, and Tyler Curtain, 321–328. London: Routledge, 2006.

Davis, Jenny. "Architecture of the Personal Interactive Homepage: Constructing the Self through MySpace." *New Media & Society*, November 2010, first published on May 4, 2010, pp. 1103–1119.

Doostdar, Alireza. "The Vulgar Spirit of Blogging: On Language, Culture, and Power in Persian Weblogestan." *American Anthropologist* 106, no. 4 (2004): 651–662.

Emery, P.G. "Nabaṭī." In *Encyclopaedia of Islam*, 2nd ed., Vol. 7. Brill, 1993.

Enkvist, Nils Erik. "Text and Discourse Linguistics, Rhetoric, and Stylistics." In *Discourse and Literature*, ed. Teun Adrianus van Dijk, 11–38. Amsterdam, 1985.

Erstad, Ola, and James V. Wertsch. "Tales of Mediation: Narrative and Digital Media as Cultural Tools." In *Digital Storytelling, Mediatized Stories. Self-Representation in New Media*, ed. Knut Lundby, 21–40. New York: Peter Lang, 2008.

Etling, Bruce, John Kelly, Robert Faris, and Palfrey, John. *Mapping the Arabic Blogosphere: Politics, Culture, and Dissent*, 2009. http://cyber.law.harvard.edu/publications/2009/Mapping_the_Arabic_Blogosphere, last accessed December 29, 2011.

Fairclough, N., and R. Wodak. "Critical Discourse Analysis." In *Discourse Studies: A Multidisciplinary Introduction*, ed. T. Van Dijk, Vol. 2, 258–284. London: Sage, 1997.

Farid, Sonia. "No More Online Publishing, Religious Police Demand Saudi Poet Busted for 'Sorcery' Poems." 2008. http://www.alarabiya.net/articles/2008/11/09/59794.html, last accessed September 7, 2009.

Fitzpatrick, Kathleen. "The Pleasure of the Blog: The Early Novel, the Serial, and the Narrative Archive." 2007. http://machines.pomona.edu/dossier/files/2009/10/fitzpatrick-blogtalk.pdf, last accessed January 27, 2012.

Friedlander, Larry. "Narrative Strategies in a Digital Age. Authorship and Authority." In *Digital Storytelling, Mediatized Stories. Self-Representation in New Media*, ed. Knut Lundby, 177–196. New York: Peter Lang, 2008.

Frissen, Valerie, and Hermineke van Bockxmeer. "The Paradox of Individual Commitment. The Implications of the Internet for Social Involvement." In *Communication Strategies*, no. 42, 2nd quarter, 2001.

Funkhouser, Christopher. "Digital Poetry: A Look at Generative, Visual, and Interconnected Possibilities in its First Four Decades." In *Companion to Digital Literary Studies*, ed. Ray Siemens and Susan Schreibman. Oxford, 2008. http://www.digitalhumanities.org/companion/view?docId=blackwell/9781405148641/9781405148641.xml&chunk.id=ss1-5-11&toc.depth=1&toc.id=ss1-5-11&brand=9781405148641_brand, last accessed January 27, 2012.

Gendolla, Peter, and Jörgen Schäfer. "Auf Spurensuche: Literatur im Netz, Netzliteratur und ihre Vorgeschichte(n)." In *Dichtung Digital*, 2002. http://www.brown.edu/Research/dichtung-digital/2002/05/08-Gendolla-Schaefer/index.htm, last accessed January 3, 2012.

Ghédira, A. "Ṣaḥīfa." In *Encyclopaedia of Islam, Vol. 8*, ed. C.E. Bosworth, E. van Donzel, W.P. Heinrichs, and G. Lecomte, 834–835. Brill, 1997.

Global Voice. "Bahrain Protests 2011." December 19, 2011. http://globalvoicesonline.org/specialcoverage/bahrain-protests-2011/, last accessed December 29, 2011.

Graham, Paul. "Web 2.0." November 2005. http://www.paulgraham.com/web20.html, last accessed November 11, 2011.

Guertin, Carolyn. "Handholding, Remixing, and the Instant Replay: New Narratives in a Postnarrative World." In *Companion to Digital Literary Studies*, ed. Ray Siemens and Susan Schreibman. Oxford, 2008. http://www.digitalhumanities.org/companion/view?docId=blackwell/9781405148641/9781405148641.xml&chunk.id=ss1-5-6, last accessed January 27, 2012.

Guth, Stephan. "fa-ġrawraqat ʿuyūnuhum bi-d-dumūʿ. Some notes on the flood of tears in early modern Arabic prose literature." In *Encounters of Words and Texts. Intercultural Studies in Honor of Stefan Wild on the Occasion of His 60th Birthday, March 2, 1997*, ed. Lutz Edzard and Christian Szyska, 111–123. Presented by His Pupils in Bonn, Hildesheim, Zürich, New York, 1997.

———. "Individuality Lost, Fun Gained. Some Recurrent Motifs in Late Twentieth Century Arabic and Turkish Novels." *Journal of Arabic and Islamic Studies* 7, no. 1 (2007): 25–49.

Hafez, Sabry. "Women's Narrative in Modern Arabic Literature: A Typology." In *Love and Sexuality in Modern Arabic Literature*, ed. Roger Allen et al., 154–174. London: Saqi, 1995.

———. "The Aesthetics of the Closed Horizon. The Transformation of the City and the Novel in Egypt Since 1990." In *From New Values to New Aesthetics Turning Points in Modern Arabic Literature, 2. Postmodernism and Thereafter*, ed. Stephan Guth and Gail Ramsay, 109–138. Wiesbaden: Harrassowitz Verlag, 2011.

Henderson, Joan C. "Tourism in Dubai: Overcoming Barriers to Destination Development." *International Journal of Tourism Research* 8 (2006): 87–99.

Hertberg Kaare, Birgit, and Knut Lundby. "Mediatized Lives. Autobiography and Assumed Authenticity in Digital Storytelling." In *Digital Storytelling, Mediatized Stories. Self-Representation in New Media*, ed. Knut Lundby, 105–122. New York: Peter Lang, 2008.

Hine, Christine, Lori Kendall, and danah boyd. "Question One: How Can Quantitative Internet Researchers Define the Boundaries of their Projects?" In *Internet Inquiry. Conversation about Method*, ed. Anette N. Markham and Nancy K. Baym, 1–32. London: SAGE Publications 2009.

Hoffmann, Sarah. "Give Us Back Our Bahrain", pen.org, June 9, 2011. http://www.pen.org/blog/?p=71, last accessed January 16, 2012.

Hofheinz, Albrecht. "The Internet in the Arab World: Playground for Political Liberalization." *Internationale Politik und Gesellschaft* 3 (2005): 79–96.

———. "Arab Internet Use: Popular Trends and Public Impact." In *Arab Media and Political Renewal: Community, Legitimacy and Public Life*, ed. Naomi Sakr, 56–79. London: I. B. Tauris, 2007.

Holes, Clive. "Gulf States." In *Encyclopaedia of Arabic Language and Linguistics Vols 1: A-ED*, ed. K. Versteegh, M. Woidich, and A. Zaborski, 210–216. Leiden, Boston and Cologne, 2006.

Indiana University. "What Is a Proxy Server?", May 3, 2011. http://kb.iu.edu/data/ahoo.html, last accessed December 29, 2011.

Jargy, Simon. "Sung Poetry in the Oral Tradition of the Gulf Region and the Arabian Peninsula." *Oral Tradition* 4, nos. 1–2, Columbia (1989): 174–188.

Johnson, Tom. "Less Text, Please: Contemporary Reading Behaviors and Short Formats," posted on January 21, 2011. http://idratherbewriting.com/2011/01/21/contemporary-reading-behaviors-favor-short-formats/, last accessed January 2, 2012.

Junge, Christian. "I Write, Therefore I Am. Metafiction as Self-Assertion in Mustafa Dhikri's 'Much Ado About a Gothic Labyrinth'." In *Arabic Literature: Postmodern Perspectives*, ed. Angelika Neuwirth, Andreas Pflitsch, and Barbara Winckler, 444–460. London: Saqi, 2010.

Jurkiewicz, Sarah. "Blogging as Counterpublic? The Lebanese and Egyptian Blogosphere in Comparison." In *Social Dynamics 2.0: Researching Change in Times of Media Convergence*, ed. N. C. Schneider and B. Gräf, 27–47. Berlin: Frank & Timme, 2011.

Kirby, Alan. "The Death of Postmodernism and Beyond." *Philosophy Now* 58 (2006). http://www.philosophynow.org/issue58/58kirby.htm, last accessed November 11, 2011.

Kirchner, Henner. "Internet in the Arab World: A Step Towards 'Information Society?'" In *Mass Media, Politics, and Society in the Middle East*, ed. Kai Hafez, 137–158. Cresskill, NJ: Hampton Press, 2001.

Kuebler, Johanne. "Overcoming the Digital Divide: The Internet and Political Mobilization in Egypt and Tunisia." *CyberOrient* 5, no. 1 (2011). http://www.cyberorient.net/article.do?articleId=6212, last accessed December 29, 2011.

Lang, Xiaomeng. "Der Dialog der Kultur und die Kultur des Dialogs: die chinesische Netzliterat." http://dokumentix.ub.uni-siegen.de/opus/frontdoor.php?source_opus=398&la=de, last accessed January 3, 2012.

Leung, Louis. "User-Generated Content on the Internet: An Examination of Gratifications, Civic Engagement and Psychological Empowerment." *New Media & Society* 11, no. 8 (2009): 1327–1347.

Leye, Veva. "UNESCO, ICT Corporations and the Passion of ICT for Development: Modernization Resurrected." *Media Culture Society* 29, no. 6 (2007): 972–993.

Lynch, Mark. "The Structural Transformation of the Arab Public Sphere." In *Voices of the New Arab Public: Iraq, Al-Jazeera, and Middle East Politics Today*, 29–88. New York: Columbia University Press, 2006.

Markham, Annette N. "Internet Communication as a Tool for Qualitative Research." November 18, 2003. markham.internetinquiry.org/writing/silver-mangalleyproofs.pdf, last accessed November 11, 2011.

Mehrholz, Peter. *Play with Your Words*, posted on May 17, 2002. http://www.peterme.com/archives/00000205.html, last accessed December 30, 2011.

Miller, Carolyn R., and Dawn Shepherd. *Blogging as Social Action: A Genre Analysis of the Weblog*, 2004. http://blog.lib.umn.edu/blogosphere/blogging_as_social_action_a_genre_analysis_of_the_weblog.html, last accessed December 26, 2011.

Miller, Robin 'Roblimo'. "Meet Saudi Arabia's Most Famous Computer Expert," 2004. http://www.linux.com/articles/33695, last accessed September 7, 2009.

Milner, Helen V. "The Digital Divide: The Role of Political Institutions in Technology Diffusion." *Comparative Political Studies* 39, no. 2 (2006): 176–199.

Mourtada-Sabbah, Nada, Mohammed al-Mutawa, John W. Fox, and Tim Walters. "Media as Social Matrix in the United Arab Emirates." In *Popular Culture and Political Identity in the Arab Gulf States*, ed. Alanoud Alsharekh, Robert Springborg and Sarah Stewart. London: Saqi Books, 2008.

Neuwirth, Angelika. "Introduction." In *Arabic Literature: Postmodern Perspectives*, ed. Angelika Neuwirth, Andreas Pflitsch, and Barbara Winckler, 41–64. London: Saqi, 2010.

Nielsen, Niels Kayser. *Welfare-Nationalism: Comparative Aspects of the Relation between Sport and Nationalism in Scandinavia in the Inter-War Years*, Ethnologia Scandinavica, 1997. www.la84foundation.org/SportsLibrary/SportsHistorian/.../sh172h.pdf, last accessed January 18, 2012.

O'Reilly, Tim. *What Is Web 2.0*, posted September 30, 2005. http://oreilly.com/web2/archive/what-is-web-20.html, last accessed November 11, 2011.

Papacharissi, Zizzi. "Audiences as Media Producers: Content Analysis of 260 Blogs." In *Blogging, Citizenship, and the Future of Media*, ed. M. Tremayne, 21–38. London: Routledge, 2007.

Pepe, Teresa. "Improper Narratives: Egyptian Personal Blogs and the Arabic Notion of Adab." *LEA—Lingue e letterature d'Oriente e d'Occidente* 1, no. 1 (2012): 547–562.

———. "When Writers Activate Readers. How the Autofictional Blog Transforms Arabic Literature." *Journal of Arabic and Islamic Studies* 15 (2015): 73–91.

Pflitsch, Andreas. "The End of Illusions: On Arab Postmodernism." In *Arabic Literature: Postmodern Perspectives*, ed. Angelika Neuwirth, Andreas Pflitsch, and Barbara Winckler, 25–40. London: Saqi, 2010.

"Protesters Storm Kuwaiti Parliament." November 16, 2011. http://www.bbc.co.uk/news/world-middle-east-15768027, last accessed December 29, 2011.

Qusti, Raid. "Court Rejects Case Against Rajaa Al-Sanea." *Arab News*, October 9, 2006. http://arabnews.com/?page=1&section=0&article=87886&d=9&m=10&y=2006&pix=kingdom.jpg&category=Kingdom, last accessed January 4, 2012.

Rafeedie, Fadia. "Review of Imagined Communities, by Benedict Anderson." http://socrates.berkeley.edu/~mescha/bookrev/Anderson,Benedict.html, last accessed in September 2000.

Ramsay, Gail. "Global Heroes and Local Characters in Short Stories from the United Arab Emirates and the Sultanate of Oman." In *Middle Eastern Literatures*, ed. Paul Starkey, Boutros Hallaq and Stefan Wild, Vol. 9 (Number 2) August 2006a, pp. 211–216.

———. "Globalisation and Cross-Cultural Writing in the United Arab Emirates and Oman." In *Literature and Literary History in Global Contexts: A Comparative Project*, ed. Gunilla Lindberg-Wada, Stefan Helgesson, Margareta Petersson, and Anders Pettersson, Vol. 4, 241–277. Berlin, New York, 2006b.

Riegert, Kristina. "Understanding Popular Arab Bloggers: From Public Spheres to Cultural Citizens." *International Journal of Communication* 9 (2015): 458–477.

Rosenberg, David. "UAE's Expat Population Surges to Reach Almost 90 Percent." April 3, 2011. http://arabnews.com/middleeast/article342321.ece, last accessed December 29, 2011.

Samir, Yousra. *A Qatari Man and His Kashkha*. http://www.qatarvisitor.com/index.phcID=412&pID=1639, last accessed January 3, 2012.

"Saudi Arabia Bans Protest Rallies." March 5, 2011. http://www.aljazeera.com/news/middleeast/2011/03/201135143046557642.html, last accessed December 29, 2011.

Stagh, Marina. *The Limits of Freedom of Speech: Prose Literature and Prose Writers in Egypt under Nasser and Sadat* (PhD thesis, Stockholm University, 1993), pp. 127–132.

Trammell, K.D., A. Tarkowski, and J. Hofmokl "*Rzeczpospolita blogów*", ["*Republic of Blog*"]. 2004, June. Paper presented at the 5th Annual Meeting of the Association of Internet Researchers, Brighton, September 19–22, 2006.

Warschauer, Mark, and Douglas Grimes. "Audience, Authorship, and Artifact: The Emergent Semiotics of Web 2.0." *Annual Review of Applied Linguistics* 27, no. 1 (2007): 1–23.

Wheeler, Deborah. "Blessings and Curses: Women and the Internet Revolution in the Arab World." In *Women and Media in the Middle East: Power through Self-Expression*, ed. Naomi Sakr, 138–161. London: I. B. Tauris, 2004.

Wittgenstein, Ludwig. *Philosophical Investigations*. Trans. G.E.M. Anscombe. New York: Prentice Hall, 1953.

York, Jillian C. "How to Alienate Business Customers without Really Trying." March 3, 2009, *OpenNet Initiative*. http://opennet.net/blog/2009/03/geo-filtering-how-alienate-business-customers-without-really-trying, last accessed December 29, 2011.

Younis, Eman. "Transcontinental Texts: Reality or Fantasy? Muhammad Sanajilah's Novel Chat as a Sample," *Hyperrhiz* 16: Essays, Spring 2017. http://hyperrhiz.io/hyperrhiz16/essays/5-younis-transcontinental-texts.html.

العدد (فصول) مجلة النقد الأدبي 79 شتاء وربيع، 2011.

Websites

OpenNet Initiative

OpenNet Initiative. "Bahrain". http://opennet.net/research/profiles/bahrain, last accessed January 25, 2012.

———. "Kuwait". http://opennet.net/research/profiles/kuwait, last accessed January 25, 2012.

———. "Oman". http://opennet.net/research/profiles/oman, last accessed January 25, 2012.

———. "Qatar". http://opennet.net/research/profiles/qatar, last accessed January 25, 2012.

———. "Saudi Arabia". http://opennet.net/research/profiles/saudi-arabia, last accessed December 29, 2011.

———. "United Arab Emirates". http://opennet.net/research/profiles/uae, last accessed December 29, 2011.

http://www.state.gov

Bahrain. http://www.state.gov/r/pa/ei/bgn/26414.htm, last accessed January 2, 2012.

Kuwait. http://www.state.gov/r/pa/ei/bgn/35876.htm, last accessed January 2, 2012.

Oman. http://www.state.gov/r/pa/ei/bgn/35834.htm, last accessed January 2, 2012.

Qatar. http://www.state.gov/r/pa/ei/bgn/5437.htm, last accessed January 2, 2012.
Saudi Arabia. http://www.state.gov/r/pa/ei/bgn/3584.htm, last accessed January 2, 2012.
UAE. http://www.state.gov/r/pa/ei/bgn/5444.htm, last accessed January 2, 2012.

Websites Misc

European Science Foundation: Individual and Society in the Mediterranean Muslim World. http://www.esf.org/activities/research-networking-programmes/humanities-sch/completed-rnp-programmes-in-humanities/individual-and-society-in-the-mediterranean-muslim-world.html, last accessed January 19, 2011.
"Internet Usage in the Middle East Middle East Internet Usage & Population Statistics." http://www.Internetworldstats.com/stats5.htm, January 2011, last accessed December 29, 2011.
"Many New European Immigrants." http://www.ssb.no/innvbef_en/, last accessed January 16, 2012.
"Population. The Newest New Yorkers." http://www.nyc.gov/html/dcp/html/census/nny_exec_sum.shtml, last accessed January 16, 2012.
"Reporters without Boarders published their last Annual Report on Saudi Arabia in 2007." http://arabia.reporters-sans-frontieres.org/article.php3?id_article=20775, last accessed May 28, 2009.
"What Is a Backlink?" http://www.wisegeek.com/what-is-a-backlink.htm, last accessed December 30, 2011.
DeFlumere, Ashley. "*Omanization.*" http://www.mtholyoke.edu/~deflu20a/classweb/omanization/omanization.html, last accessed November 29, 2011.
http://arabizi.wordpress.com/, last accessed January 17, 2012.
http://theory.org.uk/, last accessed December 29, 2011.
http://www.Internetworldstats.com, last accessed January 30, 2012.
http://www.markosweb.com, last accessed January 30, 2012.
http://www.searchenginehistory.com/, last accessed December 29, 2011.
http://www.sheikhmajidawards.com/about-sheikh-majid-media-award.aspx, last accessed January 4, 2012.
http://www.websitelooker.com, last accessed January 30, 2012.
http://www.mixpod.com/, last accessed January 30, 2012.
oman.net. http://www.omanet.om/english/misc/omanise.asp, last accessed November 29, 2011.
Technorati.com, last accessed January 3, 2012.

BIBLIOGRAPHY

YouTube

computingstudies1. *Virtual Private Networks (VPNs)*, April 6, 2010. http://www.youtube.com/watch?v=jJdW0_yB9vo&feature=related, last accessed December 29, 2011.

Gauntlett, David. *Participation Culture, Creativity, and Social Change*, November 29, 2008. http://www.youtube.com/watch?v=MNqgXbI1_o8&feature=related, last accessed November 11, 2011.

———. *Transforming Audiences 3—Introduction by David Gauntlett (Sept 2011)*, August 22, 2011. http://www.youtube.com/watch?v=VQp3q_z47ys, last accessed January 3, 2012.

Hicham. http://worldtv.com/hicham_tv, last accessed December 26, 2011.

Reason TV. *Cory Doctorow on The War on Kids, Boing Boing, & His Next Novel*, July 15, 2010. http://www.youtube.com/watch?v=LLf3nldagXc , last accessed November 11, 2011.

teaminbiz. *Princess Ameerah Seeks to Improve Saudi Womens' Rights*, September 23, 2011. http://www.youtube.com/watch?v=gxVJ9PnikI8, last accessed November 29, 2011.

SELECTION OF ONLINE LITERARY TEXT SOURCES

Blogs

http://7osen-man.blogspot.com
(All Accessed June 2011)

June 3, 2011 كلمة
http://7osen-man.blogspot.com/2011/06/blog-post.html.

May 25, 2011 ماذا نأكل
http://7osen-man.blogspot.com/2011/05/blog-post_25.html.

May 8, 2011
http://7osen-man.blogspot.com/2011/05/blog-post.html.

March 28, 2011 لعبة الحياة
http://7osen-man.blogspot.com/2011/03/blog-post.html.

January 24, 2011 كلام
http://7osen-man.blogspot.com/2011/01/blog-post.html.

January 18, 2011 عالم خيالي
http://7osen-man.blogspot.com/2011/06/blog-post_18.html.

http://al-zain.blogspot.com
(All Accessed February 2011)

February 6, 2011 الى حين استجمع شتات نفسي
http://al-zain.blogspot.com/2011/02/blog-post.html.

January 23, 2011 قصاصات ورق .. له
http://al-zain.blogspot.com/2011/01/blog-post_23.html.

January 25, 2011 نكشه
http://al-zain.blogspot.com/2011/01/blog-post_16.html.

January 3, 2011 وبدايات 2010 خواتيم
http://al-zain.blogspot.com/2011/01/2010-2011.html.

December 12, 2010 غرس الوطن
http://al-zain.blogspot.com/2010/12/blog-post_12.html.

November 25, 2010 هلاوس المد واتزان الجزر
http://al-zain.blogspot.com/2010/11/blog-post_25.html.

October 31, 2010 ليلة الجمعة.. سبمبوت .. استكانه
http://al-zain.blogspot.com/2010/10/blog-post_31.html.

October 28, 2010 شفيهم؟؟
http://al-zain.blogspot.com/2010/10/blog-post_28.html.

October 26, 2010 الخطابه أم فلان
http://al-zain.blogspot.com/2010/10/blog-post_26.html.

October 25, 2010 أين نحن اليوم من البارحة
http://al-zain.blogspot.com/2010/10/blog-post_25.html.

October 17, 2010 حديث الزين .... هرطقة
http://al-zain.blogspot.com/2010/10/blog-post_17.html.

October 6, 2010 بوست كلش ماله داعي
http://al-zain.blogspot.com/2010/10/blog-post_06.html.

October 5, 2010 حديث الزين ... طفو
http://al-zain.blogspot.com/2010/10/blog-post_05.html.

October 3, 2010 حديث الزين ... عروج
http://al-zain.blogspot.com/2010/10/blog-post_03.html.

http://t7l6m.com
(All Accessed August 2011)

جمعيتنا مُغلقة August 8, 2011
http://t7l6m.com/2011/08/08/%D8%AC%D9%85%D8%B9%D9%8A%D8%AA%D9%86%D8%A7-%D9%85%D8%BA%D9%84%D9%82%D8%A9/.

(2)السفر نائما July 25, 2011
http://t7l6m.com/2011/07/25/%D8%A7%D9%84%D8%B3%D9%81%D8%B1-%D9%86%D8%A7%D8%A6%D9%85%D8%A72/.

السفر نائما July 24, 2011
http://t7l6m.com/2011/07/24/%D8%A7%D9%84%D8%B3%D9%81%D8%B1-%D9%86%D8%A7%D8%A6%D9%85%D8%A7/.

الصيف وعطلة الربيع July 15, 2011
http://t7l6m.com/2011/07/15/%D8%A7%D9%84%D8%B5%D9%8A%D9%81-%D9%88%D8%B9%D8%B7%D9%84%D8%A9-%D8%A7%D9%84%D8%B1%D8%A8%D9%8A%D8%B9/.

القنفه: الثالث والأخير June 21, 2011
http://t7l6m.com/2011/06/21/%D8%A7%D9%84%D9%82%D9%86%D9%81%D9%87-%D8%A7%D9%84%D8%AB%D8%A7%D9%84%D8%AB-%D9%88%D8%A7%D9%84%D8%A3%D8%AE%D9%8A%D8%B1/.

القنفه:الثاني June 19, 2011
http://t7l6m.com/2011/06/19/%D8%A7%D9%84%D9%82%D9%86%D9%81%D9%87%D8%A7%D9%84%D8%AB%D8%A7%D9%86%D9%8A/.

القنفه June 16, 2011
http://t7l6m.com/2011/06/16/%D8%A7%D9%84%D9%82%D9%86%D9%81%D9%87/.

ذلك المشروب June 15, 2011
http://t7l6m.com/2011/06/15/%D8%B0%D9%84%D9%83-%D8%A7%D9%84%D9%85%D8%B4%D8%B1%D9%88%D8%A8/.

كحل June 13, 2011
http://t7l6m.com/2011/06/13/%D9%83%D8%AC%D9%84/.

http://www.salatmaiwa.com
(All Accessed June 2011)

فوشيا_الأخير June 15 2011
http://www.salatmaiwa.com/2011/06/blog-post_15.html.

April 6, 2010 أنفك منك ولو..
http://www.salatmaiwa.com/2010/04/blog-post_05.html.

March 22, 2010 بتتامين؟
http://www.salatmaiwa.com/2010/03/blog-post_5155.html.

http://fawaghi.maktoobblog.com/
(All Accessed June 2011)

June 25, 2011 شرفات الليل
http://fawaghi.maktoobblog.com/1609731/%D8%AD%D9%85%D9%89-%D8%A8%D8%A7%D8%B1%D8%AF%D8%A9/.

April 22, 2011 حمى باردة
http://fawaghi.maktoobblog.com/1609689/%D9%85%D9%86-%D8%A3%D8%AD%D8%AC%D8%A7%D8%B1-%D8%A7%D9%84%D8%B4%D8%BA%D9%88%D8%A7%D8%B1-%D9%80-%D8%AD%D8%AC%D8%B1-%D8%A7%D9%84%D9%82%D9%85%D8%B1/.

July 25, 2010 من أحجار الشغوار ـ حجر القمر
http://fawaghi.maktoobblog.com/1609689/%D9%85%D9%86-%D8%A3%D8%AD%D8%AC%D8%A7%D8%B1-%D8%A7%D9%84%D8%B4%D8%BA%D9%88%D8%A7%D8%B1-%D9%80-%D8%AD%D8%AC%D8%B1-%D8%A7%D9%84%D9%82%D9%85%D8%B1/.

http://www.bothayna.net/
(All Accessed May 2011)

May 4, 2011 مسكونون
http://www.bothayna.net/home/index.php?categoryid=13.

December 21, 2009 سام والفاصوليا
http://www.bothayna.net/home/index.php?categoryid=14&p2_articleid=196.

December 14, 2009 الضفدعة والأمير
http://www.bothayna.net/home/index.php?categoryid=14&p2_articleid=197.

December 7, 2009 من أجل أن ينتصر الخير
http://www.bothayna.net/home/index.php?categoryid=14&p2_articleid=193.

http://www.muawiyah.com
(All Accessed November 2009)

November 17, 2009 الوخزة..
http://www.muawiyah.com/search/label/%D9%82%D8%B5%D8%B5%20%D9%82%D8%B5%D9%8A%D8%B1%D8%A9.

3حنق October 30, 2009
http://muawiya.com/2009/10/3_30.html.

سرنمة على طريقة وليد النبهاني October 26, 2009
http://www.muawiyah.com/2009/10/blog-post_8940.html.

2حنق October 25, 2009
http://www.muawiyah.com/2009/10/2_25.html.

———, 2009] 1حنق[
http://www.muawiyah.com/2009/10/1_25.html.

البؤر المصابة بالعفن October 11, 2010
http://www.muawiyah.com/2010/10/blog-post_11.html.

.. قلة الشغل مصيبة October 9, 2010
http://muawiya.com/2010/10/blog-post_3723.html.

.. ويؤثرون على أنفسهم September 25, 2010
http://www.muawiyah.com/2010/09/blog-post_25.html.

.. عن أبي فيصل أخيراً August 15, 2010
http://www.muawiyah.com/2010/08/blog-post_15.html.

. أحكام خطرة لمن يكرهون الحياة June 13, 2010a
http://www.muawiyah.com/2010/06/blog-post_13.html.

. أحكام خطرة لمن يكرهون الحياة June 6, 2010b
http://www.muawiyah.com/2010/06/blog-post_13.html.

مداخلات مقال الكحول [منتدى الحارة العُمانية] June 2, 2010
http://www.muawiyah.com/2010/06/blog-post_8164.html.

.. هرب آخر June 15, 2010
http://www.muawiyah.com/2010/06/blog-post_15.html.

.. نوستالجيا June 8, 2010
http://www.muawiyah.com/2010/06/blog-post_08.html.

.. كن بخير .. يا صديقي May 25, 2010
http://www.muawiyah.com/2010/05/blog-post_25.html.

انبطاط فؤاد May 7, 2010
http://www.muawiyah.com/2010/05/blog-post_07.html.

.. هدوء April 13, 2010
http://www.muawiyah.com/2010/04/blog-post_13.html.

:ثرثرة عابرة عن خزقةٍ مهمة April 10, 2010
http://www.muawiyah.com/2010/04/blog-post_10.html.

http://baabalshams.blogspot.com/
(All Accessed April 2010)

April 9, 2010 مهمشون
http://baabalshams.blogspot.com/2010/04/blog-post.html.

March 4, 2010 قوقعة
http://baabalshams.blogspot.com/2010/03/blog-post_4260.html.

February 23, 2010 أرض نارية
http://baabalshams.blogspot.com/2010/02/blog-post_23.html.

February 18, 2010 بديلا لما لم نعشه معا
http://baabalshams.blogspot.com/2010/02/blog-post_18.html.

http://believe-a.blogspot.com/
(All Accessed October 2010)

October 2, 2010 أول مشاركه مع مجلة !
http://believe-a.blogspot.com/2010/10/blog-post_02.html.

October 1, 2010 وَجَعٌ
http://believe-a.blogspot.com/2010/10/blog-post.html#links.

September 3, 2010 إنك تعلم وهم لا يعلمون
http://believe-a.blogspot.com/2010/09/blog-post.html#links.

August 25, 2010 إني مسني الضر و أنت أرحم الراحمين
http://believe-a.blogspot.com/2010/08/blog-post.html#links.

July 3, 2010 وُجهةٌ أخرى
http://believe-a.blogspot.com/2010/07/blog-post.html#links.

http://eclipse9932hd.blogspot.com
(All Accessed May 2009)

May 10, 2009 تحت المدينة
http://eclipse9932hd.blogspot.com/2009/05/blog-post_10.html.

June 9, 2009 يوم كئيب جداً واجد كثيراً ُ
http://eclipse9932hd.blogspot.com/2009/06/blog-post.html.

May 23, 2009 السبت ولد حلال
http://eclipse9932hd.blogspot.com/2009/05/blog-post_23.html.

August 14, 1998 (sic) الزمــــن
http://eclipse9932hd.blogspot.com/2009/04/blog-post_04.html.

August 12, 1998 (sic) خفايا القيصر
http://eclipse9932hd.blogspot.com/2009/04/blog-post_01.html.

http://www.lair.ws
(All Accessed May 2010)

May 1, 2010 قلب الصنم
http://www.lair.ws/ar/?p=189.

February 28, 2010 قلب .. إثمن العبور
http://www.lair.ws/ar/?p=163.

March 18, 2006 ميت على قيد الحياة – هذيان
http://www.lair.ws/ar/?p=22.

May 1, 2006 أنت بتدخل الجنة !
http://www.lair.ws/ar/?p=23.

February 26, 2006 إرجعي للحياة يا "هيا" لإقتص لك من وزارة التربية والتهديم
http://www.lair.ws/ar/?p=17.

January 26, 2006 التبعية .. وحلم الإستقلالية !
http://www.lair.ws/ar/?p=13.

December 28, 2005 فيروزيات باللون الأبيض -1
http://www.lair.ws/ar/?p=11.

December 20, 2005 أنا ليبرالي ولكن محافظ !
http://www.lair.ws/ar/?p=10.

November 19, 2005 نافذة الغياب !
http://www.lair.ws/ar/?p=6.

November 22, 2005 والله الجفا برد !
http://www.lair.ws/ar/?p=7.

July 18, 2005 ها أنا هنا !
http://www.lair.ws/ar/?p=2.

http://othersandme.blogspot.com
(All Accessed October 2010)

October 10, 2010 غياب قسري
http://othersandme.blogspot.com/2010/10/blog-post.html.

September 13, 2010 حنين
http://othersandme.blogspot.com/2010/09/blog-post.html.

May 20, 2010 رأفة بحالك
http://othersandme.blogspot.com/2010/05/blog-post_20.html.

May 2, 2010 أعطني مكيال حنان
http://othersandme.blogspot.com/2010/05/blog-post.html.

ليلة سعيدة أيها الرجل السعيد April 2, 2010
http://othersandme.blogspot.com/2010/04/blog-post.html.

وتبقى أنت الوحيد في عيني March 13, 2010
http://othersandme.blogspot.com/2010/03/blog-post.html.

كلاكيت "خامس" مرة February 19, 2010
http://othersandme.blogspot.com/2010/02/blog-post_19.html.

في غفلة منك February 27, 2010
http://othersandme.blogspot.com/2010/02/blog-post_27.html.

نادين البدير - أنا وأزواجي الأربعة December 29, 2009
http://othersandme.blogspot.com/2009/12/blog-post_29.html.

مد يديك December 26, 2009
http://othersandme.blogspot.com/2009/12/blog-post_26.html.

لا شيء سواك في عيني November 2, 2009
http://othersandme.blogspot.com/2009/11/blog-post.html.

لأنك مطر... ولأنني ربيع October 17, 2009
http://othersandme.blogspot.com/2009/10/blog-post.html.

ليلى والذيب March 6, 2009
http://othersandme.blogspot.com/2009/03/blog-post.html.

طريق بلا قارعة January 10, 2009
http://othersandme.blogspot.com/2009/01/blog-post.html.

قلب واحد December 22, 2008
http://othersandme.blogspot.com/2008/12/blog-post_22.html.

خطر لي August 16, 2008
http://othersandme.blogspot.com/2008/08/blog-post_16.html.

أيها الموت.. اجمع قبحك وانصرف August 10, 2008
http://othersandme.blogspot.com/2008/08/blog-post_10.html.

فتنة August 5, 2008
http://othersandme.blogspot.com/2008/08/blog-post.html.

حين يشهق جلدي June 6, 2008
http://othersandme.blogspot.com/2008/06/blog-post.html.

لن يموت الطنطل May 18, 2008
http://othersandme.blogspot.com/2008/05/blog-post.html.

ذبحة صدرية April 22, 2008
http://othersandme.blogspot.com/2008/04/blog-post_22.html.

ذات دفء April 1, 2008
http://othersandme.blogspot.com/2008/04/blog-post.html.

في تداعيات اللحظة March 11, 2008
http://othersandme.blogspot.com/2008/03/blog-post_11.html.

سكر January 13, 2008
http://othersandme.blogspot.com/2008/01/blog-post.html.

إمرأة مغلفة December 20, 2007
http://othersandme.blogspot.com/2007/12/blog-post_20.html.

رجلان November 24, 2007
http://othersandme.blogspot.com/2007/10/blog-post_26.html.

خريف في حضن المنام November 9, 2007
http://othersandme.blogspot.com/2007/11/blog-post_09.html.

في حضرة الحب November 2, 2007
http://othersandme.blogspot.com/2007/11/blog-post.html.

قهوتي تشتاق September 16, 2007
http://othersandme.blogspot.com/2007/09/blog-post.html.

عيناك September 4, 2007
http://othersandme.blogspot.com/2007/08/blog-post_20.html.

ملاك August 25, 2007
http://othersandme.blogspot.com/2007/08/blog-post_25.html.

كذب ولكن August 18, 2007
http://othersandme.blogspot.com/2007/08/blog-post_18.html.

قهقهة ودموع July 7, 2007
http://othersandme.blogspot.com/2007/07/blog-post_07.html.

الواحد لا يقبل القسمة July 23, 2007 One does not accept division
http://othersandme.blogspot.com/2007/07/blog-post_23.html.

عالم مخصي June 16, 2007
http://othersandme.blogspot.com/2007/06/blog-post.html.

أحجية June 9, 2007
http://othersandme.blogspot.com/2007/05/blog-post_30.html.

هل توقف الزمن بهم في الثمانينات؟ May 13, 2007
http://othersandme.blogspot.com/2007/05/blog-post_13.html.

شوية حش May 5, 2007
http://othersandme.blogspot.com/2007/05/blog-post_05.html.

جناحان وأنت April 27, 2007
http://othersandme.blogspot.com/2007/04/blog-post_27.html.

كلنا محمود April 16, 2007
http://othersandme.blogspot.com/2007/04/blog-post_16.html.

من وين من البحرين؟ October 5, 2006
http://othersandme.blogspot.com/2006/10/blog-post_05.html.

ثقافة انتحاري September 23, 2006
http://othersandme.blogspot.com/2006/09/blog-post_23.html.

BLOGS MISC

June 2, 2006 "Back and Blocked"
http://eveksa.blogspot.com/2006/06/back-and-blocked.html, last accessed December 29, 2011.

FORUMS

http://www.alamuae.com
(All Accessed December 15, 2009)

!.. أولاد الأفاعي ..! أحداث غريبة تقع لفارس !
http://www.alamuae.com/story/showthread.php?t=378.

.. بقايا أنثى مجروحـه
http://www.alamuae.com/story/showthread.php?t=393.

أوطــانك غربتي
http://www.alamuae.com/story/showthread.php?t=396.

حب في الـيونان
http://www.alamuae.com/story/showthread.php?t=391.

ليه عمري مالقى لبرده دفى الا دفاكي ؟؟؟؟.
http://www.alamuae.com/story/showthread.php?t=395.

إالـسر المـخفي ..؟
http://www.alamuae.com/story/showthread.php?t=385.

هـم قصـةٌ لا تـشـترى
http://www.alamuae.com/story/showthread.php?t=389.

القصص القصيرة
http://www.alamuae.com/story/forumdisplay.php?f=3.

نســيت أنساك
http://www.alamuae.com/story/showthread.php?t=377.

هو و هي يوم اجتمعوا
http://www.alamuae.com/story/showthread.php?t=330.

ود ..بتزوج
http://www.alamuae.com/story/showthread.php?t=379.

http://www.gulf-gate.net
(All Accessed December 6, 2009)

نذاله الاولاد وين وصلت ادخل وشوف October 2009
http://www.gulf-gate.net/vb/386164-post1.html.

صفحاتي هنا : مساحتي November 2009
http://www.gulf-gate.net/vb/t19851.html.

فجأة اصبحت بلا فائدة November 2009
http://www.gulf-gate.net/vb/t19271-2.html.

(All Accessed December 15, 2009)

قصة مفيدة فيها عبرة وعض December 2009
http://www.gulf-gate.net/vb/t20364.html.

قصتي الحزينة :::: جديدي:::: November 2009
http://www.gulf-gate.net/vb/t19427.html.

شباب3دور و 75قصة ولا كل القصص.. December 2009
http://www.gulf-gate.net/vb/t20084.html.

قصة راعي التاكسي December 2, 2009
http://www.gulf-gate.net/vb/t18932.html.

طفل احضر تراب الجنة November 22, 2009
http://www.gulf-gate.net/vb/t19402.html.

بعد ماتقروها قولولي ايت قصه ادهشتك October 21, 2009
http://www.gulf-gate.net/vb/t18761.html.

http://www.omanxa.com
(All Accessed December 15, 2009)

مشاهدة النسخة كاملة August 28, 2010
http://www.omanxa.com/vb/archive/index.php/t-18161.html.

November 26, 2009 British Airways
http://www.omanxa.com/vb/showthread.php?p=180729.

November 27, 2009 الليل, حطي, طحت
http://www.omanxa.com/vb/showthread.php?t=13437.

October 30, 2009 فتـــــاة قالت لسوداني............
http://www.omanxa.com/vb/showthread.php?t=13047.

July 21, 2009 بنت17سنة
http://www.omanxa.com/vb/showthread.php?t=11678.

March 11, 2009 لا تسمع من طرف واحد ...
http://www.omanxa.com/vb/showthread.php?p=177558.

November 17, 2009 ن زرعت الامانه فستحصد الثقه
http://www.omanxa.com/vb/showthread.php?t=13317.

Forums Misc

July 31, 2010 !.. رجل // في قاعة الزفاف
http://shjn-h.com/vb/showthread.php?p=23593.

———, 2010 لعسى الأيام ... تجمعنا
http://www.ksayat.com/showthread-t_78197.html.

August 6, 2009 كيف قتلت ؟/القصة الكاملة للفتاة الاماراتية التى عثر عليها في بئر مقتولة
forum.uaewomen.net/showthread.php?t=476260,
last accessed January 30, 2012.

November 20, 2011, "British Airways."
http://www.alabudaiah.com/vb/showthread.php?p=17807,
last accessed January 26, 2012.

Index[1]

A
Abbas, W., 129
Abdel Aal, G., 61, 108
Abdul-Jalil, Z., 38n31, 117n15, 128n62
Achaari, M., 121
Albabtain, A.A., 59, 59n38, 116
Alem, R., 121
A-list bloggers, 65
Alyaqout, H., 53
Alzain, 20, 21, 26, 36, 100
Amar, P., 103
Arab E-Writers Union, 22, 55
Arabic blogs, 26
Arabic digital literature, 11, 16
Arabic literary blogs, 4, 31
Arabic online literary texts, 23
Arabic online literature, 32, 34, 82
Arab Spring poems, 22n23
Arab Uprisings, 5, 10, 22, 34, 128
Arendt, H., 62
Art online, reposting and remixing of works of, 68–78
Audience, 6, 7, 10, 11, 18, 23, 34, 38, 40, 43, 45, 47–49, 51, 55, 56, 61, 64, 69, 70, 78, 88, 100, 107, 110, 118, 120, 127–130, 135–137, 140–142, 144
   communication with, 79
   educating, 93
   foreign, 94
   online, 63
   role of, 65–68
Aupers, S., 95n28
Autofictionality, 4, 13, 19, 32, 35, 46, 64

B
Bahrain, 9–11, 116, 117, 119n19, 122, 123
Baker, L., 131n74

---

[1] Note: Page numbers followed by 'n' refer to notes.

© The Author(s) 2019
N. Lenze, *Politics and Digital Literature in the Middle East*,
https://doi.org/10.1007/978-3-319-76816-8

Banāt al-Riyāḍ, 38, 41, 41n42, 45, 45n50, 102, 105, 106, 120
Bauman, Z., 95, 96n29
Beauty standards, 82, 90, 97, 101, 112
Beck, U., 95n28
Beck-Gernsheim, E., 95n28
Ben Ali, Z.E.A., 116
Benkler, Y., 53n19, 53n20, 80n3, 114, 114n2, 127n59
Bloggers, 10, 11, 18, 20, 21, 55, 57, 60, 65, 66, 82, 88, 100, 117, 118n19, 124, 126, 129, 142
  female, 63, 64
  participation of, 51
Blog literature, 4, 38, 45
Blog posts, 15, 17, 21, 25, 26, 29, 31, 41–43, 79, 82, 83, 93, 100, 103, 111, 112, 129, 131, 140, 142, 143
Blogs, 3, 5–7, 12, 13, 15, 17–21, 23, 26, 31, 32, 35–37, 50–52, 52n13, 56, 57, 59–61, 63–65, 68, 80–82, 94, 97, 107, 111, 114, 124, 126, 127, 129–131, 137, 140–145
Bohman, J., 60, 60n39, 62, 62n49, 63, 63n52
Boker, U., 62, 63n51, 64n56
Booth, M., 5
Bouazizi, M., 116
Bradley, G., 95, 95n27
Bronner, E., 117n11
Bruns, A., 127, 128n60
Brynen, R., 108n45

C

Censorship, 7, 10, 13, 49, 54, 58, 59, 113, 114, 119–121, 124–126, 130, 137, 144
Chat, 22
Colloquial Arabic in forums and blogs, 37–42
Colloquial language, 34, 37, 38, 42n46, 44, 136, 141
Comments, 31, 57, 65, 67, 77, 101, 102, 129, 135, 136
Cooke, M., 98n34
"Correct/eloquent" (*faṣīḥ*) Arabic, 38
Critical discourse analysis (CDA), 8, 8n19, 13, 25, 79
Crystal, D., 17, 17n5, 21
Cultural citizenship, 7
Cultural production online, 48
Curtain, T., 63

D

Dada movement, 52
Dār al-Nāshirī, 53
Dar Merit, 12
Davis, J., 81, 81n6, 82
al-Dawsari, R., 129
de Beer, P., 95n28
de Koster, W., 95n28
Dean, J., 63
Decreus, F., 38n30
Dialectical-relational approach, 37
Digital culture, 6–9, 13
Digital literature
  multimedia elements, 18–23
  setup of online literary texts on blogs and forums, 17–18
  text layout and multimedia elements, 16–17
  visual setup, 15–16
Digital media, 34, 48, 51, 66, 109, 113, 114, 144
Digital natives, 49, 110
Digital novels, 17, 23
Digital poetry, 22, 32, 39
Digital short stories, 94

Digital storytelling, 33
Digital texts, 2, 13–16, 18, 32
   online, 23
Doctorow, C., 68, 131
Doostdar, A., 38, 38n32
DU, 125, 125n51

E

Egypt, 1, 9, 12, 37, 39, 57–59, 79, 95, 111, 114, 115, 117, 128, 137
   culture and tradition in, 103
   decision-making processes in, 116
   internet censorship in, 122–127
   political activism in, 10
Egyptian bloggers, 40, 46
Egyptian blog literature, 38
Egyptian blogs, 5, 35, 38, 46
Egyptian dialect, 40
Egyptian Movement of Change, 10
El-Ariss, T., 2, 2n1, 4–6, 5n8, 8, 12, 12n32, 12n34, 33, 33n17
Emery, P.G., 34n22
Enkvist, N.E., 48, 49n3
Erstad, O., 119, 119n22
Etisalat, 125, 125n51
EURAMAL conference, 45, 45n50
European Science Foundation, 96

F

Faier, E., 19n11
Fairclough, N., 37, 37n29
Femininity, 81, 98, 102, 103
Figures of Fantasy (Paasonen), 81, 81n4
Fiore, Q., 131n72
"Forms of techno-writing,", 2
Forums, 3, 6, 7, 10, 13, 15–21, 23, 25, 31–46, 50, 52, 56, 59–61, 64, 65, 68, 69, 77, 78, 80–82, 90, 92, 94, 97, 102, 107, 110–112, 114, 116, 128, 130, 131, 135, 136, 140–145

Fox, J.W., 49n5, 109n49
Friedlander, L., 42, 42n45, 62, 62n46, 136, 136n77
Frissen, V., 95n27
Funkhouser, C., 2n2, 16n1, 39, 39n35

G

Gasser, U., 49n4
Gauntlett, D., 6, 6n14, 53, 53n18, 54, 54n25
Gender
   narration of, 106–112
   roles, 98–106
Gendolla, P., 52, 52n17
Genette, G., 7, 31
Gesamttexte, 13, 17, 21
Ghassoub, M., 103
Gill, R., 129n65
Glazier, L.P., 32, 32n12, 58n34
Golley, N.H., 98n34
Goodreads, 52, 52n14
Graham, P., 50n9
Grimes, D., 13, 48n2, 49, 49n6, 60n41, 61n43, 65, 65n61
Guertin, C., 52, 52n16, 58n35, 61, 61n44, 62, 62n50, 66, 66n65
Gulf Countries, 9–12, 39, 79, 80, 103, 114, 116, 118, 118n19, 120, 136
   internet censorship in, 122–127
Günther, D., 16n2
Guth, S., 4, 31n10, 96, 96n32, 97, 101n39

H

Habermas, J., 62
Haddad, J., 121, 121n29
Hafez, S., 4, 31, 31n10, 36, 98–99n35
Harré, R., 80n2

Haykal, M.H., 100
Hayles, N.K., 32, 32n11, 41n43
al-Hejery, E.S., 119
Held, D., 108n45
Henry, C.M., 108n45
Hermes, J., 7
Heroes
  in blog posts, 82
  depicting, 93–94
  gender roles, 98–106
  narration of gender and normativity of traditions, 106–112
  perspectives on online identity, 81–82
  portrayal of, 2, 4, 79–82, 94, 97, 98, 108, 110–112, 143
  portrayal of individualisation, 94–98
  representation of, 143
Hibbard, J.A., 62, 63n51, 64n56
Hicham, 21, 21n21
"Ḥiṣṣa and the Taxi Driver" blog post, 39n36, 40, 42, 92–94, 102, 105, 106, 108, 110
Hoffmann, S., 117n14
Hofheinz, A., 125, 125n52
Hofmokl, J., 53n21
Holes, C., 39, 39n34, 45, 45n51
Houtman, D., 95n28
How Was She Killed? blog post, 18, 36, 60, 82, 90–92, 98, 101, 105, 112
Hypertext literature, 16

I
Identity representation, 4, 13, 45, 82, 111, 112, 114
Imagined Masculinities, 103
ʿImārat Yaʿqūbiyān, 45
Individualisation, 79, 80, 111, 143
  portrayal of, 94–98

Information and Communication Technology (ICT), 94, 94n26, 95, 95n27, 109, 110, 113, 114, 116, 116n9
  global and local influence on, 127–129
Instagram, 51, 135, 145
Intellectual property, 60, 78, 114, 130–137, 142, 144
Intermediality, 16, 52
Internet censorship, 113
  in Gulf Countries, Lebanon, and Egypt, 122–127
Internet service providers (ISPs), 123, 123n45, 125
Internet Service Unit (ISU), 119, 120, 125
Istikhdam al-Hayah, 127

J
Jargy, S., 34, 34n20
Johnson, T., 32n14
Jubrān, J.K., 101
Junge, C., 4, 35, 35n23, 36, 141
Jurkiewicz, S., 7, 7n18

K
Kaare, B.H., 33, 34n19, 35, 35n25
Keen, A., 51, 51n12
Kefaya movement in Egypt, 10
Khamis, S., 11, 11n27
Kibar, M., 21
Kifaya movement, 117
Kirby, A., 49, 50, 50n7, 66, 66n64, 142, 142n2
Kirchner, H., 124n49, 125n53
Klötgen, F., 16n2
Kolk, M., 38n30
Koster, F., 95n28

Kuwait, 10, 52, 53, 59, 79, 82, 103, 115, 117, 119n19, 122, 123, 137
Kuwaiti blogs, 82

L

Lebanon, 1, 9, 10, 39, 58, 59, 95, 111, 114, 115, 118, 137
  internet censorship in, 122–127
Lenze, N., 38n31, 117n15, 128n62
Leung, L.W., 6, 6n13, 48n1, 50, 50n10, 51n11, 54n22
Leye, V., 116, 116n9
Links, form of communication, 57
Literary forums, 23
Literary texts, authoritarian regimes on, 113, 117–122
Louw, E., 122n32
Lovink, G., 57, 57n33, 116, 116n10
Lundby, K., 33, 33n18, 34n19, 35, 35n25, 42n45, 62n46, 119n22, 136n77
Lynch, M., 120, 120n27

M

Mahfouz, N., 38
Mahne, N., 13, 16, 17n4, 21
Maktoob, 52
al-Manfalūṭī, 101
Markham, A.N., 55, 56n30
Maywah, S., 88
McLuhan, M., 114, 114n4, 131, 131n72
Media make-up, 2, 14, 26
Miller, C.R., 17, 18, 18n6
Miller, R., 119, 119n23
Milner, H.V., 114n1
Mixpod, 21n19
Modern Standard Arabic (MSA), 2, 13, 37–44, 46, 122, 141
Moghadam, V.M., 110, 110n52

Morocco, 21, 57
Mourtada-Sabbah, N., 49n5, 109, 109n49
Muawiyah, 21, 41, 64
Multimedia
  applications, 15, 21–23, 52
  elements, 15–23, 34, 140
al-Mutawa, M., 49n5, 109n49
MySpace, 81, 81n5

N

Nabaṭī poetry, 34
Nada, 64
Naji, A., 127
Nashiri, 52, 53, 107, 122
Nawwab, N.I., 108, 108n46
Neuwirth, A., 4, 4n4, 6n11, 35n23
Nordenson, J., 17, 117n13

O

Oman, 4, 9, 10, 123
Online censorship, 59, 124, 125
Online digital text, 23
Online distribution, 52, 53, 55–56, 66, 78
  anonymity, intellectual property, and redistribution of stories, 130–136
  authoritarian regimes on literary texts, 117–122
  challenges of, 113–115
  global and local influence on ICT, 127–129
  impact of online media on political conditions, 115–117
  internet censorship in Gulf Countries, Lebanon, and Egypt, 122–127
Online identity, 81–82

Online literary texts, 12, 23, 35, 41n42, 55, 70, 79, 97, 98, 102, 106–108, 111, 112, 114, 130, 139, 142, 143, 145
  on blogs and forums, setup of, 17–18
  interactivity in, 49–50
  language in, 37
Online literature, 1, 6, 8, 9, 11, 15, 21, 23, 32, 33, 33n16, 35, 40, 41, 41n42, 46, 55, 58–62, 65, 66, 79, 80, 94, 99n35, 106, 107, 111, 113–115, 117, 122, 124, 139–141, 144, 145
Online media, on political conditions, impact of, 115–117
Online participatory culture, 48, 55, 61
Online publishing, 52–54, 113, 128, 137, 142, 144
Online short stories, 15, 93, 143
  dialogues in, 42–46
Online writing, economic developments in, 11–12
Open Net Initiative, 122
Oral poetry, 34
Orange movement, 117
O'Reilly, T., 50, 51

P
Paasonen, S., 13, 81, 81n4, 82
Palfrey, J., 49n4
Panovic, I., 38n31
Papacharissi, Z., 63, 63n54
Participatory culture, 2, 13
  authors of online literature, 58–62
  dynamics public and private, 62–65
  interaction, and Web 2.0, 48–53
  interpersonal experience, time, and space, 55–57
  links as a form of communication, 57–58
  reposting and remixing of works of art online, 68–78

  role of audience, 65–68
  user-generated content, 53–54
Pepe, T., 4, 5, 5n6, 5n7, 11, 11n28, 12, 12n30, 12n33, 35, 35n24, 37, 39n33, 80, 111, 141, 141n1
Pflitsch, A., 4, 4n4, 5, 6n11, 35n23
Poetry, 12, 21, 34, 64, 108, 111, 117, 145
Poster, M., 130, 130n69
Public and private, 13, 64, 141
  spaces, 62, 78
  spheres, 47
Public sphere, 7, 62–64, 118
Punzi, M.P., 56, 56n31, 109, 109n48

Q
Qatar, 118n19, 123, 124

R
Radarurl, 20, 20n18
Ramsay, G., 4, 4n5, 5, 17, 31n10, 40, 41n40, 64, 65, 80, 111
Redistribution of stories, 77, 130–137, 144
Remixing, 13, 47, 57, 61, 65, 136, 141, 142, 144
  of art online works, 68–78
Repostings, 19, 34, 36, 37, 114, 131–136, 140, 142, 144
  of art online works, 68–78
Riegert, K., 7, 7n15, 7n17, 10, 10n24, 11, 11n29, 62, 65
Roosevelt, E., 20
Rugh, W.A., 118, 119, 119n20

S
Saghie, H., 96, 96n30
Said, E., 6
Salem, M., 117, 129
Salloukh, B.F., 108n45

Samir, Y., 103, 103n40
Sanajleh, M., 22, 23
al-Ṣāni, R.A., 38, 41n42, 120
Saudi Arabia, 9, 10, 59, 64, 116, 117, 118n19, 119, 120, 122, 124, 126–127, 136
  gender segregation, 95
  online censorship in, 125
Saudi Eve, 126, 127
Schäfer, J., 52, 52n17
Schriwer, C., 38n31, 117n15, 128n62
Self-censorship, 13, 118, 118n19, 119, 123, 137, 144
Self-referentiality, 32, 35
Al-Shehabi, O., 117, 117n12
Shepherd, D., 17, 18, 18n6
Short stories, 2, 4, 15, 17, 19, 25, 32–46, 69, 80, 90, 92, 95, 102, 103, 105, 110, 111, 128, 131, 135, 136, 140, 141, 143
  digital, 94
  online, 93
Simanowski, R., 16, 16n3
Sinclair-Webb, E., 103
Slackman, M., 117n11
Snir, R., 3, 3n3, 41, 42n44
Social actors, 8, 81, 106
Social censorship, 59, 119, 144
Social norms, 35, 79, 100, 104, 106–112, 136, 143
Springborg, R., 49n5, 108n45, 108n46, 109n49
Stagh, M., 118, 125, 125n54
Starkey, P., 4, 121, 121n31
State censorship, 54, 59, 119
Storytelling, 32–46, 108, 140
Sultanate of Oman, 118n19

T
Tagalog, 39
Tarkowski, A., 53n21

Al-Tarrah, A.A., 103, 103n41
al-Ṭayyib Ṣāliḥ, 83
Torstrick, R.L., 19, 19n11
Trammell, K.D., 53n21
Tumblr, 26, 26n2, 52
Twitter, 20n14, 51, 52, 64, 135, 145

U
Ulrichsen, K., 108n45
User-generated content, 10n26, 48, 50–54, 58, 68, 78, 127

V
van Bockxmeer, H., 95n27
van Eynde, K., 103
Video poetry, 16, 17, 22, 23
Virtual Private Networks (VPNs), 123n44, 124
Visual setup, 13, 15–16

W
Walters, T., 49n5, 109n49
Warhol, A., 144
Warschauer, M., 13, 48n2, 49, 49n6, 60n41, 61n43, 65, 65n61
Web 2.0, 10, 10n26, 20, 47, 49–53, 58, 77, 78, 127, 141
Wertsch, J.V., 119, 119n22
Wesch, M., 69, 69n69, 77
"Western" literary theory, 5
What Shall We Eat? blog post, 82, 85–88, 98, 99, 102, 103, 106, 107, 112
Wheeler, D., 10, 10n23, 128, 128n61, 128n62
Williams, R., 56
Winckler, B., 4, 6, 35n23
Wodak, R., 8, 13, 25, 25n1, 37n29
Writing styles, 25, 26, 35–37

X

Xeroxing, 53
 culture, 78
Xiaomeng Lang,
 55n27

Y

Younis, E., 22, 22n23, 23n29,
 34, 34n21

Your Nose Belongs to You, So What?
 blog post, 82, 88–90, 97, 101, 112
YouTube, 15, 16, 22, 22n22, 23, 34,
 68, 69, 123
Yunxiang Yan, 95n28

Z

Zaynab, 100
Zero Comments (Lovink), 116

CPSIA information can be obtained
at www.ICGtesting.com
Printed in the USA
LVHW07*1937160518
577418LV00019B/438/P